RESOURCE UNLIMITED

Resource Unlimited

Edited by —

William L. Hendricks

Published by the Stewardship Commission of the Southern Baptist Convention,
Nashville, Tennessee 37219.

Contents

Introduction

It may well be that beauty is, indeed, in the eye of the beholder and that reality is what we make of it. The human outlook is the wellspring and source of man's motivation. Therefore to be unhindered in outlook, uncramped by restrictions, and unfettered by anxiety is a desirable posture for approaching life. Such a life, lived in such an outlook, might well be called a "resource unlimited."

The major question in all of this is can man of himself engender and sustain such an outlook? The despair of our society and the collapse of many "American dreams" in the swamps of social and spiritual despair seems to say man cannot, of himself, attain or sustain the life characterized by a positive resource unlimited.

It is the genius, and the promise, of Christian faith that man can and ought to live life in such a fulness and with such freedom. The gospel is precisely the good news that to human resource has been added the resource of God himself. The resource of God himself is God himself siding with man in Jesus Christ and recreating resources for men by the power of the Holy Spirit.

Nor is the resource of God non-material or other worldly. Every resourceful Christian life should be founded on the scandalously particular and this worldly promise of Jesus Christ: "I came that they may have life, and have it abundantly" (John 10:10 RSV). The Holy Spirit is the effective agent of this promise, and the world in which we live is our present context for the fulfilment of the promise.

What is lacking in modern Christianity is the audacious joy of life characterized by resource unlimited. Such life is aware that the resource is God's resource—how else could it be unlimited? It is a corollary that the joy of using such resource is accompanied with the responsibility of stewardship toward God. It is both a mark of confidence and a feeling of obligation to entitle a book of Christian stewardship, *Resource Unlimited*.

1

The Occasion

Occasions arise because of needs and because of planning. The need which occasioned this work was a conviction on the part of the Stewardship Commission of the Southern Baptist Convention that Southern Baptists must become increasingly and effectively aware of the fullest meaning and implications of Christian stewardship. From the occasion created by this need there came an occasion carefully planned and prepared which, it is hoped, will help to meet the need.

This planned occasion was the National Stewardship Seminar held at Glorieta Baptist Assembly, April 27-30, 1971. The cross section of Southern Baptist leaders attending was diverse and delightful. Professors, pastors, administrators, executive secretaries, and denominational personnel came together with openness and a vision of what more we may and must do in our time to deepen the response of the people of God to the needs of the church and the world.

The beauty of the surroundings was conducive to the sessions of worship and study. Numerous sessions were held involving addresses, dialogue, and discussion. Fourteen formal addresses were given. They comprise the sections of this book.

The composition of the seminar, the concern which went into planning it, and the whole-hearted cooperation of the participants resulted in a "different kind of meeting." There was much business, but it was more than business as usual.

Taking seriously the obligations of good stewardship, the Commission is seeking to make available and usable the wealth of material and insights shared by the participants in the seminar. Hence this book about stewardship is itself conceived and executed as a venture in stewardship.

The Format

The fourteen chapters are highly individualized contributions from Baptist leaders and scholars who were given the awesome assignment of reflecting seriously, and in depth, about Christian stewardship. Their contributions are, except for some emendations for the sake of stylistic uniformity, exactly as presented. Outlines, where they accompanied the chapters, are placed at the end to preserve a coherence in reading. In some instances chapter titles were assigned by the editor, hopefully in integrity to what the author was attempting to present. The accompanying list of contributors will identify the authors more fully.

The three sections of the book also grew out of the seminar proceedings. But the reasons for and value of these sections occurring as they do is more than procedural. The brief editorial comments at the beginning of each section will explain more completely the substantial reasons for these divisions. It is significant to place first the theological context for stewardship. From this the rationale of stewardship as trusteeship under the ownership of God is expressed. Only then is it appropriate to discuss the procedure of stewardship, especially as it relates to the practice of tithing.

Possible Uses of This Work

It is true that "of the making of books there is no end." A book on stewardship, which takes seriously its subject, needs to be more than just another book. It is hoped that this volume will be so. There are many purposes for projecting this work and many uses to which it may be put. Some of them are as follows:

(1) This work may serve as a source book in stewardship studies.

(2) The work calls attention to the theological and rational grounds for Christian stewardship.

(3) This work is intended to set the practice of stewardship in the proper focus of an adequate theological basis. Therefore—

(4) Practical and methodological programs of Christian stewardship may find this work helpful as an underlying philosophy and guide for adequate stewardship plans, promotion, and techniques.

(5) The pulpit minister and stewardship committee of local congregations, as well as the denominational officers charged with stewardship and financial affairs, will find this work a major source book in matters of biblical, theological, and historical insights on stewardship.

(6) The work may well serve as a text for formal instruction in Baptist colleges and seminaries and other institutions which offer classes in this, often grossly neglected, area.

(7) It is hoped, most fervently, that the book will help in educating laymen in the depth and challenge of Christian stewardship.

The book is designed as part of a larger stewardship emphasis among Southern Baptists to "Live the Word." Surely it is fitting that in the living of the Word we will catch the vision of the Word of God who is God's stewardship (*oikonomia*) for us. To know this is to be aware of and responsible for the "resource unlimited" that God has freely and joyfully given his people.

William L. Hendricks

Section I

The Context of Stewardship

Even the sublime becomes ridiculous when it is expressed in isolation from a proper context. All of us have been victims of conversations and, worse, disputations that didn't make sense. They didn't make sense because the participants weren't talking about the same thing, weren't listening to each other, and weren't concerned for truth so much as for vindicating their own position. What was needed was a context where meaning was assigned to terms, issues were clarified, and mutual awareness and understanding were evidenced. Context is where things take place, where issues are joined and where decisions are made and implemented.

Everything that happens happens in a context. The question is whether the context of a thing is chaotic and inappropriate or ordered and worthy. The more significant the subject, the more essential is an appropriate context. When men discuss God, or a matter pertaining to God's ways with men, it is vital to insure a context adequate to the topic. In seeking a context for a discussion of Christian stewardship four questions must be answered (1) what perspective is best—general or particular? (2) what starting point is best? (3) what are the proper questions to ask about this subject? (4) what model or image is fitting to illustrate the idea?

Perspective: Choosing a Large Enough Canvas

Perspective is the way things appear in relationship to one another. To have a lifelike image or perspective of a thing is a prerequisite to reproducing it. Engineers and architects must have a perspective on how things will look or relate to one another. The artist especially must be able to visualize what he intends to paint before he does so. It is of great consequence to an artist that he choose a canvas large enough for whatever he intends to paint.

4

Religious discussions, of all types, have often lacked perspectives. It is sad to see significant and grand doctrines painted verbally on three by five cards. In much of our talk about God, and particularly is this true in the realm of God and stewardship, we are guilty of crowding too much onto too small a canvas.

Of course the opposite problem is a reality too. One can paint a small item on an enormous canvas and thereby lack perspective. Often this is done when a discussion of Christian stewardship is limited to tithing or the methodology of stewardship campaigns.

The question of perspective has to do with whether one wants a large panorama or a small detail. Shall we talk about a context for Christian stewardship which is general or particular? Hopefully, we will be able to do both. But, obviously, we cannot do both at the same time. A decision must be made; and, in the planning for the conference where these discussions first occurred, the decision was to discuss the large general context first and then to place the particular discussions in that framework. The decision has proved a wise one; for the interpretation of particulars, as is so often the case, proved intriguing and complicated. If we had painted the particular "flower of tithing" first, we might never have filled out the canvas. As it was, we began at the borders with broad, background brush strokes.

A Starting Point

Even when one decides to begin a general discussion, he has to start at some particular place. A starting place may be chosen arbitrarily for many topics, but Christian stewardship requires special attention at this point. The problem is simple, but a decision in the matter is difficult. When one speaks of Christian stewardship, should he begin with creation, redemption, providence, or eschatology? That is, shall we discuss things as they were intended to be—before the fall one might say. This would be to start with an idealized view of creation. Or should we start at the end, that is by discussing an idealized view of eschatology—what God ultimately will do. Perhaps, taking our clue from God's providential care of his creation, we could discover meaningful ways to be his co-laborers in a theological task of preservation. Despite the value of these three approaches we have taken a fourth one. No evangelical Christian would overlook the necessity of beginning every discussion about God at the point where his Word initiated conversation with us, namely in redemption.

The group which first structured the discussion also felt the pull of a starting point. As in all Baptist occasions, uniformity was neither re-

5

quested, required, nor forthcoming.

It seems to the editor that there is a way of balancing the starting point so that justice may be done to the starting point and adequate perspective may be achieved.

Our starting point for a discussion of Christian stewardship will be creation as seen from the viewpoint of redemption. This means that we are first those who have been grasped by God and, in reflecting on the meaning of this, we observe that the God who grasps men in Jesus Christ has fashioned man and the world. Expressed theologically this is to say that the redeemer God is the creator God.

It might seem that, logically, Scripture and history begin with creation. But, internally neither Scripture would have been written nor history have divine overtones if it were not for the ultimate priority of God's redemptive purpose.

All of the chapters of this section show a sensitivity about how or when to start our discussion.[1] They all treat, in individual ways, those questions which are right and appropriate to ask if one is to have an adequate concept of Christian stewardship.

Asking the Right Questions

Since we have agreed to start with a general context and to begin from the viewpoint of creation as seen from the standpoint of redemption, we must now ask those questions that will form the context for our study.

In a world like ours why should Christian stewardship be different from the way in which things naturally occur and men ordinarily behave? The answer is simply, ours is a fallen world. Is the fallenness of our world God's last word on the subject? By no means! God has a plan to reclaim his fallen world. In effecting this plan, redemption, we have a clue as to the why of creation. God created all things good. Therefore all belongs to God. Material is good, and the Christian gospel is the focus through which we may establish and defend the goodness of God's material creation. The incarnation of Christ sacralized matter, and the redemption effected in Christ asserts the creation rights of God over all things. The covenant of God with men, which began historically with Israel, is culminated in Christ. In this context our questions of stewardship must be employed so as: to give a rationale for stewardship (Ashcraft); to view stewardship in the light of redemption (Summers); in order to assert the why and wherefore of things (Taylor); and establish the place of material things in the purpose of God and the life of man (Green). By beginning from our awareness of redemption we can thus move back to creation and have a context for a discussion of Christian stewardship which is both adequate in scope and distinctively Christian in character. This way is wise, for in choosing the broad context we are able to image and give content to a model of Christian stewardship that is able both to challenge believers to total stewardship and to provide a context worthy for stewardship, the significant interaction of God, man, and material things.

An Adequate Model

A model is important because it provides a visual or mental image which enables men to accomplish desired goals. The hero worship of super athletes may or may not be desired models which young boys accept. The fashion industry sustains itself very well by establishing models of proper style in dress. At a deeper level, Christian piety has always imaged Jesus Christ as its model.

It is problematic, that in discussions of Christian stewardship, tithing only has been suggested as the model which is adequate for "imaging" the full meaning of Christian stewardship. When this has happened, the part has been substituted for the whole, one small rose has been out of perspective on a vast canvas.

To put the matter a different way, Christian stewardship may be conceived on the model of paying one's bills. More preferable is the model of Christian stewardship as an entire life style of grace. It is salutary, and necessary, to pay one's bills. But it is seldom fun or joyful or done with enthusiasm. So it is with Christian stewardship, when it is expressed along the model of "legal duty." Infinitely more desirable is the model of stewardship as a life style of grace.

Theologically these models may be expressed in terms of law and grace. Both have a place. Law may be the form whose substance is grace. Better expressed, grace is the larger focus from which the law makes sense. Our four authors of this section show admirable awareness of the necessity of discussing redemption and creation, actuality and the ideal, grace and law, the Spirit and the letter. They have given us a context whose perspective is sufficiently wide enough to ask the right questions about Christian stewardship and whose model is challenging enough to image stewardship as a life style rather than a legal obligation.

[1] At the seminar the questions "Why did God create things?" and "What is the role of material things in the life of man?" were treated

first by authors Green and Taylor. The adoption of the starting point listed above places first the questions "What did sin do to thwart God's purpose for material things?" and "Does God have a plan to reclaim his purpose for material things?" This replacement has the advantage of asking first the questions of reality, as we face it—a fallen world, and then reasoning back to the divine intention of why things were created and what their ideal use might be. The editor does not break faith with the spirit of all four papers which reflect, from an unapologetic Christian stance, that creation must be seen from the viewpoint of redemption.

A Theological Rationale for Christian Stewardship

J. Morris Ashcraft

The concept of Christian stewardship grows out of the belief in God as Creator. The Christian man understands himself as a creature of God with a special responsibility to God. The whole of Christian life is a matter of stewardship to God. Christian faith begins in an experience in which man acknowledges God's sovereignty in his life; it proceeds under God's providence and judgment; it culminates in man's final submission to God's judgment on his life. Christian stewardship must always be understood in the context of the doctrine of God as Creator, since any other approach will lead to misunderstanding.

Churches are engaged in a very important enterprise and must have financial resources if they are to be responsible. Great harm can result, however, if churches follow lines of expediency to achieve immediate goals at the risk of overlooking the context and foundation of Christian stewardship. For instance, it is possible to employ Malachi 3:10 as a legalistic requirement and secure funds while destroying the idea of stewardship.

True Christian stewardship is based on a personal commitment to God through Christ and an understanding that God is Creator. Its implications can be understood and taught, but the educational and persuasional approach may take longer than other approaches. The conviction expressed in this paper is that in the Christian task we must work on the basis of faithful presentation, education, persuasion, and genuine response. This will require theological understanding.

I have been asked to deal with two questions. They are: (1) What did sin do to thwart God's purpose for material things? and (2) Does God have a plan to reclaim his purpose for material things? I propose to deal with these questions in the light of the Christian doctrine of creation and redemption, because I believe the only adequate view of material things and human responsibility is based on this doctrine.

I. The Doctrine of Creation

God as Creator. The first sentence in the Bible should be read, "In the beginning GOD created the heavens and the earth," because it is a theology rather than a cosmogony. The statement affirms that God is the originator, sustainer, and absolute ruler of all that is. It means that prior to his creative act, only God was. Therefore, creation is completely dependent upon God both for its origin and for its continued existence. Furthermore, creation is distinct from God; it is neither an emanation from God nor a part of God; it cannot aspire to becoming divine without committing the worst sin of which it is capable. If God is the Creator of the world, we are obliged to say that the world is good, and the writer of Genesis correctly said exactly that. But, God forever remains God, holy and transcendent over, and distinct from, his creation.

The Christian view of creation does not depend upon an exegesis of Genesis 1 and 2. Christians know the God of creation through his revelation of himself in his Son, Jesus Christ, the Word of God. "In the beginning was the Word, . . . and the Word was God . . . all things were made through him, . . . And the Word became flesh and dwelt among us, . . . (John 1:1-14 RSV). Christians are convinced that "in him all things were created, in heaven and on earth, . . ." (Col. 1:16 RSV), and that "in him all things hold together" (Col. 1:17 RSV). We know God through his Son "through whom also he created the world . . ." who not only disclosed God to us but upholds "the universe by his word of power" (Heb. 1:1-3 RSV). Christians meet God in Jesus Christ the Lord and thereafter know the God of Creation who is the same as God in the Old Testament (Gen. 1, 2; Acts 17:24). But the starting point is Jesus Christ. Christians have come to know God in Jesus Christ. They know his sovereignty; he is Lord. The Christian view of God as Creator stands on the foundation of Jesus Christ.[1]

Creation. The term "creation" suggests origin in the purpose of the Creator. Through Christ we know what the Creator is like. God is good; creation is good. Even when corrupted by man, creation is intrinsically, intentionally, or potentially good. Yet, it remains distinct in its existence. Biblical faith will have no part of metaphysical dualism which always finds a way to brand matter as evil, or with metaphysical idealism which always devises a way to blur the distinction by making the world divine. Biblical faith insists that creation is God's work, essentially good, yet distinct from and dependent upon the Creator.

Man as Creature. In biblical faith man is a creature along with

10

other creatures, but he is distinct from them because he was created in "the image of God." Man is, therefore, distinct both from God and other creatures. His "in-between" position can be precarious. He must not lose the distinction between himself and God and seek to be his own God. He must not lose the distinction between himself and other creatures. The former is rebellion, as in Genesis 3; the latter makes man a part of the animal world and all responsibility disappears. Man must not lose the distinction and become degraded into idolatry as in Romans 1 and 2. Man's destiny is "in-between" God and the world. He obeys God and is responsible for the world.

The Earth Is the Lord's. The Hebrews believed that "The earth is the Lord's and the fullness thereof, the world and those who dwell therein; for he has founded it . . ." (Psalm 24:1-2 RSV). The patriarchs had God's promise that he would give them the land of Canaan, but somehow the title forever remained in God's name. Israelites held temporary ownership and were forbidden to sell the land permanently. "The land shall not be sold in perpetuity, for the land is mine; for you are strangers and sojourners with me" (Lev. 25:23 RSV). Modern men, and particularly those of us discussing "God's plan for material things," should be reminded that it still belongs to God. We may exploit it, corrupt it, pollute it until no birds, fish, animals, or men can live on this planet, but somehow God's title remains valid after ours have expired. It is unlikely that God cares whether the gold is strewn along the stream beds in California or neatly stacked in bars in Fort Knox. His title is secure in either instance. Even if man were to accumulate "his" treasures and launch them to outer space aboard his most powerful rockets, God would not even have to make a note in his records. Man feverishly stores, "invests," and hides his treasures, but the earth is the Lord's, even the banks of Zürich and Geneva.

God Gave Us This Land. When the Israelites summarized their faith, they told what God had done for them and that ". . . he brought us to this place and gave us this land, . . ." (Deut. 26:9 RSV). They were not permitted to forget their dependence on God and were admonished, "Beware lest you say in your heart, 'My power and the might of my hand have gotten me this wealth.' You shall remember the Lord your God, for it is he who gives you power to get wealth; . . ." (Deut. 8:17-18 RSV). Belonging to God was the same as having a "portion in" the Lord and the land which he gave.[2] When the Israelites sinned against God beyond the limit of his forbearance, they lost the land; they went into captivity. Their deliverance included a restoration to the land as in the cases of the Exodus from Egypt and the Return from Babylon. When they were right with God and with

11

their fellowmen, each family dwelt in peace on its plot of land "every man under his vine and under his fig tree" (1 Kings 4:25 RSV).

The great prophets who saw clearly the sins of men and the consequent punishment, envisioned a day in which God's redemption would be complete. They described that redemption in terms of a bountiful earth. The "plowman shall overtake the reaper . . . the mountains shall drip sweet wine . . . they shall plant vineyards and drink their wine, and they shall make gardens and eat their fruit. I will plant them upon their land, and they shall never again be plucked up out of the land which I have given them, says the Lord your God" (Amos 9:13-15 RSV). Certainly a bountiful earth and material prosperity were not seen as a curse but as a gift from God.

II. The Consequences of Sin for Creation

In spite of the knowledge that all of creation is good, there are many reminders in the Scripture that wealth and things may become the occasion for sin. The prophets condemned the rich because they oppressed the poor in order to gain wealth. The author of Proverbs (28:22) exposed the superficiality of the "miserly man" who "hastens after wealth, and does not know that want will come upon him." Job wrestled with the problem of material prosperity as an index into God's favor or disfavor.

The New Testament writers had much to say about material wealth. "For the love of money is the root of all evils; . . ." (1 Tim. 6:10). John used the term "world" on occasions to designate the creation in revolt against God and warned the Christians, "Love not the world, neither the things that are in the world" (1 John 2:15), indicating that love for God and love for the world were mutually exclusive.

Jesus warned men about making their treasure the earthly kind which is transient (Matt. 6:20ff.). He indicated that man could be so anxious about "the cares of the world and the delight in riches" that the word of God would be choked in him and he would perish (Matt. 13:22). He observed that wealth appeared to prevent men from entering the kingdom (Mark 10:23). He even said, "It is easier for a camel to go through the eye of a needle, than for a rich man to enter the kingdom of God" (Matt. 19:24).

How are we to understand the apparent contradiction of a good world in which material things are sources of danger? The problem is in man.

The Fall. The account of the fall of man (Gen. 3), though not frequently mentioned in the Scripture, stands in the background of our problem of understanding creation. Man was made for better

12

things. Something dreadful happened. Man fell. Whether through pride, self-assertion, unbelief, rebellion, or inordinate love of self, man sinned so seriously that he was excluded from the Garden. It is implied that prior to the fall, man enjoyed both God and the bounty of his creation. Thereafter, sinners look back with a haunting memory that long ago something happened which disarranged all creation. Coleridge, in his "Rhyme of the Ancient Mariner," portrays a sailor who thoughtlessly killed an albatross and thereby incurred the hostility of all creation. He and his comrades shared the awful doom, the curse, the despair of existence in a world which branded them as outlaws. Biblical faith portrays man as a fugitive from the God who made him, estranged from God, his fellows, and himself. Instead of Eden with its joy and bounty, he knows a world under a curse with thorns and thistles. This fall speaks of a contradiction deep in the soul of man (Rom. 7). Man knows right but does wrong; he knows about God but flees from him.

Having lost the security of belonging to God, man grasps for security in things. In disappointment he grasps for more and begins to grasp from his fellowmen things they need which he cannot use. This is fallen existence. When man and the things of creation are separated from the Creator, fallenness results.

The Curse. Biblical faith looks upon the consequence of sin as a curse on the land (Gen. 3:14ff.). This idea has nothing to do with the occult area of spells, hexes, or black magic which is having a revival in our quasi-enlightened age. As a result of sin, man, woman, and nature enter a hostile land with fear, toil, suffering, thorns and thistles.

Creation, disturbed by sin, attempts to reject the foreign element; a kind of chaos results; it is irrational and contradictory. For instance, modern man has the means for curing many illnesses such as smallpox, but he cannot do so because his political structures, national greeds and fears, and selfishness stand as immovable barriers. He knows that war is a very ineffective way for dealing with international disputes, and in our time it is mass suicide, but we go on supporting a bankruptive military-economic enterprise whose products and plans would horrify the permanent inhabitants of the apocalyptic lake of fire. This is living under a curse. The country which produced Martin Luther and the Reformation produced the gas chambers in which 6,000,000 Jews died. Millions of Christians, as dedicated and considerate as we are, stood nearby feeling helpless to halt the horrible slaughter. This breathing the air filled with the smoke of burning human bodies is living under a curse. We marvel at our technological advances such as those which made the moon exploration possible, but we cannot clean our air, land, and water. We face extinction at the hands of our progress. This is living under a curse.

Chaos. The Hebrew word "to create" does not require the translation "out of nothing" but the theological context in the Bible does require this idea. Other non-biblical creation stories present the idea of creation as bringing order out of chaos. The biblical faith employs this motif in many ways. Sin brings about a reversion to chaos. The orderliness of Eden gives way to flight, hostility, fear, suffering, thorns and thistles. Cain kills Abel for the way he worships God. Sinful existence is chaotic; redeemed existence is a restoration of God's sovereignty over man and creation. This chaos is personified in the personage of Satan (who appears only three times specifically in the Old Testament: Zech. 3:1; Job 1:6; 1 Chron. 21:1, but often in the New Testament). This demonic power threatens man; he even tempted Jesus. Paul and John both speak of this great enemy who masquerades as the "god of this world" (2 Cor. 4:4; John 8:44). Creation becomes a demonized world to sinful man. John in the Apocalypse portrays the final destructive chaotic campaign of this old Dragon (Satan, devil, serpent) against the Lamb of God. Creation is symbolically subjected to horrible natural catastrophes but the Lamb defeats the Dragon and casts him into the lake of fire for eternity. There is a new heaven and a new earth (Rev. 21:1) in which creation is again fully obedient to God.

Loss of the Land. Man's unfaithful use of God's creation results in his loss of it. The parents of the race are expelled from Eden; Hebrews sin until they are taken away in the Babylonian Captivity. Salvation is a restoration to the land—God's creation.

III. Redemption Restores Creature and Creation to the Creator

In Christian theology the doctrines of creation and redemption are intertwined; neither can be discussed adequately without the other.

Redemption Reverses the Consequences of Sin. In both Hebrew and Christian literature, salvation is a restoration of man to God and to his fellowman. Again, man trusts and obeys God and loves and respects his fellowman. The estrangement resulting from sin is replaced by the filial relationship in which man calls God "Abba Father" (Rom. 8:15; Gal. 4:6) and man his brother. Redemption overcomes the fall and removes the curse. The world again becomes God's creation; man again receives the land as a gift from God; he rules over the land and it serves him instead of cursing him. The chaos in Creation gives way to the orderliness God intended.

Redemption Results in a "New" Creation. It is regrettable that Isaiah did not fully interpret his strange passage about the age which would come with the "shoot from the stump of Jesse." In any event, he portrayed a kind of harmony within God's creation which would replace the hostility of sinful existence. Whether he means the animals, or that animals symbolize men of peace and men of prey, he portrays a "new creation" (Isa. 65:17) in which the wolf will dwell "with the lamb," the leopard with the kid, the calf, the lion, "and the fatling together." "They shall not hurt or destroy in all my holy mountain: for the earth shall be full of the knowledge of the Lord, as the waters cover the sea" (Isa. 11:1-9).

Jesus spoke of a "new world" when he spoke of the kingdom of the Son of man (Matt. 19:28). Paul often returned to the theme of a "new creation" when he described the transformation of sinful men who believed in Christ (2 Cor. 5:17; Gal. 6:15; Eph. 2:15; 4:24).

Paul also spoke in cosmic terms of "creation" which shared both in the consequences of man's sin and in his redemption therefrom. Although interpretation is uncertain, he appears to think that all of creation is involved in Christ's redemptive work.

> For the creation waits with eager longing for the revealing of the sons of God; for the creation was subjected to futility, not of its own will but by the will of him who subjected it in hope; because the creation itself will be set free from its bondage to decay and obtain the glorious liberty of the children of God. We know that the whole creation has been groaning in travail together until now; and not only the creation, but we ourselves, who have the first fruits of the Spirit, groan inwardly as we wait for adoption as sons, the redemption of our bodies. (Rom. 8:19-23 RSV)

John knows not only of the "new birth" for individuals (John 3:3) but also of a "new creation" which includes a new heaven and earth (Rev. 21, 22). The world in its alienation from God fell under the sway of satanic power. The Lamb through suffering defeats the demonic power, destroys chaos, and restores creation. In this new creation God will dwell with men; men will obey and love God. Sorrow ends; God wipes away all tears; joy prevails. A new Eden with the river of life and the tree of life provide abundant life for men. The nations are healed by the leaves of these trees; there is nothing accursed in the new creation. God reigns forever and ever.

IV. Responsibility for Creation

The discussion of Christian stewardship should be conducted within the doctrine of creation. This keeps us related to Creator as well as to the world. It also prevents a misunderstanding of the world.

All Christians must deal with the practical problem of their relationship to the world. Those of us who teach and preach the Christian faith have the additional problem of giving a rational statement of that relationship. Christianity has suffered great harm from erroneous interpretations of the world. Some have sought to reject the world on the ground that it is evil and have persuaded themselves and others that some form of asceticism is the only way to live for God. The monastery is the most obvious form of such asceticism, but it is no more real than a form of "other-worldliness" so characteristic of Protestant life and thought. H. Richard Niebuhr's *Christ and Culture* [3] remains the classic summary of the five ways Christians have sought to be related to the "world." The "world" here is not the physical universe but the artificial environment man has imposed upon the world of nature. This volume reveals the uneasy truce, the open conflict, the life with tension, the capitulation of Christian faith to culture, and the effort of Christianity to transform culture. The problem is not with the material universe but with the "world" as man has reshaped it. This brings us to the definition of "world."

Meaning of "World." There are three words in the New Testament which become "world" in English. They are *kosmos* (world or universe), *aiōn* (age), and *oikoumenē* (the inhabited world in contrast to the uninhabited). Of these terms the word *kosmos* is the most important and has been most seriously misunderstood. It can mean the whole universe, this planet, people in general, the world at enmity with God, or the world which God loved and has sought to redeem.[4]

When John speaks of the "world" hating God and God's people, he is not speaking of the physical universe, but of fallen humanity. This world, or this evil age, is not synonomous with creation. It is creation under sin—in revolt against God. "God so loved the world that he gave his only begotten Son . . ." (John 3:16). Zoroastrian and Gnostic thought may look upon the material universe as evil; Christian theology cannot do so. Biblical teaching knows no criticism of material things; it condemns only man's misuse of them. It condemns man's exploitation of nature and men.

When Creation Becomes "World." All human existence involves a relationship with the world. Existentialist theology offers a significant interpretation of such human existence. Heidegger defined human existence as "being-in-the-world." He distinguished between authentic existence and inauthentic existence. Man lives authentically when he recognizes that he is "in" the world but maintains his distinction "from" the world. He lives inauthentically when he loses this distinction. Rudolf Bultmann has used these two terms as synonyms for life "accord-

16

ing to the spirit" and life "according to the flesh." He argues that John and Paul employ the same idea of "world" as fallen creation. He uses the sub-title "The Perversion of the Creation Into 'the World.' " [5] Fallen man attempts to live life out of the false security of this world. Christian man lives in the same material universe; but he lives out of the resources of God's creation, and he lives by faith.

A correct interpretation of Christian stewardship requires a correct and Christian understanding of God's creation. Man is a creature in God's world and is responsible for his own life and for creation (Rom. 1:25; 8:19, 20, 21, 23, 39; 1 Cor. 11:3).

A number of contemporary scholars have attempted to correct the unchristian attitude toward the material world [6] and the present age. They follow Dietrich Bonhoeffer who pleaded for a religionless Christianity [7] or a Christianity secularized from its religious moorings. Their solution may be more damaging in some aspects than the problem they seek to correct, but their effort brings to our attention that Christianity has manifested an unfriendly attitude toward the world it seeks to bring to God's salvation. This perhaps could be corrected if we could regain the Christian view of creation. Christian must cease speaking disparagingly of their world; it is God's world—or should be.

Christian Responsibility for Creation. This is our Father's world; he has given us dominion over it (Psalm 8). We should have claimed it for God. The exploitation of the earth, the pollution of its water, air, and land should have aroused Christian indignation long before the current alarm over environmental dangers. Frank Stagg [8] is correct in his observation that faulty theology has contributed to our loss of respect for nature which has resulted in exploitation and destruction by the depletion of the "soil, pollution of air and water, and the erosion of the earth's vast resources." He rightly maintains that we need to "recover the biblical doctrine that the Creator and the Redeemer are one and the same. . . . We need to recover the biblical doctrine of the material universe, that it is God's good gift to man, to be enjoyed, cultivated, and preserved, to be neither worshiped nor despised."

A genuine doctrine of Christian stewardship is based on this understanding of creation. All too often Christians have been concerned with siphoning off of the wealth of the world enough to keep their institutions thriving even if it meant compromise with the forces of the exploitation of nature. Churches can be as grasping in their quest for material benefits as the pagan world around them. Our concern is not with getting our share of the profits for the church. "The cattle on a thousand hills" are already the possession of our God. He owns the world and all that is in it. It is highly unlikely that he keeps his ledgers

17

on the basis that ten percent is his and ninety percent is ours. All is his. God is not concerned with our bookkeeping about his wealth. God is concerned that we be responsible for the whole of creation. This means the care of it and the proper distribution of its resources to those who need them. Obviously, the churches must have money if they are to carry on their work; they will have no difficulty in securing it if they can present their understanding of man's place in God's creation.

V. God's Plan—A New Creation

The only plan God has for reclaiming his creation, insofar as I know, is his plan of redemption. It is most clearly seen in Jesus Christ. It has both individual and corporate aspects, is both present and future. I am very suspicious of stewardship teaching which threatens people that God will "take" their money through illness or accident unless they give the right proportion to the church. I am much happier with the idea that all we are and have belong to God and that meaningful life is a responsible stewardship to God. Furthermore, I am convinced that a required "ten percent" tithe may be an exhorbitant demand of the widow subsisting on Social Security, and a shabby stewardship for the affluent Christian whose children are now independent. That Christian family may well afford, and enjoy doing so on a sound theological basis, to give twenty, or thirty, or fifty percent to Christian causes. I am convinced that it cannot be "Christian" stewardship regardless of the amount unless it originates in a Christian commitment and continues as a result of Christian growth.

A New Birth. Christian stewardship begins in the experience John calls a "new birth" (John 3:3) and Paul calls a "new creation" (2 Cor. 5:17). This experience is personal and individual. A man hears the Word of God, under the convicting power of the Holy Spirit, and in the context of a community of Christian believers. He comes through repentance toward God and faith in the Lord Jesus Christ to a new kind of life. With his sins forgiven, he now lives under the sovereignty of God and the lordship of Christ and in fellowship with the Holy Spirit. The "world" is God's creation again; man is God's steward again. One may get "funds" on some other basis, but Christian stewardship must begin in this experience of salvation. This is God's plan. He sent Jesus Christ. Now, he sends us.

The Church. Personal faith in Jesus Christ is never a lonely or completely "individual" affair. One hears the gospel from the church as it proclaims and witnesses. The "new birth" is in relationship to the family of God. Whether we call it "The Church" or "the churches," the "People of God," the "Body of Christ," the "Fellowship of the Holy

18

Spirit," or "a baptized body of believers," it is a part of God's plan. In this fellowship we are nourished on the Word of God and by the prayer and care of fellow Christian brothers and sisters. Here we are taught and learn about God, creation, and our part in God's creation. This is God's plan. We must learn what the church is, and be it. The immediate need for funds must be understood and taught in this light. Without this understanding, the effort is useless.

The Consummation. Christian faith demands a decision and commitment now, but it also points to the future. "Hope" is that precious word which binds us to God's plan for the future. We expect God's final redemption to be achieved in the consummation. We live in this hope. But, we know that we shall stand before God and give an account of what we did with what we had. This is true stewardship as taught in the parables of our Lord. We expect God's new creation at the end of time. We hope to hear the Lord say, "Well done! Good and faithful servant." This is a part of God's plan.

Conclusion

We believe that God is Creator of the world. This material world with all of its resources is his and has been entrusted to us. Our very nature is seen only in our being responsible to God for creation. Only in responsible stewardship do we realize our destiny. Our sinful rejection of God led us to the exploitation of creation and fellow creatures. Restoration to God means a new relationship to creation and the joyful acceptance of responsibility for its proper use.

The nature of Christian life is accurately summed up in the theme of Christian stewardship. The refusal to accept dominion over creation and the consequent responsibility is a denial of faith in God and a rejection of being human.

Responsible Christian stewardship is possible only on the basis of a sound personal experience of salvation and an informed understanding of the doctrine of creation. Such stewardship can be known and practiced only in the fellowship of God's people. Through education and persuasion we seek to enlist others in matters of practical stewardship.

Churches and their organizations certainly have the right to expect their members to support financially their tasks and endeavors. They are justified in conducting aggressive campaigns of education and persuasion in order to achieve these goals, provided they do not neglect or violate the doctrinal foundation of such stewardship response. A "get rich quick" scheme in the church may be just as detrimental as one conducted in business on the shady side of the law.

While giving to one's church is a very small part of the whole theme of Christian stewardship, it is, nevertheless, an important part. We should never hesitate to inaugurate stewardship emphases and to encourage hearty response. We can build a very persuasive case for asking people to give sacrificially to the church which is carrying out Christ's commission. We should make no apologies for asking Christians to practice genuine Christian stewardship. However, we need to remind ourselves of the theological reasons for doing so and be guided accordingly. People should give not proportionately, and cheerfully, but for the right reason.

FOOTNOTES

[1] Emil Brunner, *Dogmatics II, The Christian Doctrine of Creation and Redemption*, trans. by Olive Wyon (Philadelphia: Westminster Press, 1952), p. 52f.

[2] Joshua 22:25; See Gerhard von Rad, *Old Testament Theology*, Vol. 1, trans. by D. M. G. Stalker (New York and Evanston: Harper and Row, 1962), pp. 196ff.

[3] H. Richard Niebuhr, *Christ and Culture* (New York: Harper & Bros., 1951).

[4] *Interpreter's Dictionary of the Bible*, p. 873; *The Theological Dictionary of the New Testament*, III, 883ff.; V, 157.

[5] Rudolf Bultmann, *The Theology of the New Testament*, Vol. II, trans. by Kendrick Grobel (New York: Charles Scribner's Sons, 1955), p. 15.

[6] Harvey Cox, *The Secular City* (New York: The Macmillan Company, 1965); Carl Michalson, *Worldly Theology* (New York: Charles Scribner's Sons, 1967); John A. T. Robinson, *Honest to God* (London: SCM Press, LTD, 1963).

[7] Dietrich Bonhoeffer, *Letters and Papers from Prison* (New York: The Macmillan Company, 1953).

[8] Frank Stagg, "Orthodoxy and Orthopraxy in the Johannine Epistles," *Review and Expositor* (Fall, 1970), p. 431.

Christian Stewardship in the Light of Redemption

Ray Summers

Presuppositions to this chapter:
1. That God is the Lord of creation
2. That God is the Lord of redemption

The biblical affirmation of these presuppositions is the foundation of the biblical doctrine of stewardship. The Bible opens with an affirmation of God's creation of the heavens and the earth (Gen. 1:1). The Bible closes with an affirmation of God's creation of the new heaven and the new earth (Rev. 21:1-5 NEB)—verse 5, "Then he who sat upon the throne said, 'Behold! I am making all things new!'" And in the middle of the Bible stands Jesus' pronouncement on the continuing work of God in his creation, "My Father has never ceased his work, and I am working too" (John 5:17 NEB).

The biblical doctrine of redemption is grounded in the biblical doctrine of creation. The God who creates is the God who *re-creates* (redeems). This is dramatically and movingly demonstrated in the juxtaposition of the two songs in the enthronement scene of Revelation 4-5. In Revelation 4:11, God on the throne is worshiped as the Lord of creation,

> Worthy art thou,
>   Our Lord and our God . . .
> For thou didst create all things . . .
>   By thy will they came to be.
>   (author's paraphrase)

In Revelation 5:9-10, the Lamb before the throne is worshiped as the Lord of redemption,

> Worthy art thou,
>   To take and to open the scroll,
> For thou was slain and by thy blood

Thou didst redeem men . . .
And didst make them a kingdom
In which every man serves as a priest.
(author's paraphrase)

So the Christian doctrine of stewardship begins with these two presuppositions: God is Lord of Creation; God is Lord of Redemption.

Introduction

1. The subjects assigned to this chapter are two:
    (1) *What did sin do to thwart God's purpose for material things?* This relates to presupposition 1 with its background in the first subject. "Why did God create material things?"
    (2) *Does God have a plan to reclaim his purpose for material things?* This relates to presupposition 2 with its relation to the second question, "What is the role of material things in the life of man?"
2. The body of this chapter will be developed under two propositions: That *sinful* man says, "mine," but *redeemed* man says, "thine."

Proposition One: *Sinful* Man Says, *"Mine"*

It is the nature of the Creator to give; but it is the nature of the creature to grasp. Jesus spoke of this in comparing the Heavenly Father whose nature it is to give with human fathers whose nature it is to keep (Matt. 7:11). When Jesus said, "You who are evil" (grasping, inclined to keep rather than to give), he put his finger on the heart of the matter, that is, the matter of a sinful heart.

I. The Origin of Sin in Man's "Yes" to God's "No"

Sin entered into human experience when man chose to follow his will rather than God's will. Whereas God said, "Thou shalt not," man said, "I will." The continuing tragic story of sin's thwarting God's purpose for the total of his creation is told in man's "yes" to God's "no" and man's "no" to God's "yes."

1. *The benevolent will of the Creator* is beautifully manifest in the creation account in Genesis 1. In the same successive order which biological science recognizes today *life* came. The *first* form of life on earth was vegetation (v. 11). *Second* came marine life (v. 20). *Third* came bird life (v. 20). *Fourth* came land animals (v. 24). *Fifth*

22

came human life (v. 26). Only when he had prepared a total environment which was suitable for supplying every necessity for human existence did God say, "Let us make man." Then follows that proud and ever-challenging assertion of man's faith-understanding of his origin, "So God created man in his own image" (v. 27). And the benevolent God put his blessing upon man, "and God blessed them" (v. 28). And God charged man with the responsibility of the appropriate use of the total of his creation. And God surveyed all that he had created, and it was good—"it was very good" (v. 31).

2. *The rebellious will of the creature* is tragically manifest in the creation account in Genesis 2-3. For man's home God prepared a garden, an oasis, the beauty spot, the life-sustaining spot of the east. In that garden God put everything which man would need, and he put man there to care for the garden and to use it for his total good. That total good included the responsibility of choice. Man had a free choice of every tree in the garden except one, "Of the tree of the knowledge of good and evil, thou shalt not eat" (Gen. 2:17). It was to that "no" from the Creator that the creature responded "yes" (Gen. 3:6, "and he did eat"). "Not thy will but my will," he said in a rebel reversal of what the second Adam would later say, "Not my will but thy will" (Matt. 26:39). The decision of the first Adam meant ruin; the decision of the second Adam meant redemption (Rom. 5:12-21; 1 Cor. 15:47-49).

3. *The curse of estrangement* is a part of what sin did to thwart God's purpose for material things. The bright beauty of the creation in Genesis 1-2 is replaced by the gloom of Genesis 3—the gloom of the creature's estrangement from the Creator. The garden is there, but man cannot enter it to walk with his God. The tree of life is there, but man cannot get past those flaming swords to eat of it. His work now becomes toil; by the sweat of his once lordly brow he eats what he can wrestle from the contending thorns and thistles. And his mate realizes her privilege of motherhood at the cost of agonizing pain. Whatever else Genesis 1-3 is, it is a theological treatise on sin.

What sin did to thwart God's purpose is spelled out in the Scriptures in many ways. It is painfully evident in the every day life of man.

II. The Continuing Result of Sin in Man's Self-Will

1. *Man versus God* could well be the organizing theme for the life of sinful man. That, too, is clearly evident in those early chapters of Genesis—let the flood of Genesis 6-8, and the shameful drunkenness of Noah who survived the flood (Gen. 9:20-27), and the tower of

Babel on the plains of Shinar (Gen. 11:1-9) illustrate.

2. *Brother versus brother* reflects that continuing result of sin. Cain murdered Abel as an outgrowth of the efforts of two men to use material things in acceptable worship of God (Gen. 4:1-16). And hostility and estrangement arose between Shem, Ham, and Japheth in their differences over how to deal with the exposure of their father in his drunkenness from misuse of material things (Gen. 9:20-27). "And the beat goes on" in a never ending discord.

3. *By natural inclination,* Paul said, men are children of wrath (Eph. 2:3). What he meant was that men do not have to be taught to sin. By their natural inclination, they do those things which bring upon them the displeasure and judgment of God. There is no more effective homily on the universality of the results of sin than Paul's summation in Romans 3:10-18. He lifts excerpts from the Psalms and Isaiah and puts them together in what appears to have been a sermon:

Sin Brings

Degradation of character, verses 10-12
Degradation of speech, verses 13-14
Degradation of conduct, verses 15-17
Degradation of motive, verse 18

Ah! There is the secret of the whole matter—degradation of motive, "There is no reverence for God before their eyes." They never look to see what God wants; they look only to see what they want. For sinful man "thine" is no criterion for decision. "Mine" is the only criterion he recognizes.

III. The Use and Abuse of Material Things

What has been and is now the effect of sin on man's use of the material world? The answer is bound up in several areas.

1. *Exploitation of natural resources* is a primary one. When Jeremiah wanted to isolate one of Israel's acts of disobedience which was bringing about the Babylonian exile, he selected as an example their exploitation of their land (Jer. 25:11, 12; 29:10). When Israel had come into the land, God had commanded them to work the land (farms, vineyards, etc.) in six-year cycles and then let it rest the seventh year (Lev. 25:1-7; Ex. 23:10-11). This was for the purpose of reminding them that the ownership of the land was vested in God rather than man. God owned it; he gave it to them as a matter of stewardship. They were to allow it to lie fallow every seventh year to build itself back up—a forerunner of the idea of crop rotation today.

Israel did not keep that law. She worked the land seven years out of seven. So Jeremiah said that God would see to it that the land got its sabbath—even if it had to get it all at once! Babylon would carry Israel away captive. This would last seventy years. In a rather general way of reckoning, that would be one-seventh of the time Israel had disobeyed God in exploiting the very land which he had put under their stewardship. The land would have its sabbath.

A similar exploitation of natural resources has brought genuine woes upon our world today. Frank McGee's television documentary, "Who Killed Lake Erie?" was a terrifying commentary on exploitation and greed. The biologist, the geologist, the sociologist, and every other concerned person who is caught up in the ecological crisis of today will do well to include the theologian on his team for solving our environmental problems.[1] Those problems cannot be solved apart from a consideration of the phenomenon of sin—man's expression of self-will. Dilution of pollution is not solution.

Indeed, some biologists are charging that the Judeo-Christian culture is responsible for the entire problem because of the God-given imperatives "have dominion over" and "subdue" the earth (Gen. 1:26, 28). *Properly understood* these imperatives are the best texts for ecological preaching—they relate to use, not abuse, of the material creation. God still *owns* the land. Man holds it only as a *stewardship*. He can abuse his stewardship and bring upon himself a worse "captivity" than Israel knew in Babylon.

2. *Exploitation of one's fellow-man through greed* is an abuse of stewardship. The Old Testament has its examples. David's greed in looking beyond his harem and coveting the one wife of Uriah led him to the shameful exploitation and murder of Uriah. Nathan's allegory of "the ewe lamb" (2 Sam. 12:1-14) was an effective way of causing David to confront his sinful exploitation. Ahab wanted to buy Naboth's vineyard, but Naboth would not sell. Jezebel shamefully exploited Naboth, had him murdered, and took his vineyard as a gift to please her pouting husband (1 Kings 21:1-16).

The New Testament has its examples. Jesus denounced religious leaders who wore the outward garb of piety (Luke 20:46), but beneath that garb they wore the heart of impiety which permitted them to "devour widow's houses" (Luke 20:47). By the oppression of defenseless widows they used their social position to rob. This is a part of the neglect of "justice and love" which Jesus had charged against the Pharisees in Luke 11:41. It recalls God's complaint against those in Israel "who join house to house, who add field to field" (Isa. 5:8 RSV). An exaggerated sense of one's own importance leads to a depreciating sense of the importance of others. The next step beyond that is conscienceless robbery by exploitation of the unfortunate.

This is not a vice which is limited to ancient Israel, nor to the Pharisees of the first century, nor to the first century. It is a violation of stewardship, of trusteeship, which sadly has its counterparts today. The daily news events abound with examples of greedy exploitation of men. It is tragic when this is associated with those who name themselves Christian. Such was the case of one well-known Christian who is also well-known as an industrialist who said to a class of Baylor students, "My relationship to Christ and to the church has nothing to do with the working conditions in my plant or what I pay my employees." To say the least, in the mind of those students that man is no longer known as a "Christian industrialist"! They know that you don't keep your "religion" and your "relationships" in separate files.

3. *Exploitation as a practice which is under God's judgment* is a recurring theme in the New Testament. Jesus' parable of the rich fool (or the big fool with the little barn!) is an example (Luke 12:16-21). The farmer made a crop which exceeded his storage space. In considering his problem, he could think of only one solution—build a bigger storage space. It did not occur to him that there were hungry people all around who could have made some very practical suggestions about a solution for his surplus! Hunger was a very stark reality in Jesus' day and it is significant that Luke, whose Gospel is the most pronounced in social concern, is the one who preserved this parable. Essentially the man's sin was one of selfish unconcern and a failure to recognize his stewardship in his affluence.

The tragedy of the rich young ruler (Luke 18:18-23) was that he prized his possessions above God's way to the transcendent life. His sadness (verse 23) at not being able to follow Jesus in selfless service to needy mankind was genuine, but it did not exceed his greed.

James warned his readers of the futility of a greed which did not make the will of God an element in planning one's business (4:13-17). And he warned of the futility of a greed which prompts injustice in the exploitation of wage earners. He said that those very wages held back fraudulently were protest cries in the ears of the God of judgment (5:1-6), but that is the way of sinful man who says only, "mine."

Proposition Two: Redeemed Man Says *"Thine"*

Does God have a plan to reclaim his purpose for material things? The answer is "yes," and the plan is "redemption." But it must be redemption in the New Testament sense of the word—redemption of the total person.

I. The Redeemed as a New Creation

Properly understood, redemption has an inevitable effect on man's use of material things. That is because material things are a part of the life of the redeemed. When I put my tithes and offerings on God's altar, it is a part of my very self which I put there. My physical energies, my mental energies, my spiritual energies, are all invested in that offering; it is a *part of me* and it says that *all of me* is on God's altar.

1. *The radical renewal of redemption* leaves no part of the life of the redeemed untouched. That is the disturbing reminder of Elton Trueblood's *The Company of the Committed.* Paul spoke of the redeemed person as "a new creation" (Gal. 6:15), one who is "created in Christ Jesus" (Eph. 2:10), one who has a "new nature, created after the likeness of God" (Eph. 4:24).

There is, therefore, no area of my life that is not under the renewal which redemption brings. My relationship to my wife is that of one who is "in Christ" (Eph. 5:25-33). My relationship to my children is that of one who is a parent "in the Lord" (Eph. 6:1). My work as an employee of Texas Baptists and Baylor University has a higher motivation as one who is "rendering service with good will as to the Lord" (Eph. 6:7). Time, possessions, abilities to work, home relationships, social relationships, business relationships—all of these have been radically renewed in my experience of redemption. It is as a redeemed man that I talk to my barber, to the man who services my car, and to the officer who writes me a traffic citation for "unredeemed" driving!

2. *The sense of being owned rather than being owner* is a part of this redemption. So Paul could say to the Corinthians, "You are not your own; you were bought with a price" (1 Cor. 6:20). To the ship's officers on his voyage to Rome as a prisoner of the Emperor Nero, Paul could speak of "the God *to whom I belong*" (Acts 27:23). This carries over into the area of stewardship. Mark Twain bought a new lawn mower. A neighbor came over and asked if he might *use* it. Mark Twain answered, "Certainly; *use* it all you want to. There is one condition, though—I never permit it to be *used* away from home!" Now, Mark Twain was simply exercising the right of ownership. *He* was the owner; *he* had the right to decide the conditions under which his property was to be used! I belong to God. God has the right to determine how his property is to be used. And that means that he has the right to determine how *all* of his property is to be used.

It is at this point that we need to consider carefully the biblical concept of the tithe.[2] A good starting place is Luke 11:42 (RSV)—

.But woe to you Pharisees! for you tithe mint and rue and every herb, and neglect justice and the love of God; these you ought to have done, without neglecting the others.

and Matthew 23:23 (RSV)—

"Woe to you scribes and Pharisees, hypocrites! for you tithe mint and dill and cummin, and have neglected the weightier matters of the law, justice and mercy and faith; these you ought to have done, without neglecting the others.

Luke has this as a part of Jesus' teaching on the caravan to Jerusalem for the Passover which ended in his death. Matthew has it as a part of his denunciation of the Pharisees on Tuesday after they arrived in Jerusalem. Matthew has the sharp additional charge, "You blind guides, straining out a gnat and swallowing a camel!" (Matt. 23:24 RSV).

According to Leviticus 27:30, when the Hebrew people occupied their permanent residence in Canaan, they were to give to God one-tenth of the flocks, herds, grain, and fruit which they produced. This was to be a part of their worship and it would be used to sustain the sacrificial services in their religious practice. Through the centuries the developing legalism required minute interpretation of the law and its application. The *Mishna* (written interpretation by the rabbis) reflects just how minute this came to be. They came to interpret "seed of the land" (Lev. 27:30) to include not only the grain in the fields, but also garden vegetables. Finally, the herbs which were grown for seasoning food came to be included. It was this scrupulous attention to legal requirement which Jesus used on this occasion. Luke has "mint . . . rue . . . every herb." Matthew has "mint . . . dill . . . cummin. . . ."

Mint was a plant produced for the use of its leaves in seasoning food. *Rue* was a plant which was also produced for its leaves. They were very bitter and were used in medicines. According to the *Mishna* the rabbis taught that it was not necessary to tithe the rue. *Every herb* is the translation of a general word for any type of garden vegetable produced for leaves, roots, or seeds.

Dill was produced largely for its aromatic seeds, but the leaves and stems were also used. In the *Mishna* it was specifically subject to tithe. *Cummin* was a dwarf plant of the carrot family, but was produced, not for its roots, but for its tiny seeds.

Both Luke and Matthew stress the meticulous care of the Pharisees in tithing. For every nine mint leaves used, one was set aside for

God. For every nine relatively large dill seeds used, one was set aside for God. Likewise for every nine tiny cummin seeds used, one was set aside for God. Just to be on the safe side [you can't always trust the interpretation of these professors!] and to run no risk of violating the law, the Pharisees even tithed *rue* which the rabbis excluded from the tithing law!

Jesus was not condemning the careful stewardship reflected in the tithing of even the least material possession. He was condemning a sense of values which had lost correct perspective where God's law of possessions was concerned. Jesus understood that the tithe was meant to teach God's *total ownership.* As the land and all that it produced belonged to God, so man in his *totality* belonged to God and *all* of him, material and spiritual, was to be used for God. God's law in Leviticus 27:30 required the tithing of material things. God's law in Micah 6:8 required that in spiritual matters man "do justice . . . love kindness . . . walk humbly" before God. Jesus' concern was that, while the Pharisees held so carefully to the *material requirement* of God, they had abandoned the *spiritual requirement.* And in Jesus' mind the *spiritual* was always primary, and the *material* secondary.

"You . . . neglect justice and the love of God." In place of this, Matthew has "you have neglected the weightier matters of the law, justice, mercy, and faith." The verbs which are translated "neglect" are different. Luke's word meant to pass along beside a thing without paying attention to it. Matthew's word meant to abandon a thing, or to give it up as an object of concern. The nouns vary. Both Luke and Matthew have "justice" in first place. Basically it meant to do that which is right in relation to one's fellowman. Luke has "love of God" as a summary of the Micah passage and Matthew has "mercy and faith" as a summary. Essentially they mean the same thing.

Jesus understood God's requirement in the Micah passage in terms of spiritual matters in man's relation to his fellowman and in his relation to God. Jesus understood, further, that these two cannot be separated. To give scrupulous attention to being right with God through the tithing of material possessions, but to abandon being right with God through justice, mercy, and love for one's fellowman was to miss both God's intent and his requirement. To do so is to follow the example of the ridiculous caravan guide who kneels at the oasis to drink; he carefully pushes to one side a tiny gnat, but carelessly swallows the camel which drinks beside him! (Matt. 23:24). How blind can a man be?

Matthew has "the weightier matters of the law." The word meant primarily that which was burdensome because it was difficult to fulfil. It had come to mean that which was "heavier" in the sense of "more important" when two objects were compared. It is much easier to try to meet God's requirement by meticulous tithing of possessions. That can come to be a matter of simple arithmetic—one out of ten, and almost anyone can divide by ten! What havoc if God had required one-thirteenth instead of one-tenth! It is much harder to try to meet God's requirement by the practice of justice, mercy, and love. That is spiritual and has to do with value judgments which can never be measured by arithmetic. But according to Jesus, it is the more important way, and to fail to do it leaves one short of God's requirement, regardless of his meticulous material stewardship.

"These you ought to have done" refers to the spiritual matters of justice and love. Neither in Luke nor in Matthew can it refer to tithing. Ought is the precise rendering of a word which involved an absolute necessity if a desired end was to be realized. The desired end —meeting God's total stewardship requirement—cannot possibly be realized if one leaves off justice and mercy in his inter-human relationship.

"Without neglecting the others." *Others* refers to the tithing of material possessions. A recognition of material stewardship before God is important, though Jesus thought that the rabbis' including vegetable seeds and leaves was being a bit overcautious! Jesus was not encouraging them to stop their tithing. He was encouraging them to see the whole picture. He was condemning only such preoccupation with the tithing of material possessions that they ignored God's primary requirement of justice, mercy, and love.

Both of these requirements are *stewardship* requirements. Apart from the positive practice of justice, mercy, and love, no man can rightly claim to have met God's stewardship requirement. Am *I* a good steward? If measured by tithing of material possessions, I am. The Internal Revenue Service through my church records and cancelled checks can bear witness to that! If measured by a demonstration of justice, mercy, and love, I don't know. I try to be. It is like an ever-beckoning goal for which I reach. God is my judge as to whether or not I am succeeding. But it is a part of my stewardship.

II. The Redeemed as God's Steward

And what is this "steward" and "stewardship" of which we speak so freely?

1. *The meaning of the New Testament word translated steward* is a "house manager" (Luke 16:2, for example). It is a compound of the noun for "house" and the verb for "to divide, distribute, or apportion."

The steward was one to whom was entrusted the responsibility of properly ordering the affairs of a business; he was a trusted and responsible servant.

Correspondingly the New Testament word translated stewardship meant a house management. When the rich man in Jesus' parable in Luke 16:1-9 ordered his steward, "Turn in the account of your stewardship," he was calling for the books or records which reflected how the servant had been carrying out his responsibility. Stewardship, then, means trusteeship. As a steward of God I am a "servant" whom God has "trusted" with "responsibilities." These responsibilities relate to his "ownership." I anticipate his calling upon me to account for the way I have handled that trusteeship. Another word for that giving of account is judgment—when the creature answers to the Creator for what he has done with the trusteeship of life. It is a solemn thought, and a thoroughly biblical one.

2. *The most basic requirement* of a steward is faithfulness. While this is implicit in Jesus' many parables about stewards, it is explicit in Paul's statement in 1 Corinthians 4:2, "It is required of stewards that they be found trustworthy"—one who is "worthy" of a "trust." So Paul regarded himself as a "steward" to whom God has "trusted" the "mysteries of God"—the redemptive truth of the gospel. So was it in the case of L. R. Scarborough when he was succeeding B. H. Carroll as president of Southwestern Baptist Theological Seminary. A part of Dr. Carroll's charge to Dr. Scarborough in his new responsibility for the seminary was "Lee, keep it lashed to the Cross." That was a stewardship, and no one who knew Dr. Scarborough ever questioned his being a faithful steward.

In closing this section on stewardship and ownership, let me encourage you to read some striking and discerning quotations from some generally unexpected sources—some football coaches.[3]

Frank Broyles, University of Arkansas: "I am happy to be a tither. My tithe helps my church conduct the Lord's work, and it helps me handle more carefully my money and all other gifts with which God has blessed me. . . . I want to be a good steward. Tithing helps me achieve this goal and therefore I recommend it."[4]

Paul Dietzel, University of South Carolina: "I became convinced that the Lord meant for us to give ten percent of what we earned because of the statement that I read which, when literally translated, says that wages are piled into ten piles and one of those piles belongs to the Lord. . . . Since that time . . . I have given the first ten percent of my wages to the Lord, and it has seemed to be the most natural thing in the world to me. He gives us so very much and we really

31

have so few things that we can give back to him. Our tithes are such a small thing." [5]

Tom Landry, the Dallas Cowboys: "To fully grasp the meaning of stewardship, a Christian must accept the fact that God owns everything. . . . In all of Jesus' references to money, one idea is supreme—attitudes. . . . All that Jesus said about money can be summed up in one word: Responsibility. . . . A person cannot be a generous steward until he acknowledges the sovereignty of God and accepts his personal responsibility to him." [6]

Personally, I hope no preacher or professor ever gets to meddling with the stewardship concepts of those men! To me, they are rather sound, biblically and practically so.

III. The Redemptive Use of Material Things

Much of the preceding discussion relates to the use of material things in redemptive ways. Perhaps, however, it is appropriate to include a brief and directive, though not comprehensive and exhaustive, treatment of the specific theme—the redemptive use of material things.

1. *In specific relation to gospel proclamation* there is much in the New Testament about the redemptive use of material things. Negatively, Jesus warned against preoccupation with material things when he sent the twelve on their first preaching mission (Luke 9:1-6; Matt. 9:35—10:1-15; Mark 6:7-13), and the seventy on their preaching mission (Luke 10:1-12). They were sent to proclaim that in the presence of Jesus of Nazareth, the kingdom of God had broken into history. That was to be their total concern. They were *not* to be concerned about material provisions. Material provisions would be supplied for them by those who received their message and shared in its proclamation by extending their homes as the base of operation for the messengers.

Positively, Paul spoke often of the use of material things in the proclamation of the redemptive message. Paul, Barnabas, and Titus were "sent on their way by the church" at Antioch (Acts 15:3). This expression meant to pay one's travel expense. So Paul anticipated that when he had had some ministry in Rome, the church at Rome would speed him on his journey to Spain, an expression meaning to pay his travel expense (Rom. 15:24). Paul instructed Titus on the island of Crete to lead the churches of Crete to "speed Zenas the lawyer and Apollos on their way; see that they lack nothing" (Titus 3:13). The churches were to equip them for their missionary travels.

Many other examples could be cited. The early church accepted it as a matter of correct stewardship that they should use their material means for the proclamation of the gospel. It was because of that understanding that the gospel of God's redemption in Jesus Christ challenged all other religions in the Roman world and essentially took that world for Christ.

2. *In specific relation to gospel application* there is much in the New Testament regarding the redemptive use of material things. It was a redemptive use of material possessions which led the church at Jerusalem to the sharing life which is recorded in Acts 4:32-37. The beloved Barnabas was singled out by Luke as an illustration of people who sold possessions in order that food and clothing needs of others in the Christian fellowship might be met. Ananias and Sapphira stand as negative and tragic examples of able church members who coveted a reputation for generosity but lacked the dedication to practice it (Acts 5:1-5). They may have been the first, they were certainly not the last, church members who lied about their giving. Dr. W. O. Carver has noted that today, if all the church members who lie about their gifts should drop dead as Ananias and Sapphira did there would be a sudden pick-up in the undertaking business!

In Acts 11:27-30, Luke sets out a good foundation for a stewardship campaign in the offering which the church at Antioch sent to relieve suffering and need in Jerusalem:

The Cause—"famine . . . the brethren in Judea," vv. 28-29
The Pledges—"the disciples determined to send," v. 29
The Amount—"everyone according to his ability," v. 29
The Payment—"and they did so," v. 30
The Finance Committee—"the elders," v. 30
The Treasurers—"Barnabas and Saul," v. 30

(Let him who is without his favorite stewardship sermon outline, cast the first stone!)

In Acts 24:17, in his defense before Felix, Paul made reference to the trip which he had made from Corinth to Jerusalem (Acts 24:21) to bring an offering to his needy brethren. The story so impressed Felix that he kept Paul in prison two years hoping to get a bribe from him or his wealthy friends (Acts 24:26-27). In his Corinthian letters Paul wrote of that offering (1 Cor. 16:1-6; 2 Cor. 9:1-15). The passage in 1 Corinthians 16 is best known and most used because it relates to the program which includes such phrases as "every one of you," "put something aside in store," "as the Lord has prospered you," etc. The more neglected 2 Corinthians 9 passage is one of the most beautiful and profound stewardship passages in all of the Scriptures.

It was an offering for the saints (v. 1), i.e., an offering in application of the Christian principle of love. It was an offering in which the example of some in giving had stimulated others to give (vv. 2-5). It was an offering which recognized that bountiful blessings come from bountiful giving (v. 6 and vv. 10-12). Had you ever noted that Galatians 6:7—"Be not deceived; God is not mocked: for whatsoever a man soweth that shall he also reap"—is a stewardship passage on "paying the preacher" (v. 6)? Compare it with this 2 Corinthians 9:6 passage.

This passage recognizes that giving is: (1) personal, "each one must do as he has made up his mind"; (2) unforced, "not reluctantly or under compulsion"; (3) joyful, "for God loves a cheerful giver." Transliterate that Greek word which is translated "cheerful," and you have the English word "hilarious." *That* is the kind of giver God loves!

The passage recognizes, too, that such giving glorifies God, acknowledges the implications of the gospel of Christ, establishes the principle of mutual helpfulness, and is stimulated by the memory of God's own "inexpressible gift" to us. Paul would have liked our stewardship slogan, "You cannot outgive God."

James (2:18-26) held that the most convincing demonstration of one's faith is his compassionate response to the need of others. To his fellow Jews who professed their orthodoxy in their confession in the Shema, "Hear ye O Israel, the Lord your God is one," James responded that such "orthodoxy" can be very empty. Even the demons are "orthodox" enough to recognize the reality of God, "and shudder," precisely, "their hair stands on end." But if one would be more orthodox than the demons, let him demonstrate his faith in giving to the needy —an application of the gospel of the kind of which Jesus spoke in his parable of the sheep and the goats. Redemptive use of material things includes gospel "application" as well as gospel "proclamation." In 1939 at a meeting of the Southern Baptist Convention in Oklahoma City, I stored in my memory bank a statement from a sermon by Dr. Perry F. Webb:

A religion that does not look out, reach out,
    lift out, and help out,
Is washed out!
That is stewardship!

Conclusion

Does God have a plan to reclaim his purpose for material things? Yes. And that plan can be summarized in two words—"you" and "yours." And when God really gets "you" he has "yours."

CHRISTIAN STEWARDSHIP IN THE LIGHT OF REDEMPTION

Presuppositions to this chapter:
1. That God is the Lord of creation
2. That God is the Lord of redemption

Introduction to this chapter
1. What did sin do to thwart God's purpose for material things? This relates to presupposition 1 (above) with its background in the subject "Why did God create material things?"
2. Does God have a plan to reclaim his purpose for material things? This relates to presupposition 2 (above) with its relation to a second subject of "What is the role of material things in the life of man?"

Body of this chapter:

PROPOSITION ONE: SINFUL MAN SAYS *"MINE"*

I. The Origin of Sin in Man's "Yes" to God's "No"
1. The benevolent will of the Creator
2. The rebellious will of the creature
3. The curse of estrangement

II. The Continuing Result of Sin in Man's Self-will
1. Man versus God
2. Brother versus brother
3. By natural inclination, children of wrath
(Develop Paul's summary, Rom. 3:10-18, of the message of the O.T. prophets)

III. The Use and Abuse of Material Things
1. Exploitation of natural resources
(Israel's refusal to let the land have its "sabbath"—special reference to Jeremiah)
2. Exploitation of fellow-man through greed
(O.T. examples; examples in Gospels; examples in Paul's epistles)
3. Exploitation under God's judgment
(Jesus' parable of the rich fool; the tragedy of the rich young ruler; James' warning concerning greed, 4:13-17, and injustice through exploitation, 5:1-6)

PROPOSITION TWO: REDEEMED MAN SAYS *"THINE"*

I. The Redeemed as a New Creation
1. The radical renewal of redemption ("all things have become new")
2. The sense of being owned rather than being owner

II. The Redeemed as God's Steward
1. The meaning of the terms "steward" and "stewardship" in the New Testament
2. The most basic characteristic of the steward—faithfulness
III. The Redemptive Use of Material Things
1. In specific relation to gospel proclamation
2. In specific relation to gospel application

Conclusion

God's plan to reclaim his purpose for material things includes both:
1. "You"
2. "Yours"

FOOTNOTES

[1] See *The Student* (January 1971), Eric Rust, "From the Garden to the Desert, the Quest for a Theology of Ecology" and R. Lofton Hudson, "Am I My Brother's Ecologist?"

[2] The following discussion on the tithe is taken from my forthcoming book *The Gospel of Luke.*

[3] *Baptist Men's Journal* (October, November, December, 1970).

[4] *Ibid.,* p. 7.

[5] *Ibid.,* p. 8.

[6] *Ibid.,* p. 9.

BIBLIOGRAPHY

Applegarth, Margaret. *Twelve Baskets Full.* New York: Harper and Brothers, 1957.

Bockleman, Eleanor. *The Stewardess.* Columbus: Warburg Press, 1957.

Fletcher, Joseph J. (ed.). *Christianity and Property.* Philadelphia: Westminster Press, 1947.

Hatch, C. W. *Stewardship Enriches Life.* Anderson, Ind.: Warner Press, 1952.

Kantonen, T. A. *A Theology of Christian Stewardship.* Philadelphia: Muhlenberg Press, 1956.

Kauffman, Milo. *The Challenge of Christian Stewardship.* Scottdale, Pa:. Herald Press, 1955.

McRae, Glenn. *Teaching Christian Stewardship.* St. Louis: Bethany Press, 1954.

Rolston, Holmes. *Stewardship in the New Testament Church.* Richmond: John Knox Press, 1966.

Smith, Roy. L. *Stewardship Studies.* Nashville: Abingdon Press, 1954.

The Why and Wherefore of Things

Jack Taylor

A. WHY DID GOD CREATE THINGS?

Introduction

It is debatable as to whether or not this question can be answered in any other than a speculative manner. From the standpoint of the external knowledge of man it is indeed unanswerable. It is an interesting question despite the fact that we cannot deal with specific scientific and tangible answers. To seek to know the sovereign mind and state the reason for sovereign actions is much more than a human mind can accomplish.

There are, however, within the implications of Holy Scripture and the character of God some helpful hints that we would do well to study as we seek to answer this question. For this reason we will seek to stay close to the Scriptures.

Our first assignment to be faced, obviously, is the definition of the term "things." We shall take for our study the position that our reference to "things" is inclusive of everything nonhuman in our existence. Thus we would include in this designation not only the inanimate things in man's surroundings but the animal world as well. This will be especially helpful when we come to suggest that man's accommodation is among the purposes of God in creating things.

Before we state some basic presuppositions relating to our study it is extremely helpful to remember the eternal nature of Christ. John says it well when he states, "Before anything else existed, there was Christ, with God. He has always been alive and is himself God. He created everything there is—nothing exists that he didn't make" (John 1:1-3 Living Bible).

Some foundational claims upon which we will build our study are:
1. God created all things.
2. The Pre-Incarnate Christ was involved in all creative processes.

3. Everything created was good.

4. Everything created, thus, had a purpose in God's universe.

It will be noticed that these same foundational claims will be vital in covering the question of what is the role of things in the life of man?

We will consider three general categories in seeking to answer the question, why did God create things. The categories are: the glory of God, the good of man, and the exaltation of Christ.

I. The Glory of God

A. H. Strong states, "Infinite wisdom must, in creating, purpose to itself the most comprehensive and most valuable of ends, the end most worthy of God and most fruitful in good." Because there is no higher glory to seek than himself, the supreme end of creation is the glory of him above whom there is no other. God is justifiably the "Supreme Egotist" committed to the seeking of his own glory. "I am the Lord, that is my name: and my glory will I not give to another (Isaiah 42:8). Rightfully, then, the psalmist declares, "The heavens declare the glory of God and the firmament showeth his handiwork" (Psalm 19:1).

George Gordon in *New Epoch for Faith* states, "God is necessarily a being of ends. The moment that one concludes that God is, it appears certain that he is a being of ends. The universe is alive with desire and movement. Fundamentally throughout it is an expression of will. And it follows, that the ultimate end of God in human history must be worthy of himself." Thus he agrees with Strong that God's glory is a primary end in the creation of things. We shall look two directions for evidence of this claim that God's glory is a primary end of creative processes: (1) The testimony of Scriptures, and (2) The testimony of reason.

1. The testimony of Scriptures

Romans 11:36 "To him, are all things."

1 Corinthians 15:28 "And when all things shall be subdued unto him, then shall the Son also be subject unto him that put all things under him, that God may be all in all."

Revelation 4:11 "Thou art worthy, O Lord, to receive glory and honour and power: for thou hast created all things, and for thy pleasure they are and were created."

Isaiah 60:21 "Thy people also shall be all righteous: they shall inherit the land for ever, the branch of my planting, the work of my hands, that I may be glorified."

Romans 9:23 "And that he might make known the riches of his glory on the vessels of mercy, which he had afore prepared unto glory."

2. The testimony of reason

It would appear logical to conclude that there are some obvious evidences that the glory of God is the chief end of creation.

Observation "A". God's glory is the only end actually and perfectly attained in the universe. Wisdom and omnipotence cannot choose an end which is destined to be forever unattained. God will have his way! Again A. H. Strong declares, "God's supreme end cannot be the happiness of creatures, since many are miserable and will be miserable forever. God's supreme end cannot be the holiness of creatures, for many are unholy here and will be unholy forever. But while neither the happiness nor the holiness of creatures is actually and perfectly attained, God's glory is made known and will be made known in both the saved and the lost. This then must be God's supreme end in creation."

Observation "B". God's glory is the end intrinsically most valuable. The good of God's creatures is insignificant compared to this. Because God can choose no greater end, he must choose for his and himself.

Observation "C". His own glory is the only end which consists with God's independence and sovereignty. If anything in the creature is the last end of God, God is dependent on the creature. But since God is dependent only on himself, he must find in himself his chief end.

Observation "D". His own glory is an end which comprehends and secures, as a subordinate end, every interest in the universe. The interests of the universe are bound up in the interests of God. The happiness or holiness of creatures is non-existent except God be sovereign and be recognized as such.

Observation "E". God's glory is the end which in a right moral system is proposed to creatures. We are made in his image. All that we are and all that is around us, then, is made to reflect the glory of the One in whose image we are created. The beginning of all religion is the choosing of God's end as our end. This means giving up happiness as a primary pursuit and choosing devotion to God as the chief end of life.

Now, before we leave this point dealing with the glory of God, let us not make the mistake of being unfair with God. The best end of man is for God to seek his own glory. We gain everything by it—he nothing except so far as it is his own will that we should gain what he desires to bestow upon us. God's love makes him a self-expressing being. This self-expression is not selfishness but benevolence. As a true poet forgets himself in his work, so God does not manifest himself for the sake of what he can make by it. Self-manifestation is an end in itself. But God's self-manifestation comprises all good to his creatures. Thus we are brought to our second reason for God creating things . . . namely,

II. The Good of Man

The crown of God's creation is man. It seems that in creation God is preparing for the consummative act of creation which is man. All things are made ready, day and night, earth and sky. The animals are created. Everything is good! Then God created man. He said to man, "Behold, I have given you every herb bearing seed, which is upon the face of all the earth, and every tree, in which is the fruit of all tree yielding seed; *to you it shall be for meat*" (accommodation suggested) (Gen. 1:29). The key statement in that verse seems to be, "I have given you. . . ."

In the expanded story of man's creation in Genesis 2, God plants a garden and places man in it. The record is that "God . . . put him in the garden of Eden to dress it and to keep it" (Gen. 2:15). God further clarified, "Of every tree of the garden thou mayest freely eat; but of the tree of knowledge of good and evil, thou shalt not eat of it" (Gen. 2:16b-17). The significant consideration for our study here is that God made all the trees of the garden available for the accommodation of man. It is also meaningful to notice that after each facet of God's creation before man it is stated, "And God saw that it was good." After man was created and given dominion over the creation God had made, it is stated, "And God saw every thing that he had made, and behold it was *very* good" (Gen. 1:31).

Not only has all that God made been made available to man but in God's economy all things given to man work *together* for his good. "And we know that all things work together for good to them that love the Lord, to them who are the called according to his purpose" (Rom. 8:28).

The ultimate question here is, "What is man's good?" It is here that we return to our first point. Man's good is God's glory. So we may say that God's glory includes this point as it will the following point. We cannot get away from God's glory. Man's chief end is to glorify God.

Man comes to this "good" in the following manner. He is not good in his unregenerate condition. He can never be good in that condition. He must be made "holy"; that is, he must be cleansed and set apart

40

for divine entry. He needs to be "born again" and in this new birth becomes the depository of divine life. The Bible literally designates saints as "holy ones." They are ones who have been entered by divine life.

When man is redeemed, that is, made again a part of God's plan, he reenters the great pattern of the universe for God's glory. He thus discovers his greatest good. He finds then that God's great order of things, these things belong to him in a new and wonderful way because he belongs to God.

III. Christ's Exaltation

Our first point centered around God's glory. It undergirds or over-shadows these last two. From the standpoint of time in God's order of things we come to the most significant part of our study. Let us look at some Scriptures which will be of help in this consideration:

> *Ephesians 1:10* "And this was his purpose; that when the time is ripe he will gather us all together from wherever we are—in heaven or on earth—to be with him in Christ, forever." (Living Bible)
> *Colossians 1:18b-19* "So that he (Jesus) is first in everything for God wanted all of himself to be in his Son." (Living Bible) The King James Version says, "That in all things he might have the preeminence."

The lordship of Christ is central in the Scripture. "For to this end Christ both died, and rose, and revived that he might be Lord both of the dead and living" (Rom. 14:9). This being true, we can safely assume that his exaltation being the end of his passion and resurrection, so the creation of things might be assumed to include the same. "That he might be Lord" is not only the only acceptable theme of man's existence but the only factor which makes "things" make sense. Examine this Scripture well: "And that every tongue should confess that Jesus Christ is Lord, to the glory of God the Father" (Phil. 2:11).

Another scriptural evidence that seems to confirm the claim that things are created to exalt Christ is found in the Scripture which says, "Christ himself is the Creator who made everything on heaven and earth, the things we can see and the things we can't; the spirit world with its kings and kingdoms, its rulers and authorities; all were made for Christ for his own use and glory. He was before all else began and it is his power that holds everything together" (Col. 1:16-17 Living Bible). Three glorious facts are made clear here:

1. Everything was made *by* Christ.

2. Everything was made *for* Christ.
3. Everything is held together in a purposeful whole by his power.

Thus we see that the end of things is the glory of Christ. This being consistent with the glory of God we have a picture of the marvelous unity of God which finds his glory, man's good, and Christ's exaltation all in accord with himself.

Conclusion

Two obvious questions face us as we conclude our study of the reason for God's creating things.
1. What happened to thwart God's purpose for things?
2. What needs to happen to restore the purpose of God amid the things he has created?

That the purpose of God has been thwarted is a fact much in evidence. The prostitution of things to God's reproach and man's shame is a sad and repeated fact in our day. It all began in man's choice to be independent. This choice was what, in fact, took place when he chose to take of the fruit of the tree of knowledge of good and evil. The two trees are ever in our gardens. Between them we are constantly choosing. We are choosing Christ or self. The choice is forever facing us. The choice to trust self is the choice to take the things that surround us and use them to our selfish advantage. This is to prostitute them. Thus there is imbalance in God's order of things. Chaos reigns. Disorder develops. There is frustration within man and within his world. The things that God placed around him have become ends in themselves instead of markers leading to relationsips with the Creator.

The restoration of the purpose of God is what salvation is all about. The work of redemption is a unifying work. With the salvation of man the whole purpose of things begins to be expressed. The glory of God is fulfilled, the good of man is accomplished, and the exaltation of Christ is brought about. Within the context of that relationship all that God made to be an ordered whole comes into focus. Thus as man submits himself to God, receives Christ as Saviour, allows the Holy Spirit to control his life, and releases the Christ within through his life there is vital and powerful *purpose*. We join God's vast plan when we are redeemed to be what we were made to become. Only within this context can things be seen to fulfil the role for which they were created. It is indeed a literal truth that Christ in our hearts is the only hope of glory (Col. 1:27). Only as Christ comes to live in our lives—*resident, reigning,* and *released*—does the order that God intended come together.

It is as the Spirit of God enters the creation of God through man and controls man's life in its totality that the purpose of things truly comes to light.

To answer the question to one's intellectual satisfaction as to the purpose of things is quite beside the point. We must not leave the subject before we declare that all spiritual experience is based on spiritual knowledge. To know the purpose of God, whether it be by implication or direct revelation, is incomplete. *Spiritual* satisfaction is the aim of this study. Jesus said, "If any man will come after me, let him deny himself, and take up his cross daily, and follow me" (Luke 9:23). It is in choosing against ourselves (denying ourselves), taking the place of death to ourselves (taking up the cross), and choosing his will in advance for our lives (following him) that we discover to our spiritual satisfaction why God created things.

B. WHAT IS THE ROLE OF THINGS IN THE LIFE OF MAN?

Introduction

Man is surrounded by things. We have defined "things" under the previous question as everything nonhuman in our existence. This would include every object, animate and inanimate, in our world. Thus all that surrounds us—plants, animals, bodies of water, the atmosphere, the elements, as well as that which we have made by our own hands—is included. It is obvious upon the very mention of the subject of things as they relate to man that we have come upon the problem which is of front-page interest in our world. The word "ecology" was an unknown word except to the dictionary until a brief time ago. The word is defined thusly: "the science concerned with the interrelationships between organisms and their environments" or "the totality or pattern of relations between organisms and their environments." Thus as we come to discuss the intended role of things in the life of man, we must in the process discuss two very important questions: (1) Assuming that the intended role of things has been all but obliterated, what has been the cause? and (2) How and when can we expect this original divine purpose and order of things to be restored?

We shall discuss the first question in the introduction and the latter one in the conclusion.

In answer to the first question we are assuming that things had a direct and divine purpose in man's existence. God created the world and all that is in it. He created the sun, the moon, the stars, and the earth. He furnished the earth very elaborately with the right kind of atmosphere, resources, animal life, elements, and planted a beautiful garden. Then he created man, just right for his world. He could breathe its air, enjoy his surroundings, live off the earth's resources, and have fellowship with God. His world was "good" and when God placed man in the world it was "very good." It seems that in man God added the consumate touch to creation. He was the crown of God's creation.

When God made man, he said to him, "I am going to equip you both physically and mentally to rule over the earth beneath your feet. I will give you mind to enjoy its mysteries and hands to subdue and utilize its resources. The one thing I will not give to you is the deep understanding of how all this will fit together. In the place of consumate knowledge I will endow you with the capacity to depend (faith) and to love. This will mean that you must put your hand in mine in total trust and my will will be your will forever." Now in this world in which man was placed he was faced with a decision. To make a legitimate decision he must have two choices. God mentioned two trees in this beautiful garden in which man was placed. One was the tree of life. Man could eat of this tree. There was also the tree of knowledge of good and evil. Man was forbidden to eat of this tree. To do so would be to assert his independence from God. The rest is history. The serpent (Satan) beguiled Eve and Adam and with eyes wide open they committed the sin that broke the fellowship of God and with it the original purpose God had for man and the things in his world. Man chose the route of his own knowledge instead of divine revelation. He was appealed to on the basis of "being a god" himself. Thus, man, by wilful choice, selected himself to be the master of his life. The results of this tragic decision are more manifold than we would ever be able to assess this side of heaven. Some of the obvious consequences were:

1. Enmity between the seed of Satan and seed of woman
2. Multiplied sorrow for the woman
3. The ground was cursed
4. Death reigned
5. Man was banished from the garden.

Thus a lower order of life than God intended was brought about on the earth as rebellious man would be assigned the task of tilling a rebellious earth in the sweat of his face. Thus we have the answer to the cause which has brought about the accumulated effect of disorder and imbalance in our world today.

Now, all of a sudden, in the latter part of the twentieth century, the interest is on a subject that has been thousands of years in the making. Man lost the privilege of dominion, and the earth was thrown into chaos and confusion. Selfish man began his rape of the great earth God gave him, exploiting it to the limit of his intelligence. He has with each succeeding generation handed the next one a more worn-out, barren, polluted world than the one before. Thus, today we have in the things God placed around us for specific purposes involving his glory, polluted air, poisoned waters, barren wastes, and purpose-less lives.

As man was properly related to the God of the universe, he began to discover the full purpose of God in things. As this relationship was broken, there came misuse, abuse, and confusion. Though God sur-rounded man with things that were good, man ceased to be good because he ceased to be godly. He then began to take good things and prostitute them to bad ends. He sought to establish his own identity as opposed to God. He now continues to seek and assert his own inde-pendence by gathering a mass of things as his own possessions. In doing so he feels, falsely so, that he has achieved security and may further shield himself against the need of God.

Let us come to discuss specifically the possible role of things in the life of man. We will observe this role under our divisions: I. The Reve-lation of God, II. The Accommodation of Man, III. The Gratification of Both, and IV. The Lordship of Christ.

I. The Revelation of God

Romans 1:20 says, "Since earliest times men have seen the earth and sky and all that God made, and have known of his existence and eternal power. So they will have no excuse when they stand before God at Judgment Day." (Living Bible)

Built within the structure of the universe is order. Even without the Scripture there is the built-in suspicion that God "is up to some-thing" . . . that he is using the earth as a great laboratory to work out a vast plan beyond all our human capacity to understand or engineer. From the smallest atom to the largest construction in God's earth there is obvious purpose and order. We dealt with the subject of God's glory in the previous section on "Why Did God Create Things?" We will refer to a portion of that study in this observation. A part of the pattern of revealed glory is that of making known his wisdom, his power, and his holy name. "He who made all things had secretly planned from the very beginning. And his reason? To show to all rulers of heaven how perfectly wise he is" (Eph. 3:9-10 Living Bible). God has affirmed himself in creation. Self-affirmation means self-communication.

Man's chief end is to glorify God. A little lad came dangerously close to the truth when he misread that part of the catechism and said, "Man's chief end is to glorify God and to annoy him forever." "Enjoy" should have been the word but too many times "annoy" is what man does. For man to discover his chief purpose he must, of course, have revelation. It is through his works that God chooses to reveal himself. The psalmist declares, "Great is the Lord, and greatly to be praised; his greatness is unsearchable. One generation shall praise thy works to another, and shall declare thy mighty acts. I will speak of the glorious honour of thy majesty, and of thy wondrous works" (Psalm 145:3-5). When the psalmist further considered God's self-disclosure he stated, "When I consider thy heavens, the work of thy fingers, the moon and the stars, which thou hast ordained; what is man, that thou art mindful of him? and the son of man, that thou visitest him? For thou hast made him a little lower than the angels, and hast crowned him with glory and honour. Thou madest him to have dominion over the works of thy hands; thou hast put all things under his feet (Psalm 8:3-6).

God's great power is evidenced throughout his creation. The weeping prophet, Jeremiah, said, "He hath made the earth by his power, he hath established the world by his wisdom, and hath stretched out the heavens by his discretion" (Jer. 10:12). Paul includes among the disclosures of God through the creative processes, "For the invisible things . . . are clearly seen, being understood by the things that are made, even his eternal power and godhead" (Rom. 1:20).

As to possession, the psalmist said, "The earth is the Lord's, and the fulness thereof; the world, and they that dwell therein" (Psalm 24:1). The man whose mind is open sees the mark of God on the things surrounding him.

Closely linked to God's revelation of himself through things is the revelation of man's responsibility to God in the things with which he has been endowed.

In the matter of stewardship, which is the care of another's possessions, God clearly reveals his capabilities as we affirm our faith. As we learn the grace of giving out of a cheerful heart, God reveals his wonderful plan of provision. "And God is able to make all grace abound toward you; that ye, always having all sufficiency in all things, may abound unto every good work" (2 Cor. 9:8).

Thus, God's self-revelation is primary in the life of man.

II. The Accommodation of Man

This division of study generally corresponds with the division in the previous section entitled, "Why Did God Create Things?"

Divine providence includes all his creation, the crown of which is man. Fundamental in the consideration of the purpose of things is the area of *normal provision.* In Genesis 1:29 is this word, " . . . to you it shall be for meat." It is a very matter-of-fact truth that all things seem to fit together until we begin to investigate more closely. It then becomes downright remarkable. Here is man, a complex creature indeed. His system demands all sorts of exacting responses from the world around him. The air, the water, the food, and his environment as a whole must be right for him to exist. Is it one great cosmic accident that the air is just the right texture, the substance the earth produces the exact requirement the need demands, or is there a great plan of providence whereby God in his glorious unity created it all with a wonderful purpose in mind? We affirm that it is the latter! God has a purpose, man is a part of that purpose. In pursuit of that purpose God provides for man's normal needs.

Innate with the framework of God's creation is the principle of mutual beneficence. If a man is a steward of another's (God's) possessions he then must respond to others' needs as that One who owns it all would. It is in giving that the universe continues. The earth is one great picture of giving. The sun gives its rays. The earth gives its fruit. The animal world produces its own kind. The earth does not lose by giving; it gains. Jesus taught a principle, vital to existence, when he said, "He that saves his life shall lose it; but he that loses his life for my sake, the same shall find it." The verse we quoted earlier is appropriate here (2 Cor. 9:8). Let us examine it in its statements.

"And God is able to make all grace abound toward you. . . ." This is not an end in itself. God has a more delightful purpose than making our reception the end of his grace. The purpose follows.

". . . that ye, always having sufficiency in all things, may abound unto every good work." There is the purpose stated. That we might be utilitarian in God's great plan for his universe.

We have considered the accommodation of man in normal provisions and in meeting the needs of others. Let us now look briefly at the matter of creature comfort. God wants his creatures to be happy and enjoy the earth. He is not a cosmic grandfather who is so out-of-sorts that he does not want anybody to enjoy anything. He delights in the joy of his creatures. Jesus was a joyous person. In John 15:11 he said, "These things have I spoken unto you, that my joy might remain in you, and that your joy might be full." Paul encourages young Timothy with this fact. "God, who giveth us richly all things to enjoy" (1 Tim. 6:17).

III. The Gratification of Both

In the process of the revelation of God and the accommodation of man, both God and man are gratified. Let us have a look at what might be properly called the "divine flow." God creates, gives, and thereby reveals. Man receives, responds responsibly, utilizes, and returns to God that designated. God is glorified, and rewards man. This gratifies both God and man. Let us observe what the Bible says about some of the rewards of God:

1. Riches and honour for fear and humility. "By humility and fear of the Lord are riches, and honour, and life" (Prov. 22:4).
2. Substance and treasures for love of God. "That I may cause those that love me to inherit substance; and I will fill their treasures" (Prov. 8:21).
3. Thorough provision for kingdom seeking. "But seek ye first the kingdom of God, and his righteousness; and all these things shall be added unto you" (Matt. 6:33).

IV. The Lordship of Christ

In considering the role of things in the life of man, we cannot leave the subject without coming to the lordship of Christ. The lordship of Christ is the pyramid peak toward which all creation moves. Observe some Scriptures, some of which we have already mentioned:

Romans 14:9 "For to this end Christ both died, and rose, and revived, that he might be Lord, both of the dead and living."
Philippians 2:9-11 "Wherefore God also hath highly exalted him, and given him a name which is above every name: that at the name of Jesus every knee should bow, of things in heaven, and things in earth, and things under the earth; and that every tongue should confess that Jesus Christ is Lord to the glory of God the Father."
Ephesians 1:10 "That in the dispensation of the fulness of times he might gather together in one all things in Christ, both which are in heaven, and which are in earth; even him."

It is within the context of the economy of things that God works out the program of Christ's lordship in the life of man.

Conclusion

In God's glorious economy he seeks the fellowship of man. Things play a vital role in the fellowship . . .

> . . . in INITIATING IT . . . by revealing himself through things;
> . . . in CONTINUING IT . . . by the accommodation of man's need and man's continued response as a steward; and,
> . . . in CULMINATING IT through the temporal and eternal gratification of both God and man through the lordship of Christ.

It is within the redemptive relationship that man begins to discover the proper role of things in his life. Only in Christ do things fit together in an ordered whole. "By him all things consist" (Col. 1:17).

In closing let us approach the answer to the second question posed at the beginning, namely, "How and when can we expect this original divine purpose and order of things to be restored?" It is the assertion of this paper that such an accomplishment is going to be brought about. There are necessarily two parts to the answer. As man discovers the blessed principles of his relationship to God through Christ he finds that a Spirit-controlled life is the beginning of the solution to the problem of ecology. It is the accumulated result of man's sin and negligence, selfishness and incapacity to finally care that has brought about the vast problem of pollution facing us. It is man's worship of materialism that keeps him from having an abandoned interest in solving the problem. However, when man discovers that his purpose, under God, is an eternal purpose, he develops respect for the creation of God and with it begins to commit himself to be a part of the solution.

All of man's schemes for cleaning up his world without any view to the will of God will fail. There may be intermittent improvement but the end of human schemes that do not reckon on God are bound to fail. That God's redemptive plans involve this old world is more than a suspicion. "For we know that the whole creation groaneth and travaileth in pain together until now" (Rom. 8:22). The Living Bible rendering of the verses surrounding verse 22:

> For all creation is waiting patiently and hopefully for that future day when God will resurrect his children. For on that day thorns and thistles, sin, death, and decay—the things that overcame the world against its will at God's command—will all disappear, and the world around us will share in the glorious freedom from sin which God's children enjoy (Rom. 8:19-21).

It is in the midst of those conditions, and ony then, that we shall fully know the original intended purpose of things in the life of man. Toward that day we now look . . . when the kingdoms of this world shall become the kingdom of our Lord and of his Christ. Then we shall know!

OUTLINE
A. WHY DID GOD CREATE THINGS?

I. The Glory of God

God is committed to his own consistency. He cannot be consistent and seek any thing other than his own glory. Thus, the primary purpose of God in creating things is the revelation of his glory.

1. His glory shown by revealing himself through things. "For the invisible things . . . of the world are clearly seen, being understood by the things that are made" (Rom. 1:20).
2. His glory shown by revealing himself through man as he is related to things.

II. The Good of Man

"And we know that all things work together for good to them that love God, to them who are called according to his purpose" (Rom. 8:28).

1. God gives all things for man. "How shall he not with him also freely give us all things" (Rom. 8:32).
2. God sees to it that all things work together for good. (Rom. 8:28).
3. God's goal for us is maturity in Christ. "That we should be to the praise of his glory" (Eph. 1:12).

III. Christ's Exaltation

1. An exaltation based on unity. "That in the dispensation of the fulness of times he might gather together in one all things in Christ" (Eph. 1:10).
2. An exaltation issuing from God's good pleasure. "For it pleased the Father that in him should all fulness dwell" (Col. 1:19).
3. An exaltation fulfilling God's purpose. ". . . that in all things he might have the preeminence" (Col. 1:18).

B. WHAT IS THE ROLE OF THINGS IN THE LIFE OF MAN?

I. The Revelation of God

1. Revelation of God's nature
   (1) Purposeful
   (2) Powerful
   (3) Possessive of all
2. Revelation of God's expectations
   (1) Man's acknowledgement of God's ownership
   (2) Man's acknowledgement of his own stewardship

SUMMARY: Romans 1:20 declares, "For the invisible things of him from the creation of the world are clearly seen, being understood by the things that are made, even his eternal power and Godhead." Thus a very primary role of things in the life of man is found in God's disclosure of himself to man through things which he has created. God then uses things to communicate his purpose and his love.

II. The Accommodation of Man

1. For normal provision. (Gen. 1:29. "And God said, Behold I have given you every herb bearing seed, which is upon the face of the earth, and every tree . . . yielding seed; to you it shall be for meat.")
2. For meeting the needs of others. (2 Cor. 9:8, 11. "And God is able to make all grace abound toward you; that ye, always having sufficiency in all things may abound unto every good work. Being enriched in every thing to all bountifulness, which causeth through us thanksgiving to God.")
3. For creature comfort. (1 Tim. 6:17. ". . . the living God, who giveth us richly all things to enjoy.")

III. The Gratification of Both

Things play a vital role in the process of mutual gratification of both God and man in their relationship. God creates and gives; man responds responsibly, properly utilizes and returns a portion; and, God then rewards.

1. God creates things and man.
2. God gives things to man as their master.
3. Man acknowledges his responsibility.
4. Man properly uses and returns a token to God.
5. God rewards.
   (1) Riches and honour and life for fear and humility. (Prov. 22:4. "By humility and fear of the Lord are riches, and honour, and life.")
   (2) Substance and treasures for love of God. (Prov. 8:21. "That I may cause those that love me to inherit substance; and I will fill their treasures.")

(3) Thorough provision for kingdom-seeking. (Matt. 6:33. "Seek ye first the kingdom of God, and his righteousness; and all these things shall be added unto you.")

IV. The Lordship of Christ

The Place of Material Things in the Purpose of God and the Life of Man

J. Leo Green

A. The Problem

In a papal Bull issued on December 25, 1961, Pope John XXIII said: "At a time when mankind is at a turning point, entering a new age, the Church is faced with tasks of immense gravity and vastness, as she was in the most tragic times in her history. We have to bring into contact with the life-giving and perpetual forces of the Gospel this modern world, a world glorying in its progress in the fields of technology and science, but suffering consequences in the temporal order, which some men have tried to regulate and organize apart from and without God. The result is that modern society is distinguished by a great material progress unmatched by similar progress in the sphere of morality. Because of this there has been a weakening of spiritual values, and from this springs the search, more or less exclusively, for worldly pleasures, which advancing technology so easily provides for all."

Observe in the Pope's pronouncement the recurrence of the key word *technology*. The modern world cannot be described apart from it. Note, too, the allusion to mankind's being at a turning point in history, the entry of a new age. This age is being called by many "The Age of Technology" or "The Socio-Technic Age." Recall, also, the Pope's reference to the moral and spiritual decline accompanying the advance of technology. To discerning people it is apparent that America is in the throes of an unprecedented moral and spiritual upheaval. For this upheaval the abuses of technology may be held, in large measure, gravely responsible. But the situation is not confined to our country. It is present in all lands where technological progress has been pronounced. A fourth thing stands out in the Pope's proclamation: "The Church is faced with tasks of immense gravity and vastness."

We are currently in the midst of a cultural crisis which affects every area of life and which marks the end of an era. Accompanying the crisis as a very vital part of it is a radical criticism of the matrix of meaning which has shaped and sustained the structures of society since the Reformation. One obvious effect of this criticism is the presence of some professed and much practical atheism among people today, even in the churches. Such atheism is characteristic of a cultural crisis.

What is the role of the church in the crisis? In the past it has sought to engage the movement of men at their spatial, temporal, and ideological centers, in order to influence and change them in the light of the purpose of God for the world. This it must now do. There is a desperate need at the present time for the confrontation of men with an articulation of a Bible-based theology and ethic for a socio-technic age.

Central to the whole situation currently facing us is the problem of man's relation to his material environment. This problem has been brought into sharp focus by the breathtaking progress of technology in mastering that environment and by some of the appalling evils accompanying that domination and its underlying materialistic philosophy.

Though the problem is acute, relatively little has been done on the religious meaning of "things" and their important place in our life and destiny. It is imperative that much, much more be done.

B. Significant Questions

Some significant questions will help us put the problem in perspective. Why did God create the world? What is the rightful role of material things in the life of man? What is the proper relation of Christian man to the world of "things"?

C. The Approach

This is to be primarily a biblical study. It will involve an examination of some relevant Scripture passages and an indication of some of the conclusions growing out of that examination.

I. An Examination of Some Relevant Scripture Passages

Because of a superabundance of material and because of space limitations, the study must be quite selective and necessarily brief. Summary statements will often have to suffice.

1. The Creation of All Things

We begin with the creation of all things. Our minds turn almost automatically to the first two chapters of Genesis. There the story of creation is preserved in two parts: 1:1-2:3 and 2:4ff. These two parts are often set in sharp contrast to each other as separate and even contradictory accounts of creation. So harsh an antithesis is unfortunate, particularly for the exposition of the passages. For, although they are different in language, style, and representation, they are basically the same in teaching [1] (except where one supplements the other). There *is* a difference in emphasis. Whereas the first account (1:1-2:3) is oriented more toward God and heaven, the second (2:4ff.) is oriented toward man and the earth. The primary stress in the first seems to be on the sovereign power of God as Creator. In the second the major emphasis appears to be on the truth that, though God is Lord of creation, his chief purpose in the creation is that there may be communion between the Creator and man, the crown of creation. The accounts are best regarded as complementary, not contradictory.

It should be kept in mind that there are many statements in the Bible concerning the Creator and the creation (e. g., Job 38; Psalms 8, 19, 104; Isaiah 40ff.; et al.). In the majority of these passages the dominant note is that of praise. When the inspired writers speak about the Creator and the creation, they burst into joyful praise at the majesty of the former and the mystery and marvel of the latter. Chapters 1 and 2 of Genesis cannot be isolated from these passages. They, too, are to be set in the context of the praise of God. One senses this as he reads the magnificent masterpiece, 1:1-2:3. It has a somber rhythm and sounds like a "heavenly liturgy."

Certain things stand out in the Genesis account. The first is that God, in his sovereign freedom and power, brought all things into being: the world in its entirety (1:1-2:3) and existence in its entirety (2:4ff.). The word rendered "create" in Gen. 1:1 (and elsewhere) is never used of human activity in the Old Testament, only of divine activity. It means "originate, bring into being something distinctly new." It can mean "make something out of nothing." [2] It refers to that which is beyond human comprehension or achievement, that which only the God of miracles can do.

The word for "God" in Gen. 1:1 (the only term for deity in 1:1-2:3, occurring 34 times in 34 verses) is *'Elohim* in Hebrew. It is a plural of intensity and may convey by implication the richness and fulness of God's nature as "a society of love" (possibly a foreshadowing of the Christian concept of the Trinity). [3] Most likely the root meaning of *'Elohim* is "strength, might, power." The word seems to signify plurality of power, or absolute, unqualified energy (cf. the modern emphasis on energy in connection with the source and essence of the universe).

The principal word for God in 2:4ff. is *Yahweh*. It is the personal name of God in his covenant relation with his people and designates him as the God who ever is and becomes present among his people, making himself known and meeting their needs.

Following the brief summary statement in Genesis 1:1-2, we are given some information concerning the order followed by God in his creative activity. That information is in general agreement with the fundamental principle of modern scientific thought, namely, orderly progression from the simple to the more complex, from the lower to the higher. In the mind of the inspired writer, there is a hierarchy of being in creation; also, creation and evolution are not mutually exclusive concepts.

As the story unfolds, we are told of the creation of light, of the formation of the firmament, of the appearance of the dry land, of the development of plant life, of the role of the heavenly bodies, and of the bringing into being of the fish, the birds, and the land animals. Each work of creation is a whole within itself, with its own function; at the same time it is related to the other systems and to the larger whole, the totality of creation.

The praise element may be implicitly present in God's contemplation of his work. Five times the statement appears: "and God saw that it was good" (1:10, 12, 18, 21, 25 RSV). All created things are good in themselves and in relation to the purpose of God.

God's creative work comes to a climax in the creation of man. In Gen. 1:26-31 this is indicated by the solemnity of the introduction, the variation of the structure, the length of the description, the threefold occurrence of the word "created" in verse 27, and the more direct and intimate involvement of God in the process. In Gen. 2:4ff. it is suggested by the emphasis on man and God's activity in relation to man. In particular, it is seen in the fact that God, the Source of life, personally fashions man from the earth and personally imparts to him his own vital breath—an honor not bestowed upon any other creature. It has been said that in the first passage man is at the peak of a pyramid; and in the second, at the center of a circle. In either case, he is the climax and crown of creation.

At the same time, it must not be overlooked that man is included in the whole of creation. In 2:5 this is brought out by a striking wordplay: 'adam, "man"; 'adamah, "ground." The force of this wordplay may be secured, at least in part, by using in close conjunction the words "earth" and "earthling." Man is a creature of clay; there is a close bond between him and the earth. In 1:22, 28 the blessing, the command to multiply, and the granting of plant life for food unite man with the animal world.

So man is a part of the rest of creation. At the same time, he is apart

56

from the rest of creation. His uniqueness is stressed by the fact that he is made in the image of God. The phrase "the image of God" is a very important phrase and has been the subject of·much study and debate. It is difficult to arrive at an exact and full meaning of it. This much is certain; the phrase is not used of any other creature. It sets man off from the rest of creation and indicates that he has a unique relatedness and responsibility to God.

Actually there are two terms employed in parallelism in verse 27: "image" (*tselem*) and "likeness" (*demut*). They are not exactly synonymous; yet it is not easy to make a sharp distinction between them. An "image" is something quite concrete, a tangible likeness, a carved or cut-out copy, a fashioned duplicate or representation. A "likeness" is something a bit more abstract—an analogy, a similarity. Men have thought that the former referred to material resemblance and the latter to immaterial resemblance. This is not to be pressed, however, for the Hebrew mind, which thought in terms of totality, did not make a clear-cut demarcation between the physical and the spiritual. The probability is that the word "likeness" tempers and interprets, makes a bit more flexible and less materialistic, the meaning the word "image" could have.

In the East the function of an image was to represent someone—a god, or a king, ordinarily. The image of a god represented the real presence of that deity. A king would set up images of himself in various parts of his realm, especially in those areas which he could not visit in person. The images were symbols of his claim to sovereign control over those areas.

As one made in the image of God, man has a representative function. He is "vizier" of God on earth—as one writer puts it, "God's vicegerent, charged with the working out of God's will, responsible to God for his stewardship." [4]

As God's representative and representation on earth, man has a certain unique relatedness to God which involves a capacity to respond to God and a responsibility to God for the response he makes. He is made not only as the image of God but also in the image of God. He is not God but is made like God. We should beware of oversimplification here in identifying this likeness with physical appearance or upright posture, with reason, with spiritual nature, or with any other one thing. "The image of God" means at least that man is representative of God on earth and that he has a unique relatedness to God.

It is obvious, in verses 27 and 28, that image and dominion are closely connected. Man is made for mastery. He is to exercise lordship over "nature" [5] under the sovereignty of God and to guide it toward its intended destiny in the purpose of God. Much of human history illustrates the tragedy which comes when man attempts, through science and industry, to exploit "nature" (created things) for the gratification of his own selfish desires and ends, rather than for the glory of God and the good of his fellowman.

Thus, man is created by God as the crown of his creation; he is created in the image of God; he is created to have dominion over created things under the sovereignty of God as a faithful son of God. Moreover, he is created for a life of joyful activity in fellowship with God. He is placed in a beautiful garden (God's gracious gift to him) in the land of Eden ("delight"). [6] He is to provide for the necessities of life, to improve his surroundings, and to protect from harm and injury that which has been committed to his care (Gen. 2:8-9, 15). But work is not enough for the fulfilment of man's life. He must have a companion. God provides a helper suitable for him. Above all, he must have communion with God. The condition of continued communion is obedience. Hence, the prohibition in 2:16. This prohibition is issued in love and indicates that "God takes man seriously as his partner." [7]

From beginning to end, in the creation account, God's relationship to man is that of sovereign. God is Lord of creation and of all his creatures, including man. As sovereign Lord, he issues commands and makes demands—in love. As God's unique representative and representation on earth, man is to live in communion and cooperation with God and to share in the life and work of God, as he exercises dominion over "nature" (control over created things). He is to perform his God-given task as a steward under divine sovereignty for God's glory and the good of men. His basic attitude toward his responsibility both to God and to man is to be one of joy. As God took delight in his work, so man is to take delight in his work. No note is quite so central in the Old and New Testaments as that of joy. This note is first struck in Genesis 1-2.

In fact, as God surveyed the entire work of creation, he was almost exultant. Note the significant variation in the final appearance of the formula: "And God saw *everything* that he had made, and *behold,* it was *very good.*" That is, "completely perfect" [8]—a world characterized by beauty, purity, and harmony (Gen. 1:31, RSV; italics mine).

If the climax of God's creative activity comes in the creation of man on the sixth day, the climax of the seven-day account of creation comes on the seventh day. The concluding paragraph (2:1-3) speaks of God's rest and of sabbath holiness. The opening statement simply informs us that all of God's original creative work was completed. The word "host" refers to the total, made up of the various component parts in the planned design of creation. It simply supplements the phrase "the heavens and the earth"—that is, the universe.

When God had brought his work to a satisfying conclusion and had inspected and approved it, he "rested" on the seventh day. He also "blessed" and "sanctified" it (i. e., made it holy). There are some profound implications here. The goal of God's creation is sabbath holiness —the sanctification of all things by God's personal presence and the participation of a responding creation in praise of the Creator. Since the usual concluding statement (such as, "and there was morning and there was evening, a seventh day") is missing here, the way is left open for that exalted, final, saving good, which God has in store for man and the world.

It is essential to recognize that Genesis 3 is dynamically related to Genesis 2. The passage (2:4-3:24) records a single story, a story of creation, rebellion, and redemption. When man disobeys the command of God, he experiences retribution. But there is a promise of salvation (3:15, the *protevangelium*) and a provision of a covering (3:21), "a modest yet mighty sign of God's forgiveness." [9] "Life which has been freely given to humans who then forfeited it, is a life which is made possible only by God's forgiveness. . . . Thus verse 21 is a modest and restrained indication of the goal of the story which began with man's creation." [10]

2. The Close Connection Between Man and "Things" in Judgment

One of the arresting concepts in the Bible, especially prominent in the Old Testament, is that of the intimate relation of man and his environment in the purpose of God. Man's sin, we learn, affects not only man himself but also his surroundings. The same may be said of the retribution which comes as the inevitable consequence of man's moral delinquency.

A classic case is seen in God's address to Adam following the latter's act of disobedience:

> Because you have listened to the voice of your wife,
>   and have eaten of the tree
> of which I commanded you,
>   'You shall not eat of it,'
> *Cursed is the ground because of you . . .*
>   *thorns and thistles it shall bring forth to you . . .*
>   (Gen. 3:17-19 RSV, italics mine).

The close connection between man and "things" in sin and judgment is disclosed in the curse pronounced upon Cain (Gen. 4:10-12) and in the dramatic story of the flood (Gen. 6:5ff.).

3. The Covenant with the Earth and All Flesh

In Genesis 9 we have the first appearance in the Bible of the very important word "covenant," a word which since the second century A. D. has been used to designate the two parts of the Bible: the Old Covenant or Testament, and the New Covenant or Testament. The word is used seven times in verses 8-17. These verses tell of the covenant which God, in his love and mercy, made with mankind. "And God said . . .: 'I set *my bow* in *the cloud,* and it shall be a sign of the covenant between me *and the earth* . . . . When *the bow* is in *the clouds,* I will look upon it and remember the everlasting covenant between God *and every living creature of all flesh that is upon the earth . . .*" (vv. 12-17 RSV, italics mine).

The nexus between man and "nature" is evident in the display of God's grace as well as in the disclosure of his wrath.

4. The Place of the Land in the Promise and in the Life of God's People

Though the chasm between creature and Creator became wider and wider because of man's arrogant self-sufficiency and increasing apostasy, God did not give up with respect to his purpose of salvation and sanctification, but, instead, he set about to bridge the chasm. Genesis 12:1-3 records the inauguration of his great program of revelation and redemption.

The call of Abram (Abraham) was accompanied by a promise, a promise that was reiterated time and again to the founding fathers. There were four major elements in the promise: the gift of a land, significant nationhood (a great name and a numerous posterity), divine protection, and a high mission in human history ("in thee shall all the families of the earth be blessed"). Of the four, the gift of the land was one of the most important (cf. Gen. 12:1, 7; 13:15, 17; 15:7, 18-21; 28:4, 13-14; 35:12; Deut. 1:8, 35; 6:10, 18, 23; 7:13; 8:1; 9:5; 10:11; 11:9, 21; 19:8; 26:3, 15; 28:11; 30:20; 31:7; 34:4).

It is obvious that two-thirds of the references cited in the preceding parenthesis are from Deuteronomy. One of three writings in the Bible making love the key to the divine life and the only work containing an extended exposition of the covenant faith of Israel, it is one of the great books of the Old Testament. Among other things, it provides a theology of the land in the life of God's people. Its major theological affirmation concerning the land is that it is the gift of God to Israel. Her taking possession of it is viewed as "an act of faith and obedience." [11] She has no real life apart from the land, for her very existence as God's elect is dependent upon it. The land abounds in benefits and blessings. These are to be received with gratitude and used with enjoyment. All members of the community are to have access to the fruits of the good land which God has given.

Though the land offers many opportunities and blessings, it also makes demands. There is a close relationship between the law and the land. The security and prosperity of the people in the land are dependent upon their loving loyalty to the covenant Lord, as expressed in their compliance with his revealed way of life for them (the holy Law). This way of life involves "a humane, just order of society and a proper, total worship of Yahweh." [12] If they rebel against God's will and way of life, they will lose the land. As the possession of the land is their prime blessing, so its loss will be their prime punishment.

The Deuteronomic history (Joshua-Kings) shows how it all worked out in experience. This great history of the people in Palestine, from their entry into the land to their expulsion from it, is presented in the framework and from the perspective of the Deuteronomic theology of the land. Israel continued in the path of disloyalty and disobedience until God finally cast her out of the land and into exile.

From Deuteronomy we can learn a great deal about the way in which God expects his people to regard material things. All things belong to him. He either created them or bestows the power to make them. He gives them in love and expects them to be used in accordance with his will. He is not only the Giver of the good things of life but also the Author of the conditions which make it possible to use them with pleasure and profit. His material gifts are to be viewed from a communal as well as an individual perspective. They are to be enjoyed by all. Above all, God, the Creator and Giver, requires that both people and possessions be employed for the achievement of his purpose. A betrayal of the divine trust leads to judgment, a loss of "the land" and the good life for all.

5. The Importance of "Things" in the Worship of Israel

Worship was central in the life of Israel. The place of worship was the tabernacle, and later, the Temple, the place of the Presence.

A basic premise in Old Testament faith was that a person should not appear before God empty-handed (Deut. 16:16-17). He should bring a gift (Deut. 26:1-11). It should be a personal and a costly gift (Leviticus 1-7; cf. 2 Sam. 24:24).

One has only to read the account of the erection and furnishing of the tabernacle (Exodus 25:31, 35-40), the story of the construction and dedication of the Solomonic Temple (1 Kings 5-8), Israel's manual of worship (Leviticus 1-27), and the Psalter to realize how very important "things" were in the worship life of God's people in Old Testament days.

6. The Prophets and the Role of "Things" in the Life of God's People

The prophets had a great deal to say about worship. Some of the greatest of them launched vigorous invectives against the cult (cf. Amos 5:21-24; Hos. 6:4-6; Isa. 1:10-17; Mic. 6:6-8; Jer. 7:1-15, 21-26). The basis of their attack was twofold: the infiltration of the cult by pagan ideas and practices, and the superstitious substitution of a proper ritual for right relationships. They did not object to the presence of the people in the Temple on appointed occasions or to their presentation of tithes and offerings. They objected to the perversion of these into a perfunctory performance, a magical mumbo-jumbo of sacrifice and ceremony by which the people sought to give God what he wanted in order to get from him what they wanted.

Though they were strongly against a cult wrongly oriented and evaluated, the prophets believed in a worship which is the means of mediating a proper knowledge of God to man and the loving devotion of man to God. Worship necessarily involved the use of "things" in the service of God and man.

The prophets were steeped in the covenant faith and law. They were quite familiar with the Hebrew conception and custom concerning land tenure. The land belonged to God. He had entrusted it to man. Man was to enjoy it and use it, with respect for the land and with a sense of responsibility to God and to the community.

We are not surprised, therefore, to find the prophets denouncing the exploitation of the land as sin. In one of his most striking sermons, Isaiah says:

> Woe to those who join house to house
>   who add field to field,
> until there is no more room,
>   and you are made to dwell alone
>   in the midst of the land (Isa. 5:8 RSV).

The evil spoken of here is that of land-grabbing, apparently a major sin in Isaiah's day (cf. Mic. 2:1-2). This practice of accumulating real estate—whether by fraud, purchase, or mortgage foreclosure—was contrary to Hebrew covenant law and the Hebrew conception of land tenure.

The greedy land-grabbers were devoid of any concern about land as a sacred, social trust. They would find, however, that their violation of covenant law would lead to judgment (vv. 9-10). The judgment portrayed is that of loneliness and barrenness—"empty hearts and empty homes." No neighbors, no cultivators! Exploitation of land, loss of production!

Isaiah has a word for our time, not only in his denunciation of the spirit of greed for earthly gain, but also in his condemnation of a particular form which this greed sometimes takes, namely, the exploiting of the land for a quick profit without concern for other people of the present and future generations. We in America, who "twice in a generation . . . have created dust bowls through excessive deforestation and failure to practice crop rotation and other conservation procedures," and who are building up large farm corporations which tend to rob rural life of its stability, ought to give heed to the prophetic word (cf. Ezekiel 34). The earth is the Lord's and should be used for his glory and the good of all men.

The concept of the close connection between man and his material environment is quite prominent in the prophets. Man's sin not only corrupts him, but also infects his surroundings. Nature suffers with him in the judgment which is the inevitable consequence of his sin (cf. Hos. 4:3; Amos 4:6-11; Jer. 4:23-28; 12:4; 14:1ff.; Ezek. 6:1ff.; Joel 1:15ff.; etc.; recall Gen. 3:17-19; 4:10-12; 6:5ff.). One of the most forceful presentations of this idea is found in Isaiah 24. Note especially verses 1, 4-6, 7-9, and 17-21. A powerful climax comes in these words:

> The earth is utterly broken,
>   the earth is rent asunder,
>   the earth is violently shaken.
> The earth staggers like a drunken man,
>   it sways like a hut;
> its transgression lies heavily upon it,
>   and it falls, and will not rise again (Isa. 24:19-20 RSV).

"From this intimate association of man and nature in their relation to the mystery of iniquity it followed that the redemption of man would be accompanied by the restoration of paradise." [13] Isaiah has the classic passage on this subject. In 11:1-9 he paints a beautiful picture of the Messiah and his kingdom. In verse 1 he speaks of the epiphany of the Messiah and in verse 2, of his equipment, his enduement by the Spirit of God with all of the abilities and qualities of a perfect ruler. In verses 3-5 he depicts the reign of the Messiah. Then comes his familiar and beloved description of the return of Eden:

The wolf shall dwell with the lamb,
  and the leopard shall lie down with the kid,
and the calf and the lion and the fatling together,
  and a little child shall lead them.
The cow and the bear shall feed;
  their young shall lie down together;
and the lion shall eat straw like the ox.
The suckling child shall play over the
    hole of the asp,
and the weaned child shall put his hand
    on the adder's den.
They shall not hurt or destroy
  in all my holy mountain;
for the earth shall be full of the
    knowledge of the Lord
as waters cover the sea (Isa. 11:6-9 RSV).

This is the poetic way of saying that when redemption is full and final there will be a restoration of the beauty, harmony, and glory of man's environment.

Ezekiel sketches a similar picture in which the concept of restoration is extended to include not only the animal kingdom but also the plant world (34:25-30). He speaks of "a covenant of peace" which God will make. Hosea also refers to an unusual covenant which will involve a remarkable chain reaction of blessing in the messianic age:

"And I will make for you a covenant on that day with the beasts of the field, the birds of the air, and the creeping things of the ground; and I will abolish the bow, the sword, and war from the land; and I will make you lie down in safety. And I will betroth you to me forever; I will betroth you to me in righteousness and in justice, in steadfast love, and in mercy. I will betroth you to me in faithfulness; and you shall know the Lord.

'And in that day, says the Lord,
  I will answer the heavens
  and they shall answer the earth;
and the earth shall answer the grain,
  the wine, and the oil,
  and they shall answer Jezreel;
  and I will sow him for myself in the land.
And I will have pity on Not pitied,

64

and I will say to Not my people,
    "You are my people";
and he shall say, "Thou art my God'" (Hosea 2:18-23 RSV).[14]

The prophets and the Hebrew people did not think of the world as a rigidly closed system. They saw it as a personal universe, God's world in which he is personally present and free to act. The regularity which characterizes it is not that of "a self-contained machine" but that of the consistency of a "faithful Creator" (1 Peter 4:19) of whose very body nature is a part. In such a world there is a dynamic relation between man's morals and nature's condition. His sin ruptures the relation. His salvation restores it.

7. Jesus and "Things"

When we come to the New Testament, we find the same conception of the vital connection between God, man, and "nature." But the nexus is viewed "in terms of man in Christ." [15]

Apart from this nexus, the Incarnation would have been impossible. "The Word *became flesh* and dwelt among us" (John 1:14 RSV, italics mine). Jesus Christ is God "biologized," God in person in our midst. Now if "matter" is essentially evil, if there is therefore no close relation between God and creation or between man and creation, this central mystery and miracle of the Christian faith could never have been. To deny this intimate relation as a believer is to become trapped in one of the earliest and greatest of all heresies, Gnosticism.[16] On the other hand, to understand Jesus, born of the Virgin Mary, as deity "plunged into matter in order to redeem it" and man, is to discover the true essence of things (see comments later on John 1:3-4; Col. 1:15-20; Heb. 2:6-9; 11:13).

As Jesus grew to maturity and began his ministry, he exhibited in his own life a complete and contagious certainty about God. For him the whole world was alive with evidences of the reality and activity of God: flowers, trees, seed, birds, children, men. His miracles were "miracles of the kingdom," "evidence that God's sovereignty was breaking in, with a new effectiveness, upon the confusion of a rebellious world." [17] He did not divorce the world of nature from the world of the spirit but indicated that they are one kingdom of which he is master. The healing of both body and spirit are necessary if there is to be wholeness for man (Mark 2:9-12). In his teachings Jesus affirmed that all things belong to God and are to be used for his glory in the carrying out of his purposes. In his life of service and sacrifice he unveiled the very essence of things. He disclosed that man's spiritual existence has its "roots in matter and in the personal nature of the world." [18] This revelation (and evaluation) is preserved in the use of water, bread, and wine in the two ordinances he instituted among his followers. "Through your own incarnation, my God, all matter is henceforth incarnate." [19]

8. The Position of Paul

Paul, the principal interpreter of the person and work of Christ, found himself in conflict with the Gnostics, the spiritual aristocrats of his day. They believed that matter is evil and that there were many intermediaries of decreasing standing between God and creation. The Gnostic heresy had gotten the Colossian Christians into quite a tangle concerning the relation of God to the material universe.

The apostle launched a polemic against that heresy in Col. 1:15-3:4. Near the beginning of his polemic he stressed the supremacy of Christ by showing his preeminence in the realms of revelation, creation, and redemption (1:15-20).

The particular part of the passage of interest to us is verses 16-17, in which Christ is spoken of in his relation to creation. Three aspects of this relation are stressed. "All things"—material and spiritual, visible and invisible (Gnosticism hits the mat!)—were created *in* him (interpretation and/or origination), *through* him (mediation), and *for* him (consummation). In him all things hang together (cohere) as an ordered system. In short, the universe becomes intelligible only when viewed in terms of God's self-expression through Christ, the Word.

Here Paul invests the life and work of Jesus in history with cosmic significance. He sees "Jesus, by character and action, embodying the essence of the universe; Jesus represents and epitomizes, initiates and completes the nature of the world whose·energies from man to the farthest star bend towards reconciliation. What has been veiled in abstraction is now unrestrictedly open to view, for the character of the universe is summed up 'in Christ' through whom it has been created and moves upon its reconciliatory way" (Col. 1:15-20).[20] All of the energies which give life to all things "meet together and acquire personal features in Jesus. Everything is gathered up into him (Eph. 1: 10). . . . He is the beginning and the goal of creation; everything emerges from him and converges upon him; he is the point of emanation and in him its harmonious climax is a *fait accompli.*" [21]

The most remarkable passage in the New Testament concerning the relation of God, man, and "things," particularly in terms of cosmic redemption, is found in the wonderful eighth chapter of Romans. Paul is speaking about those who are "in Christ Jesus" and about their duty to live according to the Spirit and not according to the flesh. The verses of special concern to us are verses 18-23. I would like to use Professor Moule's paraphrase of these verses that we may get the impact of them:

> For I reckon that the sufferings of the present time are negligible, compared with the splendor that is destined to be revealed for us. For creation, with eager expectancy, is waiting for the revealing of the sons of God. For creation was subjected to frustration, not by its own choice but because of Adam's sin which pulled down nature with it, since God had created Adam to be in close connection with nature. But the disaster was not unattended by hope—the hope that nature, too, with man, will be released from its servitude to decay, into the glorious freedom which characterizes man when he is a true and obedient son of God. For, up to the present time, we know that the whole of creation joins together in common groaning and agony; and not only creation in general, but we Christians too—even though we have the Holy Spirit as a foretaste of that hope—groan inwardly in our longing for that adoption as sons which means the release of our bodily existence from decay . . . .[22]

This passage plainly indicates that man has a responsibility under God for his environment (created things). It tells us that when man fails to assume his responsibility, that environment is subject to frustration and decay, and that when he finds his proper place as a son of God in Christ, the dislocations in his environment will be reduced and ultimately, when redemption is complete, will be removed.

9. The Teaching of Hebrews
The author of Hebrews applies the gospel of the Incarnation in the same direction by declaring that it is Christ who, by God's grace and by his own vicarious death, restores man to a true relationship with God and all created things (Heb. 2:6-9).

10. The Picture in Revelation
In Revelation 4 and 5 we have a picture of heavenly worship in the New Jerusalem. The worship is directed to "him who is seated on the throne . . . and who lives forever and ever:"

> Worthy art thou, our Lord and our God,
> to receive glory and honor and power,
> for thou didst create all things,
> and by thy will they existed and
> were created (Rev. 4:11 RSV).

Standing near the throne is a Lamb. He takes a scroll from the one seated on the throne. A new song breaks forth:

> Worthy art thou to take the scroll and
>   to open its seals,
> for thou wast slain and by thy blood
>   didst ransom men for God
> from every tribe and tongue and
>   people and nation,
> and hast made them a kingdom and
>   priests to our God,
> and they shall reign on earth (Rev. 5:9-10 RSV).

Then "myriads of myriads and thousands of thousands" join in the paean of celestial praise, saying: "Worthy is the Lamb who was slain, to receive power and wealth and wisdom and might and honor and glory and blessing" (Rev. 5:12 RSV). The inspired writer injects: "Then I heard *every created thing in heaven and on earth and under the earth and in the sea, all that is in them*" (Rev. 5:13 NEB, italics mine). This "ecumenical song" bears eloquent testimony to the biblical hope of "nature's inclusion within the processes of salvation." [23]

Commenting on Rev. 5:13, John Calvin said: "It is absolutely certain, that both irrational and inanimate creatures are [here] comprehended. All, then, which is affirmed is, that every part of the universe, from the highest pinnacle of heaven to the very center of the earth, each in its own way, proclaims the glory of the Creator." [24] In short, we have a sanctification of all things through the presence of the living God in a creation which joins in praising him and "the sabbath guest," our Saviour.

II. Some Conclusions Drawn From the Biblical Study

Having made a brief survey of some of the relevant Scripture passages, we now seek to discover some of the light shed by the study on the subject under consideration.

1. The Starting Point
First, God is the Creator, Controller, and Completer of all things. This is the starting point. All of life is from him, through him, and in him.

2. The Purpose of God in the Creation of "Things"
Second, the biblical perspective appears to be that God created

"things" for two closely related reasons. In the first place, he created "things" *to serve his sovereign purpose: the sanctification of all things through his presence*. Herbert Richardson says: "God's end in creation is the sanctification, or spiritualization, of the world." [25] This end or aim is revealed in the establishment of the sabbath. We saw, in the examination of the creation story in Gen. 1:1-2:3, that there is a heirarchy of being in the creation, the later being the higher—moving from light to day and night to water and land to plants and animals to man. Man is the last and highest of God's creatures. To man, created in God's image on the sixth day, is given the right of dominion over every other created thing.

Though man is the highest of all beings in "nature" (all that was created during the first six days), the account in Genesis indicates that there is a dimension in the world higher than man: the sabbath of God. "Just as the land and its vegetation and animal life are good in themselves, but find their proper ordering in serving the good of man, so man is good in himself, but finds the chief and proper use of his life when he serves the holiness of the sabbath. For man is made for sabbath holiness. His end is not in himself, but in the holiness of God, which, through the sabbath, is established in the world as the final joy of all created things." [26] Ralph Waldo Emerson spoke of the sabbath as "the jubilee of the whole world." [27] Abraham Heschel refers to it as "the taste of eternity or eternal life in time, "an example of the world to come." [28] So, created things are subject to man, and man is subject to the sovereignty and sabbath of God.

Why did God create the world? That is the first question. The second is, Why did he become man? Only as we deal with these questions in this order can we arrive at a proper understanding of the work of Christ and the ministry of the Holy Spirit. "God created the world for sabbath holiness." This means that he "must personally enter the world and dwell therein . . . . The sabbath is, so to say, the world's aptitude for the incarnation." [29]

Jesus declared himself to be the lord of the sabbath, the one for whom it was made. "The incarnation proceeds from God's original intention for the creation. God created the world so that the sabbath guest, Jesus Christ, might come and dwell therein. That is, the world was created for the sake of 'Emmanuel, God with us.'" [30] Thus the coming of Christ "fulfills the purpose of God in creating the world"—i.e., the sanctification of all things.

In the second place, God created "things" *to serve the needs of man, the focal center of his purpose*. All other "things" are less than man and are created for his sake and ordered for his good (cf. Gen.

1: 26ff.; Psalm 8:4-8). Since man's rebellion against God resulted in his alienation from God and his environment, redemption was necessary, if God's ultimate purpose of sanctification was to be achieved. Thus we have the inauguration of God's plan of salvation in the election of Israel, first made known in the call of Abraham and then confirmed in historical event in the Exodus and the making of the covenant.[31] A part of the plan was the gift of the land.

Then, in the fulness of God's time, we have the incarnation, God present in person in Jesus Christ. To say, as we did above, that the Sabbath of God is "the world's aptitude for the incarnation" and that "sanctification is the chief reason for the incarnation" is not, in any sense, to detract from the redemptive work of Christ but to disclose the condition that gives it real meaning. "The world has been made for the manifestation of the Glory of God in the person of Jesus Christ." [32] Jonathan Edwards said: "The world was made for the Son of God especially . . . . What He sought as His last end was God's last end in the creation." [33]

Paul, John, and the author of Hebrews indicate that God's creative and redemptive word is carried out and can be comprehended only in Jesus Christ (see passages examined previously).

But God is not only "for" us in redeeming grace in Jesus Christ. He is also "in" us in sanctifying power in the indwelling Spirit. As the coming of Christ in the flesh fulfills the "sabbath" requirement, so the coming of the Spirit fulfills the requirements of both sabbath and incarnation.

3. The Place of "Things" in the Life of Man

Having said something about the biblical teaching concerning the starting point and God's purpose in creating all things, we now consider the place of "things" in the life of man.

(1). The relation of "things" to man

We look first at some aspects of the relation of "things" to man.

a. Man's existence

The Bible teaches that the material world is essential to man's existence. It is necessary for the sustenance of the body and for the stability of the mind and the emotions. Man's dependence on the world of "things" is a part of the purpose of God.

b. Man's enjoyment

The word "Eden" (in Hebrew) means "delight, happiness, bliss." In the Old Testament, the relationship between the faithful Israelite and the earth is dominated by joy. Like his God, the true believer rejoiced in the beauty, mystery, and importance of all created things. The creation was a good creation to be enjoyed in gratitude and trust.[34]

Jesus shared this joy. We find it, too, in the pictures of the fulness and finality of salvation. God's intention is that man appreciate and enjoy "things."

c. Man's enrichment

Man is impoverished by a lack of a variety of perceptual contacts with the surrounding world of "things"; he is enriched—or can be— by the presence of such contacts, in a number of ways.[35] Perhaps the greatest enrichment comes through an increased awareness of the reality and majesty of God. "Nature" is a medium of revelation (cf. Psalms 8, 19, 104; Job 38-41; etc.). We have two "Bibles": the inspired Scriptures and the created order of things.

d. Man's expression

The material world provides an instrument for self-expression. Through "created things" man can express his creative abilities in work (Genesis 1-2, etc.), and his devotion to God and his kingdom in worship (Gen. 4:1ff.; Deut. 26:1ff.; Lev. 1-7; etc.).

(2). Man's relation to "things"

The biblical study would suggest that man's relation to "things" should be marked by at least three characteristics.

a. A realization that he is a part of the whole creation

First, man must recognize that he stands apart from the world of "things" *and* that he is very much a part of that world (cf. Genesis 1-2). This is exceedingly important.

Moreover, the Bible teaches that there should be a grateful acceptance and joyful affirmation of life in its entirety. It makes no room for a world-denying asceticism. All things are "very good." [36]

Along about the second or third century A. D., the church began to lose its biblical heritage concerning creation and man's relation to it. It must regain it.

b. A reverence for all of life

Second, the biblical view is that man is to have reverence for all of life. This means an appreciation of *any* expression of life, based on scientific, aesthetic, and religious grounds. A tree, for example, is to be looked upon as an essential to "the photosynthetic process," a thing of beauty, and the handiwork of God. Loren Eiseley, a prominent presentday anthropologist and naturalist, says: "For many of us the biblical bush still burns, and there is a deep mystery in the heart of a simple seed." [37] Edmund Sinnott, another modern scientist, in speaking of the marvels and mysteries of man and mind and matter,

71

observes: "Before these, an attitude of wonder and reverence, so out of fashion in these days of certainty, can hardly be avoided." [38] In *Silent Spring*, Rachel Carson quotes C. J. Briejer, director of the Dutch Plant Production Service: "We need a more high-minded orientation and a deeper insight, which I miss in many [scientific] researchers. Life is a miracle beyond our comprehension, and we should reverence it even when we have to struggle against it." [39]

It sounds as though these people have been reading the Bible (cf. Psalms 8, 19, 104, 139, etc.; Matt. 6:25-33; 10:29; Rom. 8:12-25; etc.)! Our world is "a complex, precise, highly integrated system of relationships between living things . . . ." [40] We should stand in awe and wonder in the presence of it!

Such a reverential appreciation of life could be the basis for an "emerging environmental ethic" so greatly needed today: "A thing is right when it tends to preserve the integrity, stability, and beauty of the biotic community. It is wrong when it tends otherwise." [41]

Reverence for all of life will not lower man but elevate him. It will make him a better person.

c. A recognition of the responsibility of stewardship

Third, man's relation to "things" should be characterized by a deep sense of his responsibility as a steward under the divine sovereignty. This brings us to the central problem of "control." So many of the difficulties we face today stem from a distortion or a perversion of the biblical doctrine of domination. Technology has made possible for man a high degree of control of his environment (created things), but a philosophy of secularism has caused him to seek to control that environment for self and with too much speed. As a consequence, too much selfish preoccupation with "things" has "thingified" him. And man, the master of "nature," has become the victim of his own victory! In dominating created things, apart from God, he has become dominated by things. He has fallen into a self-made trap (cf. pollution, poverty, population explosion, pesticides, commercialized distraction, a barbaric desecration of the beauty of nature, a duke's mixture of adolescence, drug addiction, drink, nervous disorders, dreadful waste, noise, the congestion of urbanization, and all the rest). Worst of all, man refuses to face the central problem: himself. He prefers "to infect other planets with his problems rather than to master them at home" [42] (including the basic problem of self and the relationship of self to God).

Technology has great potential for good as well as evil. It is simply moving too fast and is full of dangers. It must be checked and, if possible, Christianized. Much depends upon a proper understanding of man's relation to his material environment. Much of this, in turn, centers around the interpretation of "control."

This brings us back to what was said about the image of God and man's dominion in the interpretation of Gen. 1:26-31. Man has a unique relatedness to God, involving the capacity to make a response to God, and responsibility for the response he makes. He is God's representation and representative, who is to exercise lordship over the realm of created things as a responsible steward, an obedient son of God, for the glory of God and the good of men (sanctification and salvation).

Two things should be stressed. The first is *restraint in the use of* "things." Man is to use but not to abuse. He is to care for that which is committed to his keeping. As indicated earlier, it is not difficult to find evidence in history and contemporary society of the terrible consequences of man's perversion of the biblical concept of control. There is a desperate need for an ecological, as well as a social, conscience.[43] We must develop such a conscience or perish!

In his recent book *Crisis in Eden,* Frederick Elder calls for a world-affirming "asceticism" which will concern itself with the preservation of "things" as well as with the possession of "things," which will place stress on quality of life rather than on quantity of existence, and which will be willing to exercise restrained acquisition and restrained procreation, for the sake of the good of all men—and things.[44]

The second thing that must be emphasized is *the relationship of* "things" to God's redemptive program. God has a great plan of revelation and redemption. Man is involved in that plan. He is a steward of all he has: his time, his talent, his money, his energy, *and* his environment. The mention of environment does not mean that we, as Christians, are to degrade or discard traditional stewardship emphases. Instead, it merely gives a new dimension to stewardship. It means that we should seek to attune ourselves to God's purpose and to use *everything* for the carrying out of that purpose.

The situation today is one of urgency. Materialism is on the march and shows no signs of slowing down. Technology is traveling the rails at terrific speed, with its riders crying, "FASTER! FASTER!" There is a crisis in our country. There is a crisis in the churches. Technology and materialism are deeply involved in this crisis. We *are* at a turning point in history. This is no time to daydream, or to dillydally, or to be indifferent or defeated. We must do something—and the time is now!

The challenge to the church in this crisis situation is to clarify and articulate an adequate theology and ethic regarding man's relation to the material world. This could serve as a meeting ground between science and religion. More significantly, it could help avert increasing dullness and deadness in our churches and certain disaster in our country. More important still, it could advance the cause of Christ throughout the world, as the gospel of the grace of God is proclaimed in all of its richness and relevance.

The church can meet the challenge. It is interesting and illuminating to note that, in one of the most recent books in the field (*Crisis in Eden*, 1970), the author designates the church as the only institution that *can* do the job.[45] He arrives at this conclusion partly through the process of elimination and partly through a recognition of the ministry, message, and motivation of the church. Christianity *is* the most materialistic of all religions and can help create a healthy, circumscribed, moderate, biblical materialism. Also, the answer to the secularization of our time is the sanctification of all things. The purpose of God, the God of the Bible, revealed supremely in Jesus and made effective through his work and the ministry of the Holy Spirit, is salvation and sanctification. All of this lies at the very heart of the faith and work of the church.

Because the church can handle the task, it must—and soon. The Scriptures—read, perhaps, with "new eyes"—can provide rich resources for the task.

FOOTNOTES

[1] E. A. Speiser, *Genesis* (New York: Doubleday & Co., 1964), p. 19.
[2] G. Von Rad, *Genesis*, trans. by John H. Marks (London: SCM, 1961), p. 47.
[3] Alan Richardson, *Genesis I-XI* (London: SCM, 1953), p. 46.
[4] *Ibid.*, p. 55.
[5] There is no word for "nature" in Hebrew, just as there is no word for "universe." "Nature" is "created things." It is not conceived of as a separate entity but in relation to God, man, and covenant.
[6] Von Rad, p. 76.
[7] Claus Westermann, *The Genesis Accounts of Creation*, trans. by Norman E. Wagner (Philadelphia: Fortress Press, 1964), p. 28.
[8] Otto Procksch, *Die Genesis* (Leipzig: Deichert, 1924), *in loc.*
[9] Westermann, p. 34.
[10] *Ibid.*
[11] Patrick D. Miller, "The Gift of God," *Interpretation*, (23, 1969), p. 456.
[12] *Ibid.*, p. 461.
[13] G. B. Caird, *The Gospel of St. Luke* (Baltimore: Penguin, 1963),

p. 121.

[14] For other similar passages, see Amos 9:13; Joel 2:18-27; Isa. 4:2; 29:17; 30:23-26; 32:15; 35; 55:12-13; Jer. 31:4-6; 33:12-13; etc.; recall Gen. 9:8-17.

[15] C. F. D. Moule, *Man and Nature in the New Testament* (Philadelphia: Fortress Press, 1967), p. 8. Used by permission.

[16] Charles E. Raven, *Natural Religion and Christian Theology* (Cambridge: University Press, 1953), pp. 2-3.

[17] Caird, p. 121.

[18] Conrad Bonifazi, *A Theology of Things* (New York: J. B. Lippincott Co., 1967), p. 203.

[19] Pierre Teilhard de Chardin, *Hymn of the Universe* (New York: Harper & Row, 1965), p. 24.

[20] Bonifazi, p. 201.

[21] *Ibid.* In the prologue to his Gospel, John asserts that all things were created as a result of God's activity in self-expression through the Word (John 1:3-4). The author of Hebrews affirms that God's creative and redemptive activity is carried on and can be comprehended only in Christ (Heb. 11:3).

[22] Moule, p. 10.

[23] Bonifazi, p. 198. "The bright strand of cosmic redemption drawn through biblical literature not only indicates an affinity and destiny common to man and things, but also attributes to matter as to man a function within the salvation structures it describes" (*Ibid.*, p. 207).

[24] *Institutes of the Christian Religion,* trans. by Henry Beveridge (Grand Rapids: Eerdmans, 1957), IV, XIV, 18; cf. also Psalm 103.

[25] *Toward an American Theology* (New York: Harper & Row, 1967), p. 112.

[26] *Ibid.,* p. 116.

[27] "The Divinity School Address," Harvard, 1838, in *Three Prophets of Liberalism,* C. C. Wright, ed. (Boston, 1961), p. 111.

[28] The Sabbath (New York: Farrar, Straus, and Young, 1951; Cleveland, 1963), p. 74.

[29] H. Richardson, p. 126.

[30] *Ibid.,* p. 130.

[31] Edmond Jacob says that the creation was for the sake of the covenant, i.e., God's "plan of love and salvation for humanity by means of Israel" (Theology of the Old Testament [New York: Harper & Row, 1958], p. 137).

[32] H. Richardson, *Ibid.*

[33] See *Dissertation Concerning the End for Which God Created the*

World (New York, 1881), II, p. 225.

[34] Cf. Genesis 1: to the Hebrew, earthly goods were to be enjoyed, partly because they were good in themselves, but primarily because they were evidences of God's favor and "blessing" and pointed to the higher good: fellowship with God. They were "pledges of a higher meaning in life" (Walther Eichrodt, *Theology of the Old Testament,* trans. by J. A. Baker [Philadelphia: Westminster, 1967], II, pp. 350f.

[35] Cf. the experiences of Admiral Richard Byrd, Dr. Alain Bombard, and St. Francis of Assisi—see Bonifazi, pp. 27ff., 160ff.

[36] For the Hebrew conception of material things and their relation to the good life, see excellent discussion in Eichrodt, II, 349-359.

[37] *The Firmament of Time* (New York: Atheneum, 1967), p. 8.

[38] *The Bridge of Life* (New York: Simon & Schuster, 1966), p. 216.

[39] *Silent Spring* (New York: Fawcett Crest Books, 1964), p. 243.

[40] *Ibid.,* p. 218.

[41] Aldo Leopold, *A Sand County Alamanac,* enl. ed. (New York: Oxford University Press, 1966), p. 240.

[42] Loren Eiseley, "An Evolutionist Looks at Modern Man," *Saturday Evening Post,* (April 26, 1958), p. 121.

[43] For a relevant example, recall the defeat of the proposal to build a nuclear reactor in the San Francisco Bay area and the reasons for the defeat—see Frederick Elder, *Crisis in Eden* (Nashville: Abingdon, 1970), pp. 100f.

[44] *Ibid.,* pp. 145ff.

[45] Elder, pp. 155ff.

BIBLIOGRAPHY

Allen, C. J., ed. *The Broadman Bible Commentary,* Vols. I-II. Nashville: Broadman Press, 1969, 1970.

Bonifazi, Conrad. *A Theology of Things.* New York: J. B. Lippincott Co., 1967.

Buttrick, George A., ed. *The Interpreter's Bible,* Vols. I,II,V,VI. New York: Abingdon, 1956.

Caird G. B. *The Gospel of St. Luke.* Baltimore: Penguin, 1963.

Calvin, John. *Institutes of the Christian Religion,* trans. by Henry Beveridge. Grand Rapids: Eerdmans, 1957.

Carson, Rachel. *Silent Spring.* New York: Fawcett Crest Books, 1964.

Commoner, Barry. *Science and Survival.* New York: The Viking Press, 1967.

Cox, Harvey. *The Secular City.* New York: Macmillan, 1965.

———*On Leaving It to the Snake.* New York: Macmillan, 1967.

Eichrodt, Walther. *Theology of the Old Testament,* Vol. I, trans. by J. A. Baker. Philadelphia: Westminster, 1967.

Eiseley, Loren. *The Firmament of Time.* New York: Atheneum, 1967.

——— *The Immense Journey.* New York: Random House, 1957.

Elder, Frederick. *Crisis in Eden.* Nashville: Abingdon, 1970.

Emerson, Ralph Waldo. "The Divinity School Address," in *Three Prophets of Liberalism,* C. C. Wright, ed. Boston, 1961.

Heschel, Abraham. *The Sabbath.* New York: Farrar, Strauss, and Young, 1951; Cleveland, 1963.

Jacob, Edmund. *Theology of the Old Testament.* New York: Harper & Bros., 1958.

Leopold, Aldo. *A Sand County Almanac.* New York: Oxford University Press, 1966.

Miller, Patrick. "The Gift of God," *Interpretation,* 23, 1969, pp. 451-465.

Moule C. F. D. *Man and Nature in the New Testament.* Philadelphia: Fortress Press, 1962.

Neibuhr, H. Richard. *Radical Monotheism and Western Culture.* Lincoln: University of Nebraska Press, 1960.

Procksch, Otto. *Die Genesis.* Leipzig: Deichert, 1924.

Queffelec, Henri. *Technology and Religion,* trans. by S. J. Tester. New York: Hawthorn, 1964.

Raven, Charles E. *Natural Religion and Christian Theology.* Cambridge: University Press, 1953.

Richardson, Alan. *Genesis I-XI.* London: SCM, 1953.

Richardson, Herbert. *Toward an American Theology.* New York: Harper & Row, 1967.

Rust, E. C. *Nature and Man in Biblical Thought.* London: Lutterworth, 1953.

——— *Science and Faith.* New York: Oxford University Press, 1967.

Sinnott, Edmund. *The Bridge of Life.* New York: Simon & Schuster, 1966.

Sittler, Joseph. *The Ecology of Faith.* Philadelphia: Fortress Press, 1970.

Speiser, E. A. *Genesis.* New York: Doubleday & Co., 1964.

Teilhard de Chardin, Pierre. *Hymn to the Universe.* New York: Harper & Row, 1965.

——— *The Phenomenon of Man.* New York: Harper & Bros., 1959.

Temple, William. *Nature, Man, and God.* New York: Macmillan, 1951.

Thorpe, W. H. *Science, Man, and Morals.* Ithaca: Cornell University Press, 1966.

Von Rad, Gerhard. *Genesis,* trans. by John H. Marks. London: SCM, 1961.

—— *Old Testament Theology,* Vol. I, trans. by D. M. G. Stalker. New York: Harper & Row, 1962.

Vriezen, Th. C. *An Outline of Old Testament Theology,* trans. by S. Neuijen. Boston: Charles T. Branford Co., 1958.

Westermann, Claus. *The Genesis Accounts of Creation,* trans. by Norman E. Wagner. Philadelphia: Fortress Press, 1964.

The Rationale of Stewardship

The context of Christian stewardship is Christian theology. The rationale, or reasons behind Christian stewardship, grows out of the theological context for Christian stewardship. Christian stewardship is possible when men view the created order from God's redemptive plan. Christian stewardship is reasonable when men reflect on God's ownership of, and man's responsibility for, the created order.

The second section of this book grows out of the first and amplifies it. The four chapters contained in this section draw out the implications of our theological context which states that God the redeemer is also the creator.

A Materialist Faith

Professor Garrett's chapter documents the fact that a Christian view of material things places a great value on the physical world and all of its components. For those who have not studied world religions or who have not reflected deeply on the Christian faith, it may seem startling to assert that Christianity is a materialistic faith. This affirmation is corroborated by a careful examination of the Bible and/ or by a look at other world faiths.

Perhaps it is exactly an other-worldly, pseudo-spiritualism which has kept Christians unrelated to the reality of the material and, therefore, unaware of the deepest meaning of Christian stewardship. Repugnance toward the physical and material implications of our faith and unwillingness to discuss finance as a "spiritual" subject illustrate our lack of awareness of what it means to acknowledge God as the maker of heaven and earth.

The recognition of the redeeming God's creator-ownership of all existence is both the context of stewardship and the deepest rationale *for* stewardship. Christian stewardship makes sense only if, despite all appearance to the contrary, "this is our Father's world." Christian other worldliness is always predicated on this worldliness. Even in matters of eschatology we expect the resurrection of the body and a new heaven and a new earth. The import of those expectations is not to try to understand God's world in physical categories so much as it is to recognize how seriously God has taken our categories of time, place, and substance. Christian faith has, as one of its major tests, the incarnation of the divine in human flesh. It is not possible to spiritualize the Old Testament in such a way as to make the God portrayed there one who is unconcerned with material. Even more, since Bethlehem, Christians find it necessary to affirm that Christianity is a materialistic faith.

What Do We Own?

The question what do we own is a loaded one. For the term *own* means to possess and it also means to acknowledge. The second section of this book is one which spells out the ownership implications and rationale of Christian stewardship. The second chapter of this section is particularly concerned with the question of what Christians own.

If the reader has followed the development of the book so far, he will already see the double answer to the question of ownership. Christians are those who own (acknowledge) that God is owner (primary possessor) of all things and that men own (possess) all things in this awareness. This is the Christian concept of ownership. Any and all things men own they own in a secondary way. A confession of man's ownership as a secondary and derived type of possession keeps us from the idolatry of possessions.

Author Hildreth spells out the implications of such a view of ownership. Since man's ownership of what he possesses is always a relative owning, he must act accordingly. Subjects as diverse (but as related) as ecology, life style, and social obligation all form valid points for discussion.

The double answer of ownership, in Christian perspective, is that men own nothing absolute but they own everything relatively. Absolute ownership is the prerogative of God. And in our relatedness to God we own all things—that is, we confess all things are God's possession and all which we have, we have before him and because of him. The rationale of stewardship extends beyond an awareness of God's concern for the material and our acknowledgement of God's ownership. The problem of the rationale of stewardship is also a problem of management. What is the economy of stewardship?

Economy: A Science or a Stance?

Words have a way of being "flattened out" in usage until they convey so much that, in turn, they convey practically nothing. Economy is one such word. We hear very much about a good or bad "economy" in our business affairs as a nation. From the broad noun economy, comes the narrower term economics. Economics may be defined as "that science which investigates the conditions and laws affecting the production, distribution, and consumption of wealth." [1]

But it would be the worst kind of mistake to identify economy with economics; even as it is utter fallacy to identify tithing and stewardship. Economy and stewardship are broad, general terms. Economics and tithing are specific terms. A failure to distinguish between economy as a term meaning stewardship of things and economics as a science dealing with measurable wealth, leads to a gross reductionism of everything to terms of wealth. Even so a tendency to identify stewardship with the commendable, but largely financial, practice of tithing is a reductionism which a study of Christian stewardship cannot afford. Economy and stewardship, which are the same term in Greek, have to do with the total management of the property of another. Given these definitions and distinctions we may answer our question as to whether economy is a science or a stance. Economy— stewardship—is a stance, a stance which recognizes the ownership of God and orders all life accordingly. It may be hoped that from the stance of stewardship (economy) there may emerge a science or methodology which will find some way to relate the stance of Christian stewardship to effective means for accomplishing it. From the stance of economy grew the science of economics. From the stance of stewardship must come the science of stewardship methodology, which will surely have much to say about tithing as one means for effecting stewardship. But we must not confuse the general term with a specific method. Author Parker has given to us valuable insights about the economy of stewardship and the practice of Christian economics.

The Beginning and the End

The final chapter of this section rounds out the discussion by giving it logical completion. The acquisition and disposition of wealth is an integral and necessary discussion in determining rationale of stewardship.

Much discussion of stewardship starts in the middle. That is, it

[1] *Webster's Collegiate Dictionary,* 5th ed.

answers the question what we do with what we have. This is a necessary part of any discussion of stewardship. But again we must remind ourselves that the part is not the whole. Concepts of stewardship must be extended in both directions. That is, one must ask how he acquires what he has and how he will ultimately dispose of it. Professor Tolbert rightly points out that this type of question is more pressing in days and circumstances of affluence than in times of poverty and deprivation. Contrasts of abundance and need—affluence and want give a prophetic urgency to modern American discussions of stewardship. The authors of this volume are acutely aware that twentieth century Baptists have freely received and are therefore responsible to give freely. Nor have we forgotten our own wide focus of stewardship. Even now, we are not talking just about money. Given our leisure time, our confluence with all society through our travels, and our influence in political and social contexts, we must consider all of life a stewardship before God and on behalf of men.

All things have begun in God and will conclude in him. Christians who are aware that life is on loan from God and that death is payment to the realm of eternity cannot fail to ask how they get and use the resources which they have in life.

From the context grows the rationale. The rationale of Christian stewardship is the reasoning which: (1) acknowledges that God is concerned for the material; that man owns (acknowledges) that all that he owns (possessions) is under the ownership of God; (2) sees stewardship as an economy of God's gifts; and (3) asks what is an appropriate stewardship in the light of the origin and end of all man's possessions. From the rationale of stewardship there must grow the practice of stewardship.

A Christian View of Material Things

James Leo Garrett

The term "material things" is a rather broad and inclusive term which is understood here to include land, bodies of water, underground, atmosphere, plants, animals, houses, buildings, clothes, adornments, furnishings, machinery, investments, money, and the like. The term "a Christian view" is used here so as to suggest that the best of biblical truth and contemporary insights are being sought so that the resultant statement about material things may be authentically Christian, but no claim is made or implied that this statement of the view is characterized by finality or is to be received with unanimity.

It is first necessary to inquire of and to provide a summary statement of the biblical teachings about material things.

I.

The biblical doctrine of creation means that all material things have their *origin* in God. In the Old Testament the divine origin of all things is conveyed by the Hebrew word *bará,* which is used only of God and of activity peculiar to God. The creation of material things other than man has a greater role in the more detailed creation account of Genesis 1 (P) than in the man-centered creation account of Genesis 2 (J). According to Genesis 1-2, to Psalm 104, and to Second Isaiah the created universe has a beginning, a sustaining continuation (Ps. 104:27-30), and an end. While Yahweh is eternal, the created universe is not eternal but derived from and dependent upon Yahweh. The cosmology of ancient Israel, especially the three-story universe, Edmund Jacob has insisted,[1] did not arise from Israel's religious affirmation about Yahweh's creative activity but was shared with the other peoples of antiquity. Psalm 104 (especially v. 24) especially presents the created universe as a unity. The creation of all things has its end—its goal as well as its termination. Second Isaiah understands the divine salvation of Israel as a new creation, and unlike the earliest affirmations about deity in the Pentateuch, moves *from* covenant *to* creation so that the idea of creation is secondary to the idea of covenant, yet covenant is only realizable within a created order. Thus God has created "for the covenant." [2] The hope of Israel is describable in terms of "the new heavens and the new earth" (Isa. 66:22).

Not only are all material things derived from and dependent upon God the Creator, according to the faith of Israel, but also these material things that make up the created universe are reckoned by God the Creator to be "*good.*" Seven distinct pronouncements of the goodness of the created are made in Genesis 1 (vv. 4, 10, 12, 18, 21, 25, 31) by the priestly writer. Then in the commission to Cyrus, Second Isaiah presents the declaration of Yahweh: "I form the light, and create darkness; I make peace (weal) and, create evil (woe), I the Lord do all these things" (45:7). No Zoroastrian dualism is to creep into Jewish beliefs! What men consider "darkness" and "woe" is to be embraced in the creative activity of Yahweh, who granted to his creatures a relative freedom. Moreover, this creative work of Yahweh produced no "chaos" but an ordered and inhabited universe (45:18-19).

The Old Testament affirms the *ownership* of all things by Yahweh as well as his creatorship of all things. In the Psalms the idea is found repeatedly. "The earth is the Lord's and the fulness thereof, the world and those who dwell therein" (Ps. 24:1 RSV). To Israel Yahweh declares: "I do not reprove you for your sacrifices; your burnt offerings are continually before me. I will accept no bull from your house, nor he-goat from your folds. For every beast of the forest is mine, the cattle on a thousand hills. I know all the birds of the air, and all that moves in the field is mine" (Ps. 50:8-11 RSV). "For the Lord is a great God, and a great King above all gods. In his hand are the depths of the earth; the heights of the mountains are his also. The sea is his, for he made it; for his hands formed the dry land" (Ps. 95:3-5 RSV). Yahweh, in answering Job and after dealing with the hippopotamus and the crocodile, declares: "Whatever is under the whole heaven is mine" (Job 41:11b RSV). In Isaiah 66:1 (RSV) Yahweh declares in similar fashion, " 'Heaven is my throne and the earth is my footstool. . . .' " The year of jubilee is predicated on the truth that the land belongs to Yahweh (Lev. 25:23). Through the prophet Haggai and in a context of the soon to be restored temple in Jerusalem the Lord of hosts declares: "The silver is mine, and the gold is mine" (Hag. 2:8).

T. A. Kantonen has called attention to the important connection between the divine ownership of all things and the divine sovereignty or rulership over all things, including the satanic rebellion and the offer to Jesus of "the kingdoms of this world" on the ground that authority over these had been "delivered" unto Satan (Luke 4:5-6) and then God's ultimate word, "The kingdom of the world has become the kingdom of our Lord and of his Christ, and he shall reign for ever and ever" (Rev. 11:15 RSV).[3]

What then is the relation of man the creature to material things, according to the Bible? First it should be noted that man is said in Genesis 1 to have been given "*dominion*" over the animal and plant creation and to have been commanded, "Be fruitful and multiply, and fill the earth and subdue it" (Gen. 1:28 RSV). Genesis 2 makes no reference to "dominion" but does refer to man's giving names to the animals (v. 20). Yet because of man's sins the earth shall bring forth "thorns and thistles" and man shall toil for his sustenance (Gen. 3:17-19). Man's dominion over plants, animals, and the resources of the material universe must always be understood as a relative or secondary dominion under the primary sovereignty of God, yet that human dominion must be recognized as real. Some have identified the image of God in which man was made (Gen. 1:27) as the very capacity for and exercise of dominion. The psalmist indeed connects man's status and his exercise of dominion: "What is man that thou art mindful of him, and the son of man that thou dost care for him? Yet thou hast made him little less than God, and dost crown him with glory and honor. Thou hast given him dominion over the works of thy hands; thou hast put all things under his feet, all sheep and oxen, and also the beasts of the field, the birds of the air, and the fish of the sea, whatever passes along the paths of the sea" (Ps. 8:4-8 RSV). Similar language about man's role appears in Job 7:17-18 and Psalm 144:3. The Epistle to the Hebrews quotes Psalm 8:4-6 and then comments, "Now in putting everything in subjection to him [man], he [God] left nothing outside his [man's] control. As it is, we do not yet see everything in subjection to him." Yet, he declares, "We see Jesus, who for a little while was made lower than the angels, crowned with glory and honor because of the suffering of death, so that by the grace of God he might taste death for every one" (Heb. 2:6-9 RSV).

God's ownership of all things and man's relative but real dominion over lower creatures lead in biblical thought to man's obligation to a responsible *management* or *use* of material things—a concept translated from the Greek New Testament οἰκονομία by the English term "stewardship." The latter term, derived from the Old English usage of "warden of the sty" or "sty-ward," has few exact parallels in other modern languages. Paul uses the term "stewardship" in reference to the gospel rather than concerning material things and declares: "Moreover, it is required of stewards that they be found trustworthy" (1 Cor. 4:2 RSV). Jesus, speaking of material things, said: "He who is faithful in a very little is faithful also in much; and he who is dishonest in a very little is dishonest also in much. If then you have not been faithful in the unrighteous mammon, who will entrust to you the true riches? And if you have not been faithful in that which is another's, who will give you that which is your own?" (Luke 16:10-12 RSV).

The Old Testament repeatedly warns against the use of material things as images of deity or as idols to be worshipped (Ex. 20:4-6, 23; 34:17; Lev. 19:4; 26:1; Deut. 4:15-19; 5:8-10; 27:15). The New Testament warns against *hoarding* or *absolutizing* material things. "No one can serve two masters. . . . you cannot serve God and mammon" (Matt. 6:24 RSV). "Take heed, and beware of all covetousness; for a man's life does not consist in the abundance of his possessions" (Luke 12:15 RSV). "For what will it profit a man, if he gains the whole world and forfeits his life?" (Matt. 16:26 RSV). Jesus' parable of the rich man and Lazarus (Luke 16:19-31) is set in the context of the difficulty which a rich man has in hearing the gospel or entering the kingdom of God. His encounter with the rich young ruler (Mark 10:17-31 and parallels) presents even more directly and clearly the necessity of choosing between the primacy of riches and discipleship, and Jesus articulated the difficulty by saying, "It is easier for a camel to go through the eye of a needle than for a rich man to enter the kingdom of God (Mark 10:25 RSV).

According to the teaching of Jesus man cannot possess material things *after death*. "Do not lay up for yourselves treasures on earth, where moth and rust consume and where thieves break in and steal, but lay up for yourselves treasures in heaven, where neither moth nor rust consumes and where thieves do not break in and steal" (Matt. 6:19-20 RSV). In the parable of the rich fool God asks the fool at the hour of his death: "Fool! This night your soul is required of you; and the things you have prepared, whose will they be?" (Luke 12:20 RSV).

Yet one saying of Jesus, his conclusion to the parable of the unjust steward, seems to indicate that man can so use material things as to have effects after his death. Jesus said: "And I tell you, make friends for yourselves by means of unrighteous mammon, so that when it fails they may receive you into the eternal habitations" (Luke 16:9 RSV).

II.

The Christian understanding of the relations of God and of man to material things has been repeatedly challenged in the course of Christian history by non-Christian or quasi-Christian views of material things. No attempt here will be made to enumerate or discuss all of these contrary viewpoints. However, three of these will be considered in some detail: the Gnostic and Manichaean views, the Hindu and Buddhist views, and the modern Western materialistic views.

Gnosticism so posited the evil of matter that the entire world, or total material universe, was regarded as being under evil or demonic powers and to have had its origin somewhat apart from the transcendent deity. Hans Jonas has summarized the Gnostic cosmology as follows:

> The deity is absolutely transmundane, its nature alien to that of the universe . . . : to the divine realm of light, self-contained and remote, the cosmos is opposed as the realm of darkness. The world is the work of lowly powers. . . . The genesis of these lower powers, the Archons (rulers), and in general that of all the orders of being outside God, including the world itself is a main theme of gnostic speculation. . . . The universe, the domain of the Archons, is like a vast prison whose innermost dungeon is the earth, the scene of man's life. Around and above it the cosmic spheres are ranged like concentric enclosing shells. Most frequently there are the seven spheres of the planets surrounded by the eighth, that of the fixed stars. . . . Basilides counted no fewer than 365 'heavens.' . . . [Moreover,] everything which intervenes between here and the beyond serves to separate man from God, not merely by spatial distance but through active demonic force. . . . The Archons collectively rule over the world, and each individually in his sphere is a warden of the cosmic prison. Their tyrannical world-rule is called *heimarmene,* universal Fate. . . . Through his body and his soul man is a part of the world and subjected to the *heimarmene.* Enclosed in the soul is the spirit . . . , a portion of the divine substance from beyond which has fallen into the world; and the Archons created man for the express purpose of keeping it captive there. . . . The goal of gnostic striving is the release of the 'inner man' from the bonds of the world and his return to the realm of light. . . . With the completion of this

process of gathering in . . . , the cosmos, deprived of its elements of light, will come to an end.[4]

In Gnostic religion and thought, therefore, man can in no sense be the steward of material things, for his salvation consists of separation from his physical body and the whole material universe. A prisoner of the cosmos, man cannot be a manager of a portion of the cosmos, for such is the function of the Archons.

The Manichaean system also regarded the universe as being evil but instead posited the eternality and independence of the realm of darkness (Ahriman) as well as of the realm of light (Father of Greatness). Conflict was provoked by the realm of darkness, and in response the Father of Greatness called forth (a) Primal man, (b) the Friend of Lights, the Great Architect, and the Living Spirit, and (c) the Messenger. Adam and Eve are formed by the Ahriman, and he deposits in them the light left in his possession. Jonas reminds us that in Manichaean thought man's body "is of devilish substance and . . . also of devilish *design*." [5] Manichaeans consequently were vegetarians, lest they consume "ensouled" animals, and were admonished to abstain from procreation, though the hearers, unlike the elect, were allowed to marry. For Manichaean thought material things could not be separated from the great cosmic struggle between darkness and light. Man's salvation consisted in ascetic practices and deliverance from darkness. To be responsible for the management of material things, therefore, was entirely alien to the Manichaean religion.

The Gnostic viewed material things as the work of the Demiurge and man's destiny as his deliverance from a material body, and the Gnostics' debt to Greek philosophical thought for these views was considerable. The Manichee eternalized the conflict of good and evil, of light and darkness, interpreted man as portions of light enfleshed in darkness, and subordinated the material world to this cosmic conflict.

Hinduism regards the material world as "a temporary, worthless illusion (Maya)." [6] Affected by the acknowledged caste system and by Karma, the cosmic power or law of justice that functions to assign souls to their status in reincarnation, the Hindu attitude toward material things proceeds from no doctrine of the goodness of creation. The ancient religion of the Vedas centered in a nature-worship in which planets and elements were prayed to and praised. From the time of the writings known as Brahmanas, restrictions have been placed on the eating of beef; thus the cow came to be looked upon as a special sacred animal. The concept of Maya was shaped in the speculative philosophy of the Upanishads with its one Supreme Being or Brahma. The world has relatively less significance for the Hindu, who has a cyclical view of history, than for the Muslim, the Jew, or the Christian. Only slowly and only in recent years have Hindu statesmen been able to evoke support for projects that alter the geographical or economic status quo.

Buddhism is a religion of the extirpation of desire through ascetical practices, an eightfold ethical "path," and the hope of a state of passionless peace called Nirvana, or after death Pari-Nirvana. Buddhism retained Hinduism's law of Karma and transmigration of souls but rejected the caste system. But to be, according to Buddhism, is to be transitory, miserable, and impersonal.[7] Insofar as material things contribute to man's desires they are presumably to be frowned upon or devaluated. Since man's body and man's activity are without specific worth in Buddhism, it is safe to conclude that man's relation to material things can have little significance at all.[8] Yet of Gautama, Reischauer has written:

> He was too much of a realist to hold that all this flux of phenomenal existence is *maya*, an illusion of the unenlightened mind. He accepted it as real and believed that this process of 'birth and death and again rebirth and death' would go on indefinitely unless the Karma energy, the blind 'will-to-be,' is stopped. Just how the universe came to be what it is or whether there is some great purpose in it all, he did not pretend to know.[9]

While the parent, Hinduism, viewed material things as unreal and illusory, the reforming daughter, Buddhism, granted reality if not value.

Western man has on the whole taken material things to be of greater significance for human life than has the man of the Orient. This difference is somewhat explicable by the Jewish and Christian affirmation of the divine creation of all things and of the value of man, including his body. But Western civilization has also been the locus for an absolutizing of material values at the expense of other values. Materialism as metaphysics had its advocates among the ancient Greeks [10] and among the eighteenth century French philosophers of the Enlightenment,[11] but it has reached much greater proportions in the modern era in the West. Two important examples may be noted: Marxist dialectical materialism and capitalist functional materialism.

It is commonly asserted that Karl Marx derived his dialectic from G. W. F. Hegel and his materialism from Ludwig Feuerbach. But Marx wrote his doctoral thesis on Democritus and Epicurus and insisted in his *Theses on Feuerbach* that materialism had been too fatalistic and should serve the cause of social revolution.[12] Matter, for Marx, was dynamic rather than inert. Moreover, history is understood as the product of the interaction of economic forces and without the existence and involvement of God. Hence the classless and utopian society envisioned by Marxism and toward which present socialism points abounds in material things, which are, it is said, to be distributed justly through the abolition of private property and the establishment of state ownership. R. N. Carew Hunt has commented on the Marxist handling of the basic question of thinking and being:

> Marx's treatment of this problem has coloured all subsequent communist thinking. He takes it, of course, as axiomatic that the material world *is* the fundamental reality, and that although it is accessible to thought, it is not constituted by it. . . . The older materialists had taught that our knowledge of the external world—and at the same time our ideas about it —was obtained by the impact of sensations upon the mind, but had regarded these sensations as passive. . . . Marx teaches that these sensations, which were held to give us faithful images of the external world, did not provide *immediate* knowledge but only stimuli to knowledge which completed itself in action. . . . Hence, he insisted that we only perceive a thing as a part of the process of acting upon it. . . . This activist theory of knowledge—known to-day as Instrumentalism—which insists that knowledge is indissolubly bound up with action (*Praxis*), is the most distinctive feature of Marx's philosophy as opposed to his theories of history and economics. . . . On the other hand, Engels, . . . went back to the older theory which held the source of knowledge to be sensations.[13]

Lenin sought to "bring Marx and Engels together by arguing that they were always in agreement, though wherever there is a divergence he invariably follows Engels." [14] Thus, to act in the cause of revolution is to be able to aid stimuli in evoking knowledge. To have knowledge of ultimate reality is to share in the dialectic processes of history. Whichever the starting point, matter, dynamically conceived, is the real. Thus, for Marxism, the world of things from atom to giant jet, from bacteria to skyscraper, or from genes to an entire society is of ultimate value as the ultimately real.

Unlike Marxism, capitalistic materialism does not proceed from the metaphysical affirmation that the material is the real. In fact it may have a loose alliance with idealistic metaphysics or theistic religion. But nevertheless in its encouragement of the acquisition and accumulation of real estate and of stocks and bonds, capitalist economics seems to bear its witness in favor of the ultimacy or supreme value of material things; at least in this present life prior to death. At this point capitalist economics stands on common ground with its arch foe, Marxism.

The Gnostic-Manichaean outlook saw material things as evil, either intrinsically, or by association with the cosmic forces of evil in conflict with the good. The Hindu-Buddhist outlook sees material things as passing and secondary phenomena, either unreal and hence illusory, or real and yet, so far as contributing to desire, more harm than good. The Marxist-capitalist outlook sees material things as the *summum bonum*, either because they are the ultimately real, or because they are reckoned to be of highest value to living man.

III.

In view of its biblical foundations and of the major contrary answers to the question of the significance of material things, what should a Christian understanding of material things mean to Christians today? Should it have the same meaning for Christians who are living amid the technology and relative affluence of the developed nations and for Christians who are living in the underdeveloped nations? The following statements constitute an effort to formulate answers.

(1) *Origin:* Christians believe, as do Jews and Muslims, that all material things were created by and derived from God. Hence material things are not eternal but are derived and temporal. Their significance, therefore, must be consonant with their origin and their destiny. Material things cannot, for Christians, be ultimate reality, but they are indeed real. Indeed it is the reality of material things and the orderliness and purposiveness of the universe that make possible the entire enterprise of modern science. Science's debt to Judaism and Christianity for such concepts was hardly acknowledged by A. Wolf when he indicted the medieval Christian Church as the "chief obstacle in the path of science." [15]

(2) *Value:* From the perspective of Christian truth one can hardly affirm unconditionally that material things are inherently moral. The pronouncements of the goodness of creation in Genesis 1 pertain to the goodness of the created order as brought into existence by God. They do not necessarily invest created things or beings with an independent and intrinsic goodness. The creation of man is embraced without the pronouncements, but the same book of Genesis presents

91

man as sinner. The usage of material things by man must be considered before their morality can be defined. Whether material things are good or evil may depend on man's usage of the same. Steel may be used to make operating room equipment for saving lives or to make weapons for killing human beings. The goodness or the evil lies in the usage. But the worth of material things in general is a corollary of the doctrine of creation.

(3) *Ownership and Dominion:* Christians by implication from creation as well as by specific biblical teaching are obliged to recognize that ultimate ownership of and dominion over all material things belong to God. "For from him and through him and to him are all things. To him be glory for ever. Amen" (Rom. 11:36 RSV). Together with and under this primary or ultimate divine ownership and dominion men participate in a secondary or relative ownership and dominion of material things through what has been called "the ownership of property." Such ownership may be collective (nation, group, family) or individual or joint (husband and wife). While subject to the mortality of human owners and to its possible sale, such ownership of property may transcend the deaths of individual men through inheritance or through collective ownership. Dominion, or at least a relative dominion, may be exercised more widely than ownership, as in the case of the seas and the atmosphere. During the history of Christianity three primary challenges have been presented to the concept and practice of individual ownership of property. One was the monastic challenge, initiated as part of a reaction against the worldliness of the contemporary Christianity and maintained through the monastic vow of poverty. The history of the Josephite monasteries in sixteenth century Russia affords clear evidence that monastic foundations can through collective ownership be marked by the same inordinate possessiveness which initially evoked the monastic vow of poverty. A second challenge was in the name of a restored Christian community in which private ownership of property by all Christians would be surrendered in favor of congregational ownership, presumably after the Jerusalem model. The Hutterian Brethren, the Moravian wing of sixteenth century Anabaptism, have been one of several examples of such communitarian Christian movements. A third challenge has been that of socialism in the nineteenth and twentieth centuries. By the nationalization of major industries and of the means of transportation and communication socialism has sought to remove or curtail the excessive accumulation of property by the few or the favored. The monastic solution centered in the monastic community, the Christian communitarian solution in the communitarian church,

and the socialistic solution centered in the national community. All three challenged the unlimited development of individual or private ownership of property. Monasticism's challenge is in the name of spirituality; Christian communitarianism's challenge is in the name of neoapostolic Christianity; socialism's challenge—of family and group ownership as well as of individual ownership—is in the name of societal justice. Nevertheless, private ownership continues in non-socialist states. Christians who exercise private and family ownership of property should recognize the ultimate ownership of God and their own responsible stewardship of that property.

(4) *Necessity:* Any valid assessment of the role of material things must consider man's need of basic sustenance: food, drink, clothing, shelter (and twentieth century man would add: medicine). Such basic sustenance must of necessity be derived from the realm of material things, as the recent East Pakistan hurricane has reminded the world. From the first century A.D. Christian love has been interpreted in terms of sharing of the necessities ($τόν$ $βίον$ $τοῦ$ $κόσμου$) with needy brothers (1 John 3:17). But Christian obedience in such instances has not always matched the needs or the mandate of love. Christians, together with many other human beings today, hold the conviction that every human being is entitled to basic sustenance and that human labor is normally the means for providing such. Such a conviction has in recent years been joined with a growing concern about an increasing world population and the availability of material resources for the sustenance of all men.

(5) *Accumulation:* The basic production or acquisition and storage of material things for the meeting of present and future needs derives from the early history of mankind, as primitive agriculture shows. Christians have reason to acknowledge the propriety of such basic accumulation. However, the protests of John Wycliffe and many others against the acquisition and ownership of much property by the medieval Western Church show that accumulation can seriously affect the well-being of the most sacred of institutions. Man, particularly in the twentieth century and especially but not exclusively in the more developed nations, is in constant danger of absolutizing material things as the *summum bonum,* either by the inordinate demand for and acquisition of the products, conveniences, and luxuries provided by modern technology or by the excessive accumulation of material things far beyond personal or family usage without exercise of responsibility to society. Christians should from time to time reassess the shape of their own obedience to God and their stewardship of material things in view of the danger that accumulation may lead to

the practice of a materialism irreconcilable with their Christian profession of faith. The saying of Jesus is relevant: "A man's life does not consist in the abundance of his possessions" (Luke 12:15 RSV).

(6) *Exploitation:* From antiquity man has been aware of those destructive natural catastrophes (earthquake, hurricane, tornado, fire, flood, etc.) that have taken human lives in considerable numbers and have devastated the realm of nature. But only in the modern period, and especially in the present generation, has mankind begun to be truly conscious of the awesome exploitation of natural resources and pollution of the environment that more populous and more technological man has brought about. Soil conservation, reforestation, replenishment of fish, and regulations to preserve wildlife have become common in the United States earlier in the present century, but now the battle against all forms of pollution and waste of natural resources has begun. Of all twentieth century men Christians should be most sensitive to the need for environmental ethics. Christian love for the brethren needs to express itself in care for the total well-being of one's contemporaries and of yet unborn generations. Martin Luther's call to Christians to "be a Christ to one's neighbor" is not alien to the present needs of a populous earth to make proper use of material things.

(7) *Christian Stewardship:* The stewardship of material things for Christians includes more than the right use and conservation of natural resources and the limitation of environmental pollution. Material things, when freely and gratefully dedicated and given to God and entrusted to the Christian "household of faith," can and should be so utilized by Christian persons in the service of Christ and the fellowship of his church as to be means and instruments employed and empowered by the Holy Spirit for Christian evangelization, Christian instruction and nurture, and Christian helping ministries. Such gifts sustain both the enablers who seek to equip all Christians for their ministries and the emissaries of the good news of Christ who plant the need for new fellowships of the reborn. With no Gnostic or Manichaean disdain, no Hindu or Buddhist detachment, and no Marxist or capitalist obsession Christians as stewards of material things —as well as of the gospel and of their total lives—can participate responsibly and joyfully in the transformation of material things into spiritual reality through Jesus Christ, his gospel, his Spirit, and his church. The medieval church used the term "transubstantiation" to describe the alleged change of "substance" of the bread and wine into the actual body and blood of Christ. But in the patristic age the offering had been produce brought by the congregation, not the wafer

and the wine elevated by the priest. Can we as evangelical Christians dare to see as the true end of Christian giving of material things (money) the "transubstantiation" by the Spirit of God of such things so given into the personal reality of redeemed humanity?

Hans Lilje, the Lutheran bishop of Hanover, wrote about World War II of the significance of Christian stewardship and declared:

> Here the insights of our American brethren in the faith have, in the perspective of church history, something like the same significance as the lessons which the German Lutheran Reformation has taught us about justification by grace, or the Communion of the Brethren [*Unitas Fratrum*] about the unity of God's children.[16]

Whether in America or elsewhere, Christians ought in the context of their possibilities as never before to practice and live out their stewardship of material things, being ever open to the ownership and dominion of the creating, redeeming God and to the needs of men and of the universe.

FOOTNOTES

[1] *Theology of the Old Testament,* trans. Arthur W. Heathcote and Philip J. Allcock (New York: Harper and Brothers, 1958), pp. 144-146.

[2] *Ibid.,* p. 137.

[3] *A Theology for Christian Stewardship* (Philadelphia: Muhlenberg Press, 1956), pp. 33f.

[4] *The Gnostic Religion: The Message of the Alien God and the Beginnings of Christianity* (Boston: Beacon Press, 1958), pp. 42-46. Used by permission.

[5] *Ibid.,* p. 227.

[6] Robert Ernest Hume, *The World's Living Religions* (New York: Charles Scribner's Sons, 1947), p. 25.

[7] *Ibid.,* p. 71.

[8] *Ibid.,* p. 77.

[9] August Karl Reischauer, "Buddhism," in Edward J. Jurji, ed., *The Great Religions of the Modern World* (Princeton, N. J.: Princeton University Press, 1947), p. 97.

[10] E.g., Leucippus, Democritus, and Epicurus.

[11] E.g., De la Mettrie, Diderot, and Holbach.

[12] Frederick Mayer, *A History of Modern Philosophy* (New York: American Book Company, 1951), pp. 428, 433.

[13] *The Theory and Practice of Communism: An Introduction* (5th rev. ed.; New York: Macmillan Company, 1960), pp. 34f.

[14] *Ibid.*, p. 180.

[15] *A History of Science, Technology and Philosophy in the 16th and 17th Centuries* (2nd ed. prep. by Douglas McKie; New York: Harper & Brothers, 1959), I, 8.

[16] Foreward to Heinrich Rendtorff, *Als die guten Haushalter* (Neuendettelsau: Freimund-Verlag, 1952), trans. and quot. by Kantonen, *op. cit.*, p. 1.

The Christian's Relationship to Material Things

Lory Hildreth

The present era in human history is property-minded. We set great store on the things which are ours. It can be aptly described as an age of expanding industry and commerce. It is a "things" civilization where things are produced and made available on a scale the human mind had never anticipated.

With these good things of earth there develop many grave, national and individual problems. In our desire for profits, trade wars develop. In our insatiable desire for material resources, misunderstandings, hate and war are bred. The "have-nots" of this world are emerging and are demanding to be heard on a scale unparalleled in human relations.

That which is so fraught with peril is, however, a legitimate concern. Material things minister to man's well-being; and food, clothing, and shelter are truly life's necessities. There is nothing unworthy about the production of these products which minister to man's sustenance. Life and civilization are supported and enriched by industrial and commercial concerns.

Material resources become vastly important when one does not have them. The proposition that the higher life is independent of possessions is not true. The lack of possessions can be just as spiritually penalizing as the abundant possession of the same. The lack of material advantages may not only lead to privation, but also to bitterness and personal antagonism.

"If any man says to me that he does not love money," writes Studdert-Kennedy, "I immediately begin to wonder, whether he is a madman, a millionaire, or a tramp, these being the only types of people I can imagine saying it with anything like sincerity." [1]

Man is not pure spirit. His earthly destiny is concerned with material things. The survival of his body as well as the cultivation of his mind are dependent on them. His spiritual life is so largely dependent upon possessions of some kind.

The major portion of man's time is spent in the acquisition of things. He is concerned about making a living, providing for his family, and preparing for the future. Man's passion to possess may become unbridled. It can breed selfishness and a calloused attitude to the needs of others.

Such a backdrop brings into focus the Christian concept of ownership. Harrell states, "The will to possess must be controlled by moral law or Western civilization is headed for disaster." [2]

The Christian idea of property confronts us immediately with what is decidedly unpleasant. We soon discover, even in casual reading, that our definition of ownership follows closely the pattern of ancient Rome. The law of ancient Rome has contributed to the progress of civilization, but it was neither God-centered nor concerned with man's responsibility for the needs of others.

Our commonly accepted idea of property reflects the same weakness as that of the ancient Roman code. In our legal system the test of ownership is not the right to use and enjoy anything. Harrell indicates, "The distinguishing mark of ownership is the owner's right to keep any other person from using it." [3]

We may purchase something and have a clear title to it. We may never use it nor enjoy it. This does not mean a forfeiture of ownership. In our town at the present time we have several houses in a state of much needed repair through nonuse and lack of concern by the property owner. If a man moved in to use one of the houses for shelter and enjoyment without the owner's permission, he would be considered a usurper and a thief.

This dilemma has led many thinking men to strive toward an application of the commandment "Thou shalt not steal" whereby each man shall have a fair share of the good things of life. They question whether or not our economic system itself does not permit a few superior ones to steal continually from many the virtues of life, liberty, and the pursuit of happiness. This approach was involved in the ancient conflict between Pharaoh and Moses: Pharaoh saw only property rights in the labors of slaves. Moses saw the right of his people to freedom and happiness.

All of these considerations confront us with the decision whether human welfare is more important than property rights.

The commandment "Thou shalt not steal" underscores the sacredness of property. The importance of ownership is vividly illustrated in the ancient story of Naboth and his vineyard. A community of

Naboths is far better than a community of tenants can ever be. His ownership, although small, gave him a real stake in the community and its progress. No doubt he took pride in what he owned and he was concerned with how it looked.

There seems to be real merit in the movements that seem to give families a small stake in the land. Trueblood says, "Stealing is evil because ownership is good." [4] A part of our moral task is to encourage ownership and to protect society against any kind of action which would tend to break down the dignity of common living.

But the dangers inherent in the idea that exclusive use is the distinguishing mark of ownership need to be reviewed.

Selfishness is immediately apparent in such emphasis. The parable of the good Samaritan illustrates this truth (Luke 10:30-37). The philosophies of each of the characters toward property and ownership are apparent.

To the lawyer who asked the question of neighborliness, property was a matter of discussion. He symbolizes the philosophical approach. He enjoyed talk as an end within itself. This type of character is too evident in our society today. We have too many talkers about life and too few who come to grips with life's issues. They prefer to keep ethical questions in the realm of the general and refuse to exercise the courage of the specific.

The philosophy of ownership in the thieves' actions is an exercise of power separated from love and justice. They counted what they possessed as theirs and what belonged to the other party would be theirs also if they could get it. Life to these robbers was nothing but a power struggle between the strong and the weak.

The expression of ownership portrayed by the priest and Levite does not present a working alternative. Theirs was the policy of non-involvement. To the fallen man they were saying by their actions: "What you have is yours, and what I have is mine; I feel no compulsion to share with you even though you may desperately need what I have."

Are we any more sensitive to human tragedy and human need? Before we berate modern man for not caring, we need to become realistic. As we bring old instruments of measurement into a new situation, we are apt to conclude that human nature is corrupt and calloused. We are weighing man's capacity for compassion on a scale which was useful only in a radically different situation.

One cannot relate to a thousand people like he could to ten. Neither can he have rapport with a whole city like he could adjust to a farm community. But we must not jump to the conclusion in this era of a population explosion that we are not to be a neighbor at all. There is no doubt that God meant for us to be related to each other in such a way that involved responsible and positive redemptive action more than just refraining from doing harm to the other person.

To approach the matter of being a good neighbor demands both personal and public endeavor. What exceeds our private limitations must be met by public team effort. Corporate influence will then become an essential tool. Politics, of the right sort, can become a form of neighborliness. This becomes an upsetting business because it may mean the turning over of time-honored prejudices.

There is also the attitude of the good Samaritan to be considered. He refused to let peripheral interests be the motivation for his action. He saw the man in need as a human being. National and racial considerations did not concern him.

He reveals the ideal attitude toward ownership for the child of God. "What I have is yours if you need it, and I will gladly share with you in your need." This spirit of sharing was strong among the early Christians. Modern Christianity could well take a lesson from *Mrs. Wiggs of the Cabbage Patch* when she said, "I just don't feel that anything is really mine until I have shared it with someone else."

Insistence on only our rights may blind us to our obligations. This is an attempt to find liberty apart from community. The early frontiersman consulted only his own interest and convenience in anything he wanted. But the frontiers have passed; our neighbor has arrived. J. Wallace Hamilton describes this new scheme of things as "a great world-house in which we have to live together." [5]

Man cannot say that anything is really his. An Old Testament passage enlightens this truth (Eccles. 5:11-20). Solomon ran the gauntlet of life's experiences. Of the things for which men strive, he drank to the full, only to learn in the end that they do not satisfy.

No man was ever more successful in acquiring wealth than Solomon. No man ever realized more than he did the utter vanity of wealth when it is sought for its own sake.

He describes the fraudulent gains of unjust lords and judges. He indicates that their returns brought much less satisfaction than they might think. They made a poor bargain after all.

They learned that "when riches increase, they increase that consume them." They could not know the refreshing sleep that comes after toilsome labor. Their hearts were always full of worry and apprehension. Robbers might drive off their flocks, investments might fail, servants might be unfaithful to their trust, official superiors could ruin them with bribes. In any event they could not take their wealth with them at death.

Charles M. Crowe takes the automobile as a symbol of the things which are ours. He asks, "Ours? It's a good question. Five million automobiles produced in the United States in any one year require 2,500,000 bushels of corn, 160,000,000 pounds of wool, 345,000,000 pounds of cotton, 10,000,000 pounds of turpentine, 12,000,000 gallons of molasses, and quantities of such things as paper, lumber, hides, wheat straw, mohair, flax seed, hog products, sugar cane, beeswax, and excelsior. Ours? All we need to do is to remember that only God can make a tree." [6]

The things which are ours belong to God. This a fundamental fact of life. Our job is not hoarding wealth or fencing it for our own pleasure, but the proper use of it in God's sight. The phrase is not open to question. Buttrick concludes, "If we treat even forests as our own, dust storms and droughts come upon us. The universe knows its rightful Lord, and rebels against impious usurpers." [7]

When man recognizes divine ownership, he no longer is a grubby, grabby animal. The command to "love thy God" is followed by "love thy neighbor." T. S. Eliot puts the question squarely before us in *The Rock*.[8]

> "We build in vain unless the Lord build with us
> Can you keep the city . . . build better
> than they that build without the Lord.
> . . . Though you have shelters and institutions,
> Precarious lodgings while the rent is paid,
> Subsiding basement where the rat breeds
> Or sanitary dwelling with numbered doors
> Or a house a little better than your neighbor's.
> When the stranger says: 'What is the meaning of this city?
> Do you huddle close together because you love each other?'
> What will you answer? 'We all dwell together
> To make money from each other?' or 'This is a community?'
> Be prepared for him who knows how to ask questions."

The Christian Use of Things

Man cannot live by bread alone. Neither can he live on this earth without bread. There is a physical side to life. God looked at the physical aspects of his creation and called them good. God made them for man's enrichment and man's development.

Christians always face the problem of appreciating the good things which God has created without becoming their slaves. A term has been coined in modern times to describe man's becoming so absorbed in things that are good but temporal that he has no concern for the things which are best and are eternal. The term is secularism.

Secularism has been called the refusal to let God be God. When man gets his gadgets, he can easily forget his God. Everything will become so natural and so biological. This is to forget that material things are creations of God, and by investing them with absolute values and ultimate concern, man falls into idolatry. ". . . and have offered reverence and worship to created things instead of to the Creator" (Rom. 1:25 NEB).

When things are in control and God is not sovereign, there develops a process of dehumanization. Machinery, organization, and technology push man from the center of things. There follows a loss of the sense of mystery and a decline of the sense of transcendence. An overemphasis on visibility blots out vision. Dollar signs become our glasses.

Secularism invades our education procedures. Religion and the Bible are barriers to secularism and to our youth learning truth as it is. This philosophy is evident in much of our contemporary literature. God's absence plays an important role.

Most writers are so dedicated to humanism that they would consider it a betrayal of their first cause even to deal seriously with the question of God. The sense of the demonic haunts the pages of a writer for whom God is manifestly absent.

Our churches are not unaffected. Lectures and harmless homilies are droned in a country club atmosphere. Sin and atonement are toned down. Jesus is sentimentalized and demythologized. Church members no longer want biblical terminology but a new idiom. We are not alert to the triviality of our petty loyalties, because God in Christ is not at the center of things.

Increasingly, Americans discontinue going to church and instead spend their weekends in pleasure seeking. "If there is no difference between "godly" and "worldly," why should one attend church regularly? If *kerugma* is not different from lectures in metaphysics, if *koinonia* can be replaced by a cocktail party, and *diakonia* by peace demonstrations, what else does one need?" [9]

A kind of terror begins to grip man when he is left alone with man, and has no invisible means of support, with no one to pray to but himself.

Will Durant wrote to some of his intellectual friends about the God who had faded out and how the empty soul of Western man wandered in the wastelands, seeking something to fill the emptiness.

In a sad and cynical book called *The Meaning of Life,* he wanted to know why progress had proved such a delusion, why the optimism of the nineteenth century had given way to the deep pessimism of the twentieth, why all the bright promises of reason and the fruits of science had been exploited for nothing but futility or destruction.

"We move," he said, "into an age of spiritual exhaustion like that which hungered for the birth of Christ. The great question of our time is not communism versus individualism, not Europe versus America, not even East versus West; it is whether man can bear to live without God." [10]

What should be the Christian's response to secularism? It should be evident that we as Christians are not to flee the secular, but to be God's agents in sanctifying this realm. We must challenge the secular way of life, occasionally supporting it, and often judging, but always in the light of another way that is open.

We must minister to the needs of men as they are and where they are in our culture and in our time. But we must beware of separating that which God has joined together. We must be careful in separating the sacred and the secular.

Robert A. Raines in *The Secular Congregation* describes the pietist-secularist controversy. He says that the pietist is church-centered and is more concerned that the essential faith be preserved than that it be relevant to the modern world. He holds fast to the church at the risk of losing the world. The secularist is world-centered. He looks for God primarily in the world. He is more concerned with the relevance of the gospel to the world than with its preservation. He holds fasts to the world at the risk of losing the church.

The pietist thinks of God's action primarily in terms of the past. He wants continuity. His mood is nostalgia, his motto is "Come weal or woe, the status quo!" The secularist thinks of God's action primarily in terms of the future. He wants change. His mood is optimism, his motto is, "Come weal or woe, go-go-go!" [11]

In this strategic chapter Raines concludes that each emphasis provides a needed corrective for the other. He feels that the tension can be creative instead of destructive. Both must see the church as God's work and God's mission in the world.

George W. Webber applies three dimensions to the purpose of the church in our time. There is the vertical dimension reminding us of the absolute dependence of the congregation upon the sustaining grace of God. This is a point of reference which stands over the secular wisdom of men.

There is the circular dimension which refers to the quality of life together in a Christian fellowship. They are united by one fact: Jesus Christ is their common Lord. There is no place for time limitations we allot to involvement in this fellowship. It is a full-time position with a life-time contract.

There is the horizontal dimension. The church exists for its mission in the world. What we do in the horizontal and circular dimensions are not pious exercises, but rather preparations directed toward our mission in the world. His work in the horizontal dimensions is sustained by his life in the vertical and circular dimensions.[12]

The Christian as he seeks "to go into all the world," which he recognizes as more than a geographical directive, will give priority to kingdom interests. Jesus instructs us that we should have regard for food and clothing, but that we should not think about them first (Matt. 6:19-33).

Some feel that it is possible for men to be free from anxiety and selfishness. When this happens, economic problems will more or less take care of themselves. Others feel that the ideal Jesus is setting forth is entirely impractical. They feel that for a person to deny anxious thought concerning material things is to throw a pious cloak over his desire for economic security.

Anxiety in Jesus' day had to do more with the basic necessities. Poverty was universal and many lived only one meal distant from death. Their care about life's necessities and covetousness for wealth undercut their loyalty to God.

In this passage Jesus draws a contrast between something strained and something effortless. Through anxiety men seem to be forcing events into patterns of their own making. He sets this over against what happens when men base their lives on the way God works.

The person who allows wealth to become his god, his organizing principle, will be rewarded by a life of anxiety and uneasiness. When he makes his god out of things, his greatest care is taking care of his god. "Moth and rust corrupting and thieves breaking through to steal" are just a few of the perils that constantly threaten the god of things.

With the birds of the air and the lilies of the field, Jesus illustrates what life is like when man allows God to work. In the place of strain, anxiety, and fear, there is joy and fulfillment. They let God be God.

Jesus seems to be saying, "Don't get entangled with worry over the necessities of life and miss the purpose of life." We need the creative anxiety concerning the will of God in crucial relationships. Man in his individual and corporate life is miserable and baffled because he will not come to terms with the living God.

George Buttrick thinks that the truth which Jesus stated should be brought to cases. "When business thinks of profits first and people second, depressions plague us. When it thinks of people first and the intent of God second, pride betrays us. . . . We place the kingdom second, and so spend more money for jails and hospitals than we would have spent on decent homes and city planning. . . . We seek pleasure first, and find nausea. We seek safety first, and find a cowardly and defenseless mind. We seek profits first, and find fratricide. It is hard for man to hammer nails upwards. He is going against the law of things." [13]

By amassing things, we do not necessarily achieve security. Jesus warns man of covetousness, because life does not consist of the abundance of man's possessions (Luke 12:15). Jesus in this warning challenges man's accepted standards of values.

To illustrate his point Jesus told a story of a man who filled his barns, and built new barns and filled them also (Luke 12:16-21). The man thought his soul could thrive on wheat, houses, and lands. He refused to nourish the life of the spirit. Luccock says that "his heart and mind had become a mere clutter of merchandise." [14]

This rich man learned too late that one's life is made secure not by things, but by triumph over things. There was no sin indicated in the productiveness of this man's fields, but his planning indicates several weaknesses. It was too self-centered. He disregarded all eternal values, consequences, and judgments. He offered his soul eat, drink, and merriment—but nothing for his spiritual existence. It is good to have money, but it is good to check occasionally to see that we also have the things that money cannot buy.

Crisis always demands spiritual qualities. We may build the big barns and neglect the essentials. We draw our strength from another source than our own will power. The attempt to be self-sufficient is vain. The moral values we hold and the spiritual power we possess are the real indications of our health and strength.

The Christian's use of things does not follow such a worldly pattern. Service rather than profit becomes his motivation. People rather than money become more important. Things serve as means to divine ends rather than as ends within themselves.

At this point also the teaching of Jesus is pertinent. He taught that the greatness of men could not be measured in terms of wealth. The service one renders, said Jesus, constitutes the measure of greatness (Mark 10:41-44).

In the context of this passage there is recorded the discussion of the twelve disciples concerning the subject of greatness. They were concerned about being first. It is interesting to note that Jesus did not condemn the disciples for desiring to be great. He continued the discussion by adding his own unique insights.

There is nothing wrong in the desire to be great. The problem lies in the means we utilize to attain this goal. At this point Jesus was ahead of them (Mark 10:32). Jesus has always been ahead. Ahead of the customs of every age, ahead of its blindness to human and spiritual values and needs.

Today he still goes ahead of our conventional morality and ahead of the minimums which we put in the places of his maximums. Jesus in a way is here challenging them by example and precept to close the gap between him and those who follow.

The great ones of that day were the ones who lorded it over all the rest (Mark 10:42). Jesus indicates that the place of greatness was not a place of authority, but a place of service. The person of greatness was not the one served, but the one serving. Here is a violent reversal of earth's measurements, the whole social pyramid is inverted. How great would our lives be if they were measured only by the amount of service we have rendered to people?

The worldly way of being great is contrary to our essential natures. We have worth because God has seen fit to make us as we are. To attain greatness by domination is to use others who have been divinely endowed with worth as means for selfish ends. Tyrannizing others does not bring joy and fulfillment.

Greatness is then a gift of God by creation and grace. Jesus, when he came to earth, "made himself of no reputation" (Phil. 2:7). He knew that he had worth already in God's eyes. This made him free of men. He did not secure greatness from them either by conformity or conquest. As we seek to conform or to dominate, we are using people as means and are dependent on them.

Knowing one's self to be "great by God," rather than having to earn it, makes us free to be a servant. We do not have to depend on servile relations to earn for us greatness.

The entire New Testament makes it clear that the people of God are a servant-people. They are called to minister to the world. The ministry is not a special function of a part of the church. It is the whole church serving. The doctrine of the priesthood of all believers means that the church is the appointed priest-nation to minister to the world.

Material wealth is thus put in its proper place, a place secondary to ministry and service. Jesus leaves no doubt that personal values are above material values. Material wealth has its place in this world, but it is made to serve men.

This means that to secure the material blessings can never be the aim and purpose of religion. This is precisely what the nature religions sought to do. Baalism would be an outstanding example. In them, religious observances made sure of the spring rains, the summer sunshine, and the autumn harvest.

Luther put this more bluntly in stating that God didn't mean for us to be fatted hogs. He was commenting on the Model Prayer and he noted that the prayer for daily bread is subordinated to the overall purposes of God; the hallowing of his name, the doing of his will, and the coming of his kingdom.[15]

The Christian Standard of Living

It is difficult to arrive at a workable definition of a standard of living. Several factors influence our thinking. One's standard has no maximum limit. Our grandparents would be amazed to see what is considered normal even in low-income American homes today. A hundred years ago, a couple being married was considered fortunate to be able to start their home life with a patch of ground, a mule, a cow, a rifle, an ax, an iron pot, some salt, gunpowder, lead, and a few blankets.

Our standards have gone up considerably since World War II. Rasmussen states: "The statistics are demonstrated everywhere. Gross National Product, average income of the American, or the type of home appliances, and automobile that the median family possesses, if not enjoys, are perhaps the most widely publicized data on our contemporary life." [16]

Paul said that having food and raiment should bring contentment (1 Tim. 6:8), but several things affect even this minimum living standard. Without reference to luxuries, there are many things which should be considered essential for the ongoing of our lives. Going beyond food, clothing, shelter, there would be the kind of transportation one could consider normal; also recreation, cultural, and educational possibilities. These are all elements in our present standard of living.

Even after one has said this, he must realize that such things as those which sustain life, the modifications required by climate and the geography in different areas of the world, make it impossible to establish a living standard for the whole world.

It is further complicated when one notes that in a given nation there are no absolute elements for a standard of living. Governmental agencies in the United States are always struggling with a poverty-level income.

J. R. Crawford, after taking these factors into consideration, defines a standard of living as "that level of wealth in material goods considered normal for a society by the majority of its members." [17]

This definition would lead immediately to Roger Shinn's conclusion that "the ethic of the past was built on the assumption of scarcity." [18] Over the long past of human history, the overwhelming majority of human beings spent their lives enslaved to the arduous routine of sheer survival. Extravagance, self-indulgence, and indebtedness were severely curbed.

But the problem is no less acute in the modern era in our nation "where doctors more often warn people about eating too much than about eating too little; where there are more agricultural surpluses than shortages; where most people have the clothing they need, if not all they want; where Americans have about 36 motor vehicles for every 100 persons; where they even have more telephones than that; where they have nearly as many radios as people—several per family on an average; where there is almost a television set for every three persons; where Americans have learned the trick of producing more and more things with fewer man-hours of work." [19]

But even in such a situation a paradox develops. Very few people consider themselves rich. They want more than the people around them. In an affluent society one thinks he must have a lot. Although three billion people of the world consider a car a luxury, in affluence, former luxuries have become necessities. Central heating, refrigerated air-conditioning, elaborate plumbing, and electric lights are considered "must" items.

Man's inner life does not remain unscathed by these value systems that surround him. It is impossible for man to insulate himself from the effects that productive machinery has on his moral climate and ways of life.

Rasmussen warns that "the massive urbanized industrial system required to produce the never ending streams of goods has revolutionized every aspect of life and is tending to produce a new kind of person." [20]

Bishop Sheen says that those who make material things a kind of God generally reveal these psychological traits. They have a passionate desire to accumulate. They are reluctant to give. They feel that the world owes them a living. [21]

They begin to confuse being with having, life with livelihood. They resolve to save themselves at all costs regardless of what others need. They create situations of dependence by refusing to work. If refused help they become aggressive. They may become neurotic, never getting beyond cradle mentality.

Abundance has become a key factor in creating our basic values. It has become a process exploiting our natural resources. The astronauts in "their giant step for mankind" have given new impetus to a critical look at our environment. Many scientists speaking from a non-biblical view assert that runaway technology, population, pollution, and consumption left uncontrolled, could spell the extinction of the human race.

God's command to have dominion over the earth has been interpreted as a blank check for the exploitation of all natural resources. The age of affluence has very much been an age of waste. The National Research Council warns that the planet Earth is running out of natural gas. Already some substances essential to society—mercury, tin, tungsten—are short. In another fifty years petroleum and natural gas may be 90 percent depleted, forbodes the council's report.

So dreadful is the air pollution problem in many cities that simply breathing is equivalent to smoking two packs of cigarettes per day. Noise pollution costs Americans four billion dollars a year by causing accidents, absenteeism, inefficiency, and health damage. Over one million oxygen-producing trees are cut down and paved over every year. We are discarding garbage in America at the rate of five pounds per person per day. Lake Erie is so near dead that only carp and sludge worms can survive its poison, and it will cost forty billion dollars to clean it up. Every year Americans dispose of seven million wrecked autos, twenty million tons of waste paper, forty-eight billion tin cans, twenty-six billion bottles and jars, three billion tons of waste rocks and mill tailings, and fifty trillion gallons of hot water.[22]

The development of a vast technology in this economy of abundance is a major culprit. Rational organizations of productivity have been created which is superior to anything man has produced in the past. But each new advance in productivity has brought with it a deeper disorganization in human life and greater violence to the environment.

Technology dominates its objects—whether things, men, peoples, or worlds—reducing the object to the predictable, powerless function in order to control it. The apparatus must be kept rolling with ever larger increases in output. Consumption becomes the key to prosperity and security, and man the producer becomes the consumer.

Man with the advent of the machine and the computer is no longer needed as a producer. Man is in danger of becoming dehumanized as work is made unimportant. He may take more pride in what he does around the house than what he did at the factory, because it is something that he does himself.

The number of computers in the United States has multiplied one hundred times in ten years. One machine can do more and do better what formerly took many men to do. Automation has taken the jobs of 400,000 coal miners since the war. In the same period 250,000 steel workers have been replaced by machines, and 300,000 textile workers have lost their jobs.

White collar workers are being pushed out by sophisticated computers. One U. S. Government department, for example, handling veterans' pensions, has cut its staff from 17,000 to 3,000 since installing electronic equipment. There is a radio factory in Chicago with a line of clicking, purring, winding robots producing 1,000 transistor sets a day—tended by only two men. A year ago 200 men were employed on the same job. In New York there is a bottling plant where 200,000 bottles a day are washed, refilled, capped, and crated. Total staff—three men! The New York telephone exchange is 20 stories high and handles millions of calls every day. It is operated by a staff of five, two on duty and three on standby. We ourselves find that by dialing 11 digits we can connect with almost anyone in the States within a few seconds. And Macy's, the world-famous New York store, has been experimenting with a robot salesgirl that sells 36 different garments in 10 styles and sizes, accepts either coin or notes, gives correct change—and rejects, with a suitably indignant scream, all counterfeit money.[23]

Not only has man become a consumer, but as a consumer, through advertising, his tastes are being created and manipulated for him.

Arnold Toynbee, the world famous historian, has these harsh words to say about advertising: "It has made a fine art out of taking advantage of human silliness. It rains unwanted goods down surfeited throats when two-thirds of all human beings now alive are in desperate need of the bare necessities of life. This is an ugly aspect of the affluent society; and, if I am told that advertising is the price of affluence, I reply without hesitation, that affluence has been bought too dear." [24]

We are indebted to Vance Packard who shows us how modern advertising is geared to man's strongest weaknesses. He did this when he described the results of motivational research. In short, this is the method of discovering why people buy what they do or vote as they do. It involves the services of several thousand social scientists with psychiatric credentials employed in a multi-million dollar industry.

He states in another book, *The Status Seekers,* that the advertising world is stimulating and exploiting the urges of Americans toward self-betterment. He goes on to show that these upward strivings of the masses soon collide with the jealousies of the elite, those who are already "in," and because of this tension a hardening of the arteries of the social system develops.

The status seeker is usually characterized by a state of restless insecurity. He is determined to advance, and his life is viewed as one endless promotion. This makes all his activity utilitarian, always seeking to enhance his opportunities for advancement.

William Hull makes a comparison in the old world culture as to how a command was obeyed without question: "Find your station in life and stay with it." Haunting questions, however, replace this imperative in America: "Do I belong? Am I accepted? How am I doing?"

In the same sermon Hull drew a significant conclusion: "The modern status seeker is caught in a kind of Purgatory between the hell of the hopelessly poor and the heaven of the entrenched rich. . . ." [25]

This desire for status has contributed to snobbishness, setting man against man, group against group. It even set the disciples quarreling, two against ten.

Thus the biblical warning that "man might gain the whole world and lose his own soul" stands painfully relevant again. Scientific progress has offered no guarantee whereby man's deprivations and frustrations may be resolved. Our questionable prosperity has brought us empty values and national disquietude. We do not have free individuals, but lost ones. We have more isolation than we do independence. Man's belief in himself has become the weakest in the very age when control of his environment is the greatest.

In this kind of situation Christians are called upon to play a decisive role in community life at every level. This action will not be merely interference but, more so, involvement. We have received no special insight that will show us what we must do in any special circumstances.

It is difficult for us to remain objective and to keep our attitude from being pre-conditioned. We live in, and are a part of, a society that demands that we go and buy. Tyrannized by status symbols, we are being led to believe that we must possess everything that is bigger, better, and newer if we are to be complete personalities.

We must somehow remain free so that our economic activity will be judged in the light of what we feel is the will of God. It is impossible to draw up a strict list of luxuries to be left out and to indicate the things that are necessary for every Christian.

As the Christian evaluates the luxury level of his life he should avoid waste, conspicuous consumption, the accumulation of goods for which he has no real need. Robert Maynard Hutchins describes our new way of getting rich: "It is to buy things from one another that we do not want, at prices we cannot pay, on terms we cannot meet, because of advertising we do not believe." [26] I would like to add, "To buy things we do not need, to go in debt because of money we do not have, to keep up with people we do not like."

To be known as a "big spender" is a questionable reputation. To be a member of the "cult of bigness" is to earn Jesus' evaluation of being called a fool. "To waste one's substance is soon to be in want."

The parable of the prodigal son aptly epitomizes our age. The prodigal mirrors our consumer complex. He became a waster rather than a worker. He confused liberty with laissez-faire. This was the quaint idea of Adam Smith's that if we follow our own self-interests, that it will automatically work out for the interests of the whole. Our modern term is "rugged individualism." The basic idea underlying this approach is that every man should be free to get what he can and to use it as he pleases as long as he keeps the rules of the game.

Adam adopted this principle in the Garden and turned it into a wilderness. In varying ways and degrees, man has been doing this ever since. He has been like a prodigal spendthrift destroying the source of his life.

We see this so clearly in our ecological crisis. We take the good earth and waste it, and the earth reflects our sins. Sheltering forests are cut or burned, and the earth answers back with roaring floods. We plow up the prairie grass lands, and the earth answers back in dust bowls, sick soil, and erosion.

We are much like the prodigal in expecting something for nothing given. Our earthly existence implies a partnership. God has provided us with raw materials and with intelligence and energy; we can transform them into bread and buildings. There must be both brain and brawn men working together with God. This a work world and we who live in it must make some return for the space that we occupy in it.

Like the prodigal—we have refused to see the importance of thinking of the other person, of living in community. Forty-five percent of American families still have incomes of less than $4,000 annually, and fifteen percent of our families live on less than $2,000 per year. Pride in our own sufficiency is blunting our concern for the "have-not" nations of the world. Rasmussen shocks us by revealing "that the

6 percent of the world's population living in America enjoy half of the world's income." [27]

This cannot be easily pushed out of the Christian's conscience. In a world where a fellowship of love is to be experienced, the cost of hate comes high. This has been the most destructive, wasteful half-century in human history. Hamilton says, "We went down into the mines, dug out their precious metal and hurled great chunks of it at each other. To preserve our oil we burned up tons of it—enough to keep our tractors going for a hundred years. To defend our homes we demolished homes, thirteen million homes in Europe, seventeen million homes in Asia; we scattered their cities and scattered their peoples on the roads, homeless and hungry—thirty million refugees!" [28]

Albert Camus, in his book *The Plague,* describes a city whose hotel was ridden by rats, thus frightening the entire population: "Are our city fathers aware that the decaying bodies of rodents constitute a grave danger to the population?"

The manager of the hotel can talk of nothing else, but he has a personal grievance too—that a dead rat should be found in the elevator of a three-star hotel seems to him the end of all things. To console him, I said, "But you know everybody is in the same boat." "That's just it," he replies. "Now, we're like everybody else." [29] It was hell to him to be like everybody else. He wanted to be different, alone, isolated. He no longer cared.

When the prodigal went back home and decided to cooperate with his father, the father gave him a fatted calf, the best robe, new shoes, and his house. What would happen in this world if we could learn to accept as brothers those whom God has accepted as sons?

Collectivism as opposed to individualism does not offer a suitable alternative. Socialism and communism represent this emphasis. The basic idea underlying both these systems is that the state should own and control for the common good every means of production and distribution. This, it is said, would eliminate the evils and waste of a competitive system.

In a socialistic state no one is free to follow his conscience in the use of his property, thus the individual would be deprived of his basic freedoms. The spirit of enterprise and initiative would be destroyed, and this destruction would lead to a denial of the opportunity for man to live creatively.

For the Marxist the only reality is an economic one. Man's struggle for bread is the determining factor of life. This materialism has fatal consequences. It results in an exclusive emphasis upon production, and there follows an overcoming of the concern for justice. With this comes the destruction of the very spiritual values which would save the system from corruption.

As we cannot accept the validity of a collectivistic economic order, we must question whether our changing economic order is in the proper hands. Our Christian faith should have an effect on the functioning of an economic order. Christian forces must build the builders of an economic order.

An economic order will be no stronger than the character of men who administer it. The functioning of our present economic order is rooted in the fact that men are honest.

The character of a man is rooted in his faith in the meaning and purpose of life. With centralization of power, with the increasing socialization of certain forms of industry and with the regimentation of life growing out of the complex society of the modern world, a high premium is put on the right kind of men being found who can be trusted with positions of power.

Christians must oppose the viewpoint which makes the economic order free from all moral and religious controls. It cannot be denied that economic aspects are an important part of a man's life. Man cannot live without bread, but man is more than an appetite. The economic order does not exist as an end in itself. It exists as a part of the larger life of man.

Christians must object to the supremacy of the profit motif. The demands for profits must not be applied in such a way that basic human rights are denied. The church needs to be aware of this profit motif. Many are led to believe that the gospel so transforms men's lives and conditions that prosperity will result. Tithing is presented in terms of ever-greater financial rewards.

Christians must protest the tendency to treat labor as a commodity. This makes the cost of labor a part of the cost of goods. Human labor becomes a commodity that is bought and sold in the market. Labor stands for the toil of human beings. He has a right to receive a fair return for this labor. This wage which he receives affects his capacity to share in the fruits of the labors of other men.

The Christian must begin to realize that his environment is not outside the domain of his religious faith. He must rethink the view that he has of himself and his world. We are indebted to Martin Buber for his description of the two basic ways a human being relates to life.

The first relationship he calls an "I-Thou" association. This is to believe that everything that is, is alive. One can so unite with anything whereby there can be a mutual disclosure of secrets. Everything

114

is alive to give and to receive. In such a setting one has as much a responsibility to give to his environment as to take from it.

The other liaison he describes as an "I-It" relationship. This is a fundamental, different way of being together. There is no sense of life between the subject and the object. A person puts himself over against the object to analyze and to manipulate. There is no moving back and forth in giving and receiving.

God created the whole universe to exist in this "I-Thou" connection. Everything is alive with the life of God. Man, therefore, can be personal with absolutely everything. But we see in the Genesis record where man in sin shifts the relationship from "I-Thou" to "I-It." Man now thinks only of himself and not of what he gives.

As a result, we have lost touch with our world. We have treated the earth as if it were something dead and worthless. We have substituted quantity for quality, substituting many things for the satisfaction of any one thing.

Being too materialistic we lack the ability to love the right way. We make up for this by loving many things superficially and have adopted a consumer-oriented disposable approach to life.

To reestablish the right relationship to our material environment demands the implementation of certain Christian principles.

Paul, as he writes concerning those who are already rich in the possession of things, reminds them that God is to be trusted. It is God who gives us the things we enjoy (1 Tim. 6:17).

We have here the understanding that the good things of this life are to be enjoyed. Paul is urging Christians to engage in the normal pleasures of life when these do not conflict with the service of God.

He did not advocate a religion based on negatives. In his Colossian letter he refers to those who say, "Don't taste that, don't touch that, don't handle that." He indicates that these ordinances may have an appearance of wisdom in promoting humility and the severe treatment of the body, but they do not have any real value in controlling physical passions (Col. 2:21-23).

In a similar emphasis, Paul writes to Timothy condemning those who forbid marriages and the eating of certain foods. He states that God has created everything good and nothing is to be rejected, but is to be received with thanksgiving (1 Tim. 4:3-6).

This is a sane and wholesome attitude toward life. The Christian should receive with thanksgiving the good things which God so richly gives. Christians should enjoy the good things that are to be found in the realms of art, literature, and music. The conveniences of modern life are to be accepted as setting man free from life's drudgeries to enable him to give his time to more creative things.

There is no gain in embracing poverty to avoid the perils of things. Rather than providing a solution of our problems, it becomes a way of escape. Christ's ideal for his followers is that they shall be in the world but not of the world (John 17:15-16). The solution is not in the renunciation of things, but in the proper use of them.

If the Christian does not need an abundance of things to be happy and contented, how much of this world's goods is required for contentment? The apostle answers, "There is great gain in godliness with contentment . . . if we have food and clothing, with these we shall be content" (1 Tim. 6:6-8 RSV).

True contentment is the cure for covetousness. When one loses his passion for material things and sees the primacy of spiritual values, he is approaching Christian contentment.

The word contentment implies independence and the capacity for getting happiness from one's own inner resources. It is a satisfaction which lives on, if need be, without any connection with external conditions.

The Christian way of life will not assure monetary gain, but a genuine Christian will enjoy real gain. He will be rich in what he is. He will be rich in discovering what he can do without.

Food and clothing sound like the very bare essentials to us today. This would terrify most of us if we were left suddenly with nothing else. Epicurus the old Greek philosopher said of himself, "To whom little is not enough nothing is enough. Give me a barley cake and a glass of water and I am ready to rival Zeus for happiness." When someone asked him for the secret of contentment, his answer was, "Add not to a man's possessions, but take away from his desires."

It is never in the power of things to bring happiness. Happiness comes from personal relationships. All the things in the world will not make a man happy if he knows neither friendship nor love.

We must also understand the narrow limits within which material goods can minister to the needs of men. Paul writes, "We brought nothing into the world, and we cannot take anything out" (1 Tim. 6:7 RSV). He seems to be saying that material things are equally irrelevant at our entrance into and our exit from the world.

Jesus illustrates this truth in the parable of the rich fool. He has God asking the farmer after he has filled his new barns and has set for himself a life of merriment, "Fool! This night your soul is required of you; and the things you have prepared, whose will they be?" (Luke 12:20 RSV).

Jesus universally applies this parable as he says, "So is he who lays up treasure for himself, and is not rich toward God" (Luke 12:21 RSV). Jesus' application posits a Christian understanding of life. A man who believes that there is no god can have no understanding of what is involved in using his goods to lay up treasures in heaven. If a man has no understanding of spiritual riches, he can hardly afford to neglect material riches. A Christian philosophy of the use of wealth must find its rootage in the whole Christian understanding of life.

Paul in his writing to young Timothy is making a plea for the permanent, the things that a man can take with him when he dies.

Barclay asserts, "Two things alone can a man take to God. He can take, and must take, himself; and therefore the great task of life is to build up a self and a character and heart and soul that a man takes without shame to God. He can take, and must take the relationship with God into which he has already entered in the days of his life . . . the secret of happiness lies in personal relationships, and the greatest of all personal relationships is the relationship to God." [30]

Rolsten concludes that, "In a world which may be described as money-mad, Christianity can perform to many people no greater service than that of teaching them to achieve contentment with the external circumstances which are part of their lot in life. In a world in which most people are dominated by false values, Christianity can teach men to realize the riches that are involved in character, in righteousness, in inner peace, in the loving service to others, and in that vast realm of spiritual values which make life worthwhile. In a world which thinks largely of material things, Christianity can point out the perishing nature of all the things that belong to this present world and the abiding realities to be found in the things which are not seen but eternal." [31]

Paul not only gave instructions concerning contentment, but he also experienced contentment (Phil. 4:11-13). The New English Bible translates his opening words in these verses: "I have learned to find resources in myself whatever my circumstances."

Paul was in everything but an ideal situation. He was in prison at the time and chained to a soldier of the Praetorian Guard. Paul says that he learned the secret of contentment. This suggests that there was a time, perhaps before he became a Christian, when he did not know the secret. In his prison experience, Paul reveals the resources of his contentment.

He had a realistic outlook upon life. The New English Bible tells that "he had been thoroughly initiated into the human lot with all of its ups and downs." Where one has only known health, prosperity, and privilege he is apt to think that such is a normal existence.

Paul had learned that in life there are certain inescapable factors. There are life's frailties hazards of environment, and the problems growing out of human relationships. He accepted the universe as God created it. John Gunther, the great American newspaper correspondent, had a son John, who died at the age of seventeen with meningitis. He left behind a private notebook in which he jotted down the lines: "Contentment with the universe. Discontent with the world."

If a person is at peace with the universe, vitally related to his Creator and facing up to reality, he is free to be discontented, creatively discontented with the domestic arrangements here on earth. This kind of realism provides Paul with the inward resources which made it possible for him to come to terms with the worst that life had to offer, as well as death.

Paul had the right priorities. In his scale of values, people were more important than things. Keeping his human relationships intact fortified him against complaint. Paul found in the Philippians' concern for him a source of joy. Usually adversity teaches us how much we need friends.

Paul also had a divine point of reference in his contentment. He had the strength of Christ which was being constantly poured in to him. He realized that his contentment was a divine achievement and that he had no sufficiency within himself. Whether he had a great deal or whether he had nothing—these made no difference. In any situation he had Jesus Christ. Living in Christ he could cope with anything.

Paul in writing to Timothy tells the rich what not to do and what to do with their material resources (1 Tim. 6:17-19). They are not to be haughty. They are not to set their hope on uncertain riches but on God. For them to be wealthy was not a sin, but a very great responsibility accompanied the possession of wealth.

They are to do good with their money. They can use wealth to minister to the needs of suffering humanity. They are to be rich in good deeds. They are to be ready to share and willing to sympathize.

If material blessings are hoarded, man's sympathy for mankind, respect for right and love, and reverence for God will be destroyed. Material riches that cater to our self-indulgence will soon possess the possessor. Money and things used for God's glory will honor God and bless the giver as well as the recipient of the gifts.

Euripides, the Greek playwright of the fifth century B.C., expressed Paul's sentiments beautifully:
    I care for riches, to make gifts

118

To friends, or lead a sick man back to health
With ease and plenty. Else small aid is wealth
For daily gladness; once a man be done
With hunger, rich and poor are all as one.

In this success-minded generation we need to be reminded of the danger of piling up the perishable. Our idea of success is determined by the treasures we lay up here on earth. Charles L. Allen says that "according to our standards of success, Jesus was one of the failures of history. He disappointed his friends and followers. His family considered him a hopeless dreamer. He was trained for a respectable trade, but he turned his back upon it. He never drew a salary, never saved any money, never owned a house in which to live. He achieved none of the status symbols that we consider so important—a flashy new car, two television sets, an honorary degree, and so on. The only status symbol he achieved was a cross on which he suffered a lonely death." [32]

Jesus still warns, "Lay not up for yourself treasures on earth!" (Matt. 6:19). Our Lord is warning against the giving of our lives for the things which are only temporary. We are citizens of two worlds and we need to remember that there is a difference between living today and living for today. Our destiny is not found in one world.

When Jesus tells us not to lay up treasures on earth, he forbids us to set our hearts on them, to accumulate them for their own sake, to make them the end of life, to use them selfishly, forgetting our obligations to others. Our real treasure must not be on earth. Jesus said, "Where your treasure is there will your heart be also" (Matt. 6:21). A man's interests are where his investments are. If everything a man desires is contained within this world, if all his interests are earthbound, he never thinks of another world and a hereafter.

How can we lay up treasures in heaven? Jesus gives us no indication here, but there are other verses which may enlighten us.

In speaking to the rich young ruler, Jesus said to him, "If thou wilt be perfect, go and sell that thou hast, and give to the poor, and thou shalt have treasure in heaven" (Matt. 19:21).

The command "to sell" and "to give" reflect a concern for the poor, but that was not Jesus' major concern. He was seeking to free the rich young man from the tyranny of riches. Jesus did not demand the surrender of property from prospective followers, but he demands of everyone the surrender of money, comfort, ambition, and anything else that hinders us from commitment to God.

It is made clear here that we lay up treasures in heaven by using our worldly resources for the good of our fellow men.

Jesus provides further enlightenment in the parable of the unjust steward (Luke 16:1-8). Many think that Jesus could not have told such a story. We must remember, however, that Jesus used such a man as an example of resourcefulness and not corruption. Jesus is wishing to convey a central truth.

The man was confronted with the results of some crooked business transactions, and he was facing a termination of his employment if they were not remedied.

From the incident Jesus challenges his disciples, "To make friends for yourselves by means of unrighteous mammon, so that when it fails they may receive you into eternal habitations."

Jesus teaches here that although money is not the true riches we may change it into such by the right use of it. To use money rightly is to remember that the supreme values always are human and spiritual.

The rascal in the story refused to be turned aside by any values which he considered secondary. He put the winning of things, the making of material provisions above everything else.

How does this compare with the conduct of the children of light —we who are to give supreme emphasis to spiritual values? When there is a clash between profits and principles, between money and men, which one do we choose?

Business has always been characterized by an attempt to foresee the future. The good businessman seeks to think far ahead and is ready for any emergency. Our economic system is dedicated to the proposition that business must win its battles by foresight and imagination.

We had better begin to examine our spiritual policies with an eye to the future. The religious man is to show the same vision as the businessman. We must realize that personal relationships are ultimate. In relating to others, we enter the realm of the absolutes. Friends made now will be the ones who will receive us "into the eternal habitations" when everything else fails. There comes a time when having a friend means more than having stocks and bonds. Let us put our money to its proper service, that of friendship and community rather than enmity and division.

The best investment for now and for eternity is in the lives of people. It will be wise for us to use now that which is entrusted to us so that in the eternity to come there will be no regret but only joy for the way in which our wealth is employed. A welcome in heaven will be experienced because of those who are there, growing out of our efforts on earth.

This surely means that a new seriousness must enter our earthly decisions. We may dedicate our money to set in motion influences which are eternal in their significance. It may be that only in the light of eternity will be measured all the good that may be accomplished because we have made our investments in the great causes of God's kingdom.

The art of Christian stewardship requires a fine sense of balance. It has its roots in a Christian understanding of the purpose of life. It involves provisions for our necessities and a reasonable provision in view of life's hazards. We are challenged to use our money for our own enrichment and the blessing of others in our investing in education and culture. There must be a balance in spending for ourselves and what is given to kingdom causes. There must be a sense of values reflected in a proper balance between the temporal and the eternal.

Stewardship as an art is difficult to master, but it will be reward enough to be able to hear the Master say, "Well done, good and faithful servant; . . . enter thou into the joy of thy lord" (Matt. 25:23).

OUTLINE

THE CHRISTIAN'S RELATIONSHIP TO MATERIAL THINGS

I. The Christian Concept of Ownership
   1. Present era of human history is property-minded
   2. Present concept of ownership
      "The distinguishing mark of ownership is the owner's right to keep any other person from using it."
      (1) This concept based on Justinian code
      (2) Rule of exclusive use leads to selfishness
          e.g. parable of good Samaritan
      (3) Insistence on only our rights blinds us to our obligations
      (4) Man cannot say that anything is really his
   3. Christian concept emphasizes owner's obligation to God and to his fellowmen
II. The Christian Use of Things
   1. Importance of rightly relating to things
      (1) When things are in control
          a. Dehumanization results
          b. Secularism results
          c. Anxiety results
          d. Insecurity results

(2) When God is in control

    a. We will not separate the sacred and the secular

    b. The amount of our possessions will be secondary to the main issues of life

2. Christian's use of things does not follow a worldly pattern

    (1) Service other than profit becomes his motivation

    (2) Service becomes the criterion for greatness

    (3) Things become servants rather than goals

III. The Christian Standard of Living

1. As related to the worldly concept

"A standard of living is that level of wealth in material goods considered normal for a society by the majority of its members."   —J. R. Crawford

    (1) What affects minimum living standard

        a. What sustains life

        b. What is considered normal in a household

        c. Modification required by climate and geography

    (2) Effect of the supposed standards on those around us

        a. Social system sets the framework in which the individual functions

        b. Effect on inner life by the value systems surrounding one

        c. Abundance as a key factor in creating our basic values

            (a) Has exploited natural resources

            (b) Developed a vast technology

            (c) Used mass communication to create and to intensify demand for things

            (d) Made us a nation of status seekers

2. As related to every day living

    (1) Some things not to be desired

        a. Avoid waste and conspicious consumption

        b. Avoid accumulation of goods for which we have no real need

    (2) Some philosophies to be avoided

        a. Laissez-faire

        b. Collectivism

3. As related to Christian influence

    (1) The Christian refuses to have the economic order free from moral controls

    (2) The Christian protests the attempts to treat labor as a commodity

    (3) The Christian seeks to establish a right relationship

with his material environment
4. As related to vital principles
   (1) Good things of life are to be enjoyed
   (2) True contentment a cure for covetousness
   (3) Material goods minister within narrow limits
   (4) Must not give lives to that which is temporary
   (5) Best investment is in lives rather than in institutions

FOOTNOTES

[1] G. A. Studdert-Kennedy, *The Wicket Gate* (Hodder and Stoughton, 1923), p. 154.

[2] Coston J. Harrell, *Stewardship and the Tithe* (Nashville: Abingdon Press, 1953), p. 18.

[3] *Ibid.*, p. 25.

[4] Elton Trueblood, *Foundations of Reconstruction* (New York: Harper Brothers, 1946), p. 88.

[5] J. Wallace Hamilton, *Horns and Halos* (Westwood, N. J.: Fleming H. Revell Company, 1954), p. 73.

[6] Charles M. Crowe, *Stewardship Sermons* (Nashville: Abingdon Press, 1960), p. 113.

[7] George A. Buttrick, ed., "Exposition, The Gospel According to St. Luke," *The Interpreter's Bible* (New York and Nashville: Abingdon-Cokesbury Press, 1951), VIII, 282.

[8] T. S. Eliot, *The Complete Poems and Plays—1909-1950* (New York: Harcourt, Brace and World, Inc., 1952), p. 103.

[9] Dr. Gregory I. Yasinitsky, "The Ism That Is Diluting Christianity," *Liberty*, (Nov.-Dec., 1968), p. 17.

[10] Cited by Hamilton, p. 38.

[11] Robert A. Raines, *The Secular Congregation* (New York: Harper and Row, 1968), pp. 3-5.

[12] George W. Webber, *God's Colony in Man's World* (New York and Nashville: Abingdon Press, 1960), pp. 45-50.

[13] Buttrick, *The Interpreter's Bible*, Vol. VII, pp. 323-24.

[14] Halford E. Luccock, *Studies in the Parables of Jesus* (New York and Nashville: Abingdon-Cokesbury Press, 1917), p. 107.

[15] Cited by Reginald H. Fuller and Brian K. Rice, *Christianity and the Affluent Society* (Grand Rapids, Michigan: William B. Eerdmans Publishing Company, 1966), p. 13.

[16] Albert Terrill Rasmussen, T. K. Thompson, editor, *Stewardship in Contemporary Theology* (New York: Association Press, 1960), p. 230.

[17] J. R. Crawford, *A Christian and His Money* (Nashville and New

York: Abingdon Press, 1967), p. 67.

[18] Roger L. Shinn, *Tangled World* (New York: Charles Scribner's Sons, 1965), p. 32.

[19] *Ibid.*, p. 25.

[20] Rasmussen, p. 228.

[21] Bishop Fulton J. Sheen, *Footprints in a Darkened Forest* (New York: Meredith Press, 1967), pp. 112 ff.

[22] Harry N. Hollis, Jr., "Can We Prevent an Ecological Armageddon?" *The Baptist Program* (Oct., 1970), p. 7.

[23] Fuller and Rice, pp. 142-143.

[24] Cited by Shinn, p. 31.

[25] From a sermon preached at Crescent Hill Baptist Church, Louisville, Kentucky, April 30, 1967.

[26] Cited by Rasmussen, p. 242.

[27] *Ibid.*, p. 247.

[28] Hamilton, p. 123.

[29] Albert Camus, *The Plague* (Australia: Penguin Books in Association with Hamish Hamilton, 1960), p. 26.

[30] William Barclay, *The Letters to Timothy, Titus and Philemon* ("The Daily Bible Study Series"; Philadelphia: The Westminster Press, 1960), p. 151.

[31] Holmes Rolston, *Stewardship in the New Testament Church* (Richmond, Virginia: John Knox Press, 1952), p. 134.

[32] Charles L. Allen, *The Sermon on the Mount* (Westwood, New Jersey: Fleming H. Revell Company, 1966), pp. 118-119.

BIBLIOGRAPHY

Allen, Charles L. *The Sermon on the Mount.* Westwood, N. J.: Fleming H. Revell Company, 1966.

Brattgard, Helge. *God's Stewards.* Minneapolis, Minn.: Augsburg Publishing House, 1963.

Buber, Martin, *I and Thou.* Edinburgh: T. and T. Clark, 1952.

Camus, Albert. *The Plague.* Australia: Penguin Books, 1960.

Conrad, Alphin Carl. *The Divine Economy.* Grand Rapids, Michigan: William B. Eerdmans Publishing Company, 1954.

Crawford, John R. *A Christian and His Money.* Nashville and New York: Abingdon Press, 1967.

Crowe, Charles M. *Stewardship Sermons.* New York and Nashville: Abingdon Press, 1960.

Elder, Fredrick, *Crisis in Enden.* Nashville and New York: Abingdon Press, 1970.

Fuller, Reginald and Rice, Brian K. *Christianity and the Affluent Society.* Grand Rapids, Michigan: William B. Eerdmans Publishing Company, 1966.

Hamilton, J. Wallace. *Horns and Halos.* Westwood, N. J.: Fleming H. Revell Company, 1954.

————. *Ride the Wild Horses.* Westwood, N. J.: Fleming H. Revell Company, 1952.

Harrell, Costen J. *Stewardship and the Tithe.* New York and Nashville: Abingdon Press, 1953.

Hobbs, Herschel H. *The Gospel of Giving.* Nashville, Tennessee: Broadman Press, 1954.

Kantonen, T. A. *A Theology for Christian Stewardship.* Philadelphia: Muhlenberg Press, 1956.

Luccock, Halford E. *Studies in the Parables Of Jesus.* New York and Nashville: Abingdon-Cokesbury Press, 1917.

McRae, Glenn. *Teaching Christian Stewardship.* St. Louis, Missouri: Bethany Press, 1954.

Powell, Luther P. *Money and the Church.* New York: Association Press, 1962.

Raines, Robert A. *The Secular Congregation.* New York: Harper and Row, 1968.

Rolston, Holmes. *Stewardship in the New Testament Church.* Richmond, Virginia: John Knox Press, 1946.

Shinn, Roger L. *Tangled World.* New York: Charles Scribner's Sons, 1965.

Sheen, Bishop Fulton J. *Footprints in a Darkened Forest.* New York: Meredith Press, 1967.

Smith, Roy L. *Stewardship Studies.* New York and Nashville: Abingdon Press, 1954.

Thompson, T. K., Editor. *Stewardship in Contemporary Theology.* New York: Association Press, 1960.

————. *Stewardship in Contemporary Life.* New York: Association Press, 1965.

Trueblood, Elton. *Foundations of Reconstruction.* New York and London: Harper and Brothers Publishers, 1946.

Ward, Hiley H. *Creative Giving.* New York: The Macmillan Company, 1958.

Webber, George W. *God's Colony in Man's World.* New York and Nashville: Abingdon Press, 1960.

Winter, Gibson. *Being Free.* New York: The Macmillan Company, 1970.

The Christian and the Economic Order

Henry A. Parker

The title of this discussion grows out of the assignment made to me in the form of questions: Does the Scripture speak to a Christian's responsibility to influence the economic order—corporate use of things, tax money, wealth, government spending, etc.? Do Christian principles apply to all economic levels? What responsibility does the Christian have to the economic order?

I. Origin of "Material Things"

1. CREATION. At the heart of the "Christian concept" of stewardship lies the basic fact that God is the Creator, Owner, Upholder, and Giver of all things.

"In the beginning God created the heavens and the earth" (Gen. 1:1).

"In the beginning was the Word, and the Word was with God, and the Word was God. All things were made by him; and without him was not any thing made that was made" (John 1:1,3).

"The earth is the Lord's, and the fulness thereof; the world, and they that dwell therein. For he hath founded it upon the seas" Psalm 24:1,2).

"The silver is mine, and the gold is mine, saith the Lord of hosts" (Haggai 2:8).

Every good gift and every perfect gift is from above, and cometh down from the Father of lights, with whom is no variableness neither shadow of turning" (James 1:17).

"For in him were all things created, that are in heaven, and that are in earth, visible and invisible, whether they be thrones, or dominions, or principalities, or powers: all things were created by him, and for him" (Col. 1:16).

The eternal question of whence came the earth and its myriads of beautiful, strange, diverse creatures is a vital one. A person's answer to this question will determine his attitude toward life, itself. In the Christian's mind, God is the great causative factor. The only cause which really explains all and against which there is not one disturbing factor is the Eternal Mind, the Infinite Creator, who is revealed in the Bible as the Lord of Creation and the Preserver of all things.

2. OWNERSHIP. J. E. Dillard reminded us that "Bible steward-ship is the acknowledgement of God's ownership, the acceptance of our trusteeship of life and possessions, and the administration of the same according to the will of God." "Christian ownership" simply means that Christ owns the things a Christian possesses.

"So God created man in his own image, in the image of God created he him; male and female created he them. And God blessed them, and God said unto them, Be fruitful, and multi-ply, and replenish the earth, and subdue it: and have dominion over the fish of the sea, and over the fowl of the air, and over every living thing that moveth upon the earth" (Gen. 1:27,28). "But who am I, and what is my people, that we should be able to offer so willingly after this sort? for all things come of thee, and of thine own have we given thee" (1 Chron. 29:14).

"But thou shalt remember the Lord thy God: for it is he that giveth thee power to get wealth, that he may establish his covenant which he sware unto thy fathers, as it is this day" (Deut. 8:18).

"Know ye not that your body is the temple of the Holy Spirit which is in you, which ye have of God, and ye are not your own? For ye are bought with a price: therefore glorify God in your body . . ." (1 Cor. 6:19,20).

A close study of history will show that man through the ages has held to the idea of God's ownership of everything. Primitive peoples, ancient or modern, never have considered the soil, the hills, plants or animals as their personal property. The area occupied by a tribe belonged to the tribal gods who allowed it to be used but never sur-rendered the title. Louis Wallace said: "The American Indian had no knowledge of absolute private property in the soil. English settlers purchased land from the Aborigines in all good faith, but the Indians did not understand that he was selling his birthright in his native country. Most of the Indian wars were over the land question. At one time, six hundred Indian braves, protected by a stockade in Eastern Connecticut, had to be slaughtered to the last man by prayer-ful Puritans, before land titles in that territory were secure. Indians believed in The Great Spirit, who gives water, air, sunshine, and soil for human life. They had no concept of private property."

A study of Hebrew history and particularly the Old Testament (see Psalm 95) will leave no doubt that the Hebrews believed God owner of all. Our early Christian forbears made a noble attempt to practice this concept in the midst of a pagan society. They were willing to share their wealth for the common good. Regardless of modern man's opinions, the Bible emphatically teaches God's ownership, and the mere possession by man.

3. THE NATURE OF MONEY—SPIRITUAL IMPORTANCE. "Money" is a charming word. Someone has said it is "as musical as dreambells sounding on the sloping hills of sleep." But isn't it amazing that when many people hear it in the sanctuary, it loses its winsomeness. To them, it becomes as jarring as musical instruments played out of tune. They are ready to gnash their teeth and say, "Money, money! That's the way it always is when I come to church." Naturally, these are not in the majority, thank God, but they are always with us. Money is the standard medium for exchange. When used in connection with the stewardship concept, we must think in larger terms that the simple amount of currency one might have available. Every material possession, though not always readily negotiable, constitutes a certain value, and is spoken of in terms of worth, dollars and cents. Luther Powell, in his book *Money and The Church,* has an excellent statement concerning the meaning of money. He says: "Money is too often looked upon as a thing of evil. For instance, due to the abuse in financial matters just prior to the Reformation, some of the Reformed churches forbad taking an offering in the services. The offering plates were kept in small shelters just inside the church gate where people placed their offerings as they left the place of worship. It is still the feeling among many that money, although desirable, carries a bit of taint because of its inherent nature. On the contrary,—the purpose for which it was created is good—to the economist, money is a *measure of value.* In Christian stewardship, it is also a *measure of value.* As long as society regulates the gold, silver, or some other precious material which guarantees that money will maintain a certain standard of values, a man will store up his time, talent and strength in the form of money. Money, then, is *value in negotiable form.* To the hungry it is food; to one who is ill, it is medicine and health; to one who is without shelter, it is a house—when a man gives his money, he is giving part

of himself." This is well stated and magnifies the spiritual importance of money, itself.

II. Possession of "Things"

1. MAN A "TRUSTEE," "STEWARD." A careful study of two New Testament words "steward and stewardship" will show that in every case the steward was one who handled the property or administered the affairs of another. It was a position of honor, trust, and responsibility. John D. Freeman, in his book *More Than Money* says: "There are treasures which God has given to each normal human being as his own. Life, personal influence, and special talents are gifts from God. While they are held in trust, they are unlike other possessions, because they belong exclusively to the holder, and are taken with him when he leaves the earth. Of course he must give an account to God for their use—when it comes to "things," the Bible teaches that they never belong to man, but are merely entrusted to him for a season, in order that his life may be made richer and more powerful in the advancement of the common welfare of all mankind." Just as Adam was the first lease-holder of the estate of God, (God committed the Garden to his care; he was only a gardener, not an owner in fee simple) even so, all men are lease-holders, caretakers, of the natural resources about them. They are temporarily in charge of the estate. The trusteeship originates with God and is limited by his divine fiat. Nowhere is this concept of man's stewardship of God's ownership more clearly stated than in Deuteronomy 8:10-18:

"When thou hast eaten and art full, then thou shalt bless the Lord thy God for the good land which he hath given thee.

"Beware that thou forget not the Lord thy God, in not keeping his commandments, and his judgments, and his statutes, which I command thee this day: lest, when thou hast eaten and art full, and hast built goodly houses, and dwelt therein; and when thy herds and thy flocks multiply, and thy silver and thy gold is multiplied, and all that thou hast is multipled; then thy heart be lifted up, and thou forget the Lord thy God . . . and thou say in thine heart, My power and the might of mine hand hath gotten me this wealth. But thou shalt remember the Lord thy God, for it is he that giveth thee power to get wealth."

2. SCRIPTURAL GIVING. The concept of Christian stewardship involves not only God as creator, a man as steward, but also demands that man acknowledge this relationship. This is done by his setting

aside a portion of his income for the extension of the kingdom. Biblical instructions involve both tithes and offerings. However, this subject will be dealt with by another author. My main motive for mentioning it here is to state that the basic responsibility applies to all. The Bible makes no distinction between the poor and the affluent, at this point. Most Christians regard the tithe as the minimum, the basis, the beginning point. His stewardship is acknowledged through the giving of the tithe into the storehouse. It becomes an integral part of his Christian life, and a part of his expression of worship of the Almighty. However, is just the Christian obligated at this point? Is anyone exempt? Carl Bates, in a pulpit message entitled "Scriptural Giving," reminds us that every man who lives in this world is a steward, whether he ever recognizes and acknowledges it or not. The evidence of his rebellion against God (sin) is seen in his refusal to recognize God as the owner and himself as the steward. Every un-saved member of the Sunday School ought to be encouraged to tithe. That would at least be a step in the right direction. The tithe is holy unto the Lord, and this means that it is His, whether it is in the hands of a Christian or a lost man. The lost man is a rebel against God. He rejects God's ownership and his stewardship. What is the difference between me and him, if I feel the same way about it?

3. GIVING "MONEY" NOT ENOUGH.   One of the fatal mistakes that men have made through centuries is to think that one can fulfill his whole duty to society and to his God by his benefactions. One passage of Scripture is sufficient to refute this misconception.

"Woe unto you, scribes and Pharisees, hypocrites! for ye pay tithe of mint and anise and cummin, and have omitted the weightier matters of the law, judgment, mercy, and faith; these ought ye to have done, and not to leave the other undone" (Matt. 3:23).

God is concerned with the entire ten-tenths of a man's possessions, and with the disposition that man makes of his money as well as his life. Mere giving, however meticulous it may be, falls short in meet-ing our obligations to God and to society.

III. The Economy Order—Man's Habitat

Any complete study of the principle of Bible stewardship must go beyond the individual and involve group implications. The situation in our world today calls for a study of the stewardship of nations, as well as the stewardship of churches and people. We need a fresh evaluation of things in their relation to persons. Actually, a proper recognition and acceptance of the principles of stewardship by the nations would make wars unnecessary, if not impossible. We return to the first point made in this message—"The earth is the Lord's." He has never given any man or nation a quit-claim deed to any part of it. The Bible tells us that God made of one blood all the nations for to dwell on the face of the earth. It is foolish to speak of one branch of the human family as supreme or superior. God intended his world for all of his people. No individual or group of individuals, no nation or group of nations has the right of preemption. All God's people should enjoy and exercise the right to life, liberty, and the pursuit of happiness. This might sound like an over-simplification of the facts, but if these truths were recognized and acted upon, there would be land, food, raiment, and shelter sufficient for all. Wars are wicked and foolish. If nations and individuals were good stewards, the causes of war would be removed and famine, plague, and physical want would cease. Our world will never find permanent peace with justice and prosperity until it heeds the will of Christ. Having said that, let us recognize the fact that this world, God's world, is the home or the living place of all of God's creatures, both Christian and non-Christian alike. Society has been defined as "the web of human relationships." Men being what they are and our world being what it is, it is a foregone conclusion that there must be some system of order or regulation of these relationships. This we speak of in terms of "state" or "government."

1. GOD AND THE PRINCIPLE OF "STATE." In our world there are numerous types or systems of government, various kinds of economic order, and in every one of them there are many Christians to be found. The basic question often asked is, "Is there a set kind of economic order that a Christian should uphold?"

"Dearly beloved, I beseech you as strangers and pilgrims, abstain from fleshly lusts, which war against the soul; having your conversation honest among the Gentiles: that, whereas they speak against you as evil-doers, they may by your good works, which they behold, glorify God in the day of visitation. Submit yourselves to every ordinance of man for the Lord's sake: whether it be to the king, as supreme; or unto governors, as unto them that are sent by him for the punishment of evil doers, and for the praise of them that do well. For so is the will of God, that with well-doing ye may put to silence the ignorance of foolish men: as free, and not using your liberty for a cloak of maliciousness, but as the servants of God. Honour all men. Love the brotherhood. Fear God. Honour the king" (1 Peter 2:11-17).

This passage alone should answer that question once and for all. Wayne Dehoney has referred to it as being "a manual for practical Christian living in a pagan world." Remember, the state under which Peter lived was a different kind of a government than we know today. He and his fellow-citizens knew absolutely nothing of the rights that we take for granted, such as freedom of speech or freedom of religion. They were denied national freedom, because they lived in an occupied, conquered country. Their every move was subject to the heavy hand of a Roman fist. They were constantly subjected to unfair, unjust, dishonest taxation. Multitudes languished in slavery—estimates run as high as three-fifths of the total population. There was no such thing as trial by jury, or the right of the accused to face his accuser and to hear the charges against him. Their state was a totalitarian state from the very outset. Yet, even under this totalitarian government, Peter wrote these words. The Christian citizen is to begin where he is, with a clear understanding of the principle of stewardship, and then do everything in his power to carry out the Lord's command that he be "salt" and "light" in the economic order where he lives.

2. PURPOSE OF GOVERNMENT. Peter clearly points out, as does Paul, that the principle of "government" has a divine function. It serves two purposes: suppressing evil and rewarding good. Laws are necessary to suppress evil as a basic part of regulating human relationships. While government is *by* man, *of* human beings, it is ordained of God. Men rule in the nations by the permissive will of God. History is not a "tale told by an idiot," but is the unfolding of the eternal purpose which God has for mankind. Back of the drama of history is a plot, and behind the plot is a director, who sees the end from the beginning. The classic expression of the divine philosophy of history was given by Paul on Mars Hill, recorded in Acts 17:24-28:

"God that made the world and all things therein, seeing that he is Lord of heaven and earth, dwelleth not in temples made with hands; neither is worshipped with men's hands, as though he needed anything, seeing he himself giveth to all life, and breath, and all things; and hath made of one every blood all nations of men for to dwell on all the face of the earth, and hath determined the times before appointed, and the bounds of their habitation; that they should seek the Lord, if haply they might feel after him, and find him, though he be not far from each one of us: for in him we live, and move, and have our being; as certain also of your own poets have said, For we are also his offspring."

Please note, the one truth which runs through this majestic utterance is the fact that God has dealings with the nations. He provides a nation's resources. This is a reminder that he is the "Creator of heaven and earth," he "made the world and all things therein," and he is "Lord of heaven and earth."

Herschel Hobbs in his book *The Gospel of Giving*, says: "Wherever a nation may be located, its resources belong to God. Whether it be rich or poor, it received its wealth from him. The fertility of the soil, the climate, the forests and rivers, the precious metals, the coal and oil —all are determined by the Lord. The wealth of given nation is not accidental; it is purposeful. To waste natural wealth is a sin—to become proud and arrogant is to invite disaster. To recognize national stewardship exalts a nation—in no sense are nations to regard their wealth other than as possessions or a stewardship from God."

Arnold J. Toynbee has said that the clue to a proper understanding of history is a spiritual one. This is simply another way of saying that God has a purpose for the nations of the earth, and history is the unfolding of that eternal purpose.

3. FUNCTIONS OF GOVERNMENT.   Since the principle of government is ordained of God, the Christian should endeavor to have a clear understanding as to the functions of government and what his relationships to that government are. For some clear comments at this point I turn to a book published in 1937, under the title of *Society: A Textbook of Sociology*, written by R. M. MacIver, at that time professor of political philosophy and sociology at Columbia University. In a discussion of the functions of state in the setting of the democratic ideal, he divides those functions as follows:

(1) Functions peculiar to the state. There are some social functions which the state alone can perform:
  A. Guarantor and guardian of the public order
  B. Secure justice
  C. Carry on international relations

(2) Functions for which the state is well adapted—more fitted to perform than any other power:
  A. Protection of citizens
  B. Preservation of natural resources
  C. Conservation and development of the personal resources of the community—education

(3) Functions for which the state is ill-adapted:

The specialized and more limited interests which unite groups within it. There are divergent and conflicting interests which properly create their own associations. To this order belong the broader cultural interests, including the religious.

(4) Functions which the state is incapable of performing:
A. Personal opinion, beliefs, morals, speech
B. Religious practices. The only power the state should exercise here is where the voice of religion becomes subversive of the public welfare.

With a clear understanding concerning the principle of government, its divine purpose, and the functions of government, the Christian, then, is in a position to have a greater insight into many of the problems involved in the larger concept of stewardship.

IV. Problems in Corporate Use of Things

One of the sensitive nerves in the Christian's concept of stewardship is of necessity the economic order in which he lives and of which he is a part. No discussion of world issues would be complete without such a consideration. John C. Bennett, in his book entitled *Christian Values and Economic Life* says: "Economic activity is an important part of human experience. It fills most of our waking hours, and to it we devote much energy and talent—it involves us in many of our most rewarding (and most difficult) human relationships —it places heavy responsibilities on us." The Christian possesses deep responsibilities, both to God and to the economic order in which he lives. T. B. Maston, in his book *Christianity and World Issues,* has an excellent discussion of this matter in a chapter entitled, "Economic Life and Relations." He says that most of the problems of the modern period are economic, to some degree, and some of the most perplexing of them are primarily economic. The Christian cannot be other than concerned about economic matters. Central and basic in his religious convictions is that of the individual's relationship to and fellowship with God, but the second commandment is of equal importance, according to the Master: "love thy neighbor as thyself." The Christian bears a relationship to God and also to his fellowman. The very genius of his religious belief is that he be concerned about his fellowman in his total life relationship. He is interested in influencing the lives of people, which means he must be concerned with economic relations and evaluations of those people, with the application of Christian moral ideals to the economic environment in which people live. His concern for people, created in the image of God, forces him to be vitally concerned about the economic order in which men live. The test of any economic practice, program, or system, is what it does for man and to men, women, and children. It is his conviction that human personality is worth more than all things material. Did not the Master say, "What doth it profit a man to gain the whole world and lose his own soul?"

Fortunately for the Christian, his religious beliefs not only provide a point of reference for his life, but also give specific guidance for many areas of life. This guidance stems from both the teachings of the Bible and the ethical implications of his faith. To be a genuine Christian means, among other things, that one is a moral person, applying more or less consistently the ethical principles of his religion to the economic as well as other areas of his life. It is of vital importance that he have a clear understanding of the meaning of "private" property and his personal responsibilities in the handling of his wealth and also in the corporate use of public wealth, tax monies, etc. I quote verbatim a discussion by Dr. Maston:

The general Christian conception is that property as such is from God and hence it is good. This idea is particularly prevalent in the Old Testament. The New Testament emphasis is more on the dangers of property and wealth, although property as such is not considered evil. The right of ownership of private property is assumed in the Bible and has been defended, in the main, by the Christian movement as a God-given right of man. However, property does not belong to man unconditionally.

The Christian view is that all belongs to God. 'The earth is the Lord's and the fulness thereof.' Every beast of the forest and 'the cattle on a thousand hills' are his. The silver and the gold belong to God. Man and all that he has belong to God. F. Ernest Johnson claims that 'the Christian doctrine of stewardship is the most radical of all the doctrines concerning property.'

The proper sense of God's ownership, if deeply ingrained into the soul of man, will at least save him from 'that hard sense of ownership that so easily becomes an obstacle to any ethical sensitivity in relation to property.' This will be true only if the Christian conception of stewardship includes more than tithing or the giving of a tenth. The Christian is responsible unto God for giving a tithe, but he is also responsible for what he does with the nine-tenths and for the methods he uses to accumulate his wealth. Wesley's famous summary concerning wealth was: 'Gain all you can. Save all you can. Give all you can.' Muelder says this means 'give all you have' and labels it radical giving and says that it is 'the only way of extracting the poison from riches.'

There is also a sense in which man is not only a steward of God but also a steward of the people. There is 'no such thing as a trustee accountable to God and society.' To a degree, man derives what he has not only from God but also 'from the people and he holds it in trust for the people.' All property is acquired, to some degree, 'under conditions which the acquirer has not himself created.' For this reason Brunner suggests that the community or the state has the right to what the individual has acquired. The generally accepted Christian view is that the community or state has such a right only if it is needed and will be used for the common good, and that if it is confiscated by the state the original owners should be adequately compensated. The state also has the obligation to protect the rights of private property as well as to define the limits of those rights. The selfish accumulation and use of property by the state would be as bad and possibly worse than such control by the individual. 'Christian ethics is fundamentally opposed to all selfish use of wealth, whether privately or collectively owned.'

The Christian position is that property should always be subservient to' human needs and welfare. 'Property is not only *from* God, but *for* man.' Rauschenbusch pointedly said 'It is the function of religion to teach society to value human life more than property, and to value property only in so far as it forms the material basis for the higher development of human life.' Whatever property the Christian may have, little or much, should be used for God's glory and the common good.

The Christian is a vital part of the social order. He pays taxes exactly as everyone else does. Because of his religious faith, he must be vitally concerned about how that tax money is used, and as far as possible, lend his influence to helping solve current problems.

1. POVERTY AND HUNGER.   To look at the problems and needs of our world can be rather depressing, but should serve as a tremendous challenge to all of us. All of us can quote statistics concerning the low per capita income of multitudes of the world's population, and are aware of the tragic fact that two-thirds of the world's population lives below the subsistence level. Men are hungry and in many areas of the world children continue to starve to death. It is estimated that half of mankind is suffering from malnutrition. In many places, the sick are without a physician, medicine, or anyone to help. It is the Christian's conviction that with a proper sense of stewardship the governments of the world could eliminate this problem overnight.

2. WAR AND OPPRESSION.   In spite of all the discussion about peace in our world, it still remains a dream which is haunted by nightmares of war. The reality of war has left incalculable destruction of material, moral, and spiritual resources of mankind. On most any direction of the compass today men live under the tragedy of either actual war or the threat of war, and yet long for liberty and peace. The loss in human life, human resources, and the inevitable lowering of moral standards in a war situation, are of basic concern to the Christian. In the face of world need, he is also greatly concerned about the expenditure of huge sums of money used for the purpose of destruction of both life and property.

3. GRAFT AND DISHONESTY.   The Christian knows that undue regard for material interests and the craving for things is at the root of much that afflicts our world today. Unless wealth can be brought under the control of a spiritual purpose, it is always destructive. We all recognize that this is true in the life of the individual, but does it not also apply in the life of a nation? Excessive, misdirected, prodigal, or harmful expenditures of money reveal that something is wrong in the heart. Graft and dishonesty in all levels of government form a blotch on the face of our national character. This is a problem that vitally concerns the child of God.

4. ECOLOGY AND POLLUTION.   An old, old problem that has been given fresh emphasis in recent years concerns man's destruction and pollution of his natural environment, as much a gift of God as anything else. Public sentiment has been so aroused that perhaps we are on our way towards solving at least some of the problems involved in this vital area. The child of God must let his voice be heard and his influence felt not only in concern over the problems, but in the use of corporate wealth to correct the problems and preserve the world's natural resources.

V. The Christian as a Citizen

1. RELATIONSHIPS—TWO KINGDOMS.   Every citizen of the United States has a great heritage. Christian citizens have added responsibilities because they are privileged to possess dual citizenship. Religion and politics are inescapable facts of life. The Christian is a citizen of an earthly kingdom, the economic order in which he lives, but he is also a citizen of the heavenly kingdom. Paul reminds us of this great truth when in Philippians he says, "For we are a colony of heaven." (Your citizenship is in heaven.) This was a figure

the Philippians could understand since Philippi was a "colony" of Rome. Both of these kingdoms have a ruler, a code of laws to govern, and both regulate citizenship. Roman citizenship was obtained in one of three ways: birth, gift, or purchase. Heavenly citizenship involves all three methods. Whereas they might resemble each other in some details, yet in quality they are quite different. Heavenly citizenship deals with character, morals, spirituality, salvation and is far more than voting, paying taxes, and obeying laws. The principle of dual citizenship is of vital importance. Since the Christian is a citizen of some country in this world, then he owes that country many things. He is a man of honor, therefore he must be a responsible citizen. At the same time, he is a citizen of heaven. There are matters of conscience and of religion and of principle in which the responsibility of the Christian is to God. Where the boundaries between the two duties lie, Jesus did not specifically say. The Christian conscience is to be the test at this important point.

2. PRIVILEGES.   The Bill of Rights delineates the privileges or blessings accruing from citizenship in this nation. These privileges take on added significance when one becomes a Christian. We name only a few: *security, fellowship, freedom.* We briefly touch on the idea of "privileges" and move immediately to a much more important consideration.

3. RESPONSIBILITIES.   When Paul says in Philippians 1:27, "Only let your conversation be as it becometh the gospel of Christ," he is referring to the duty of citizens to the commonwealth in which they live. The Bible has a great deal to say about some of these responsibilities.

(1)   Support with taxes.   Common sense dictates that every human being bear some relationship to a government. Even our Lord had to face this matter. One day he was confronted with the loaded question, "Should a religious Jew pay taxes to Rome?" Actually, *everyone* from 14 to 65 had to pay a poll tax to Caesar, simply for the privilege of existing. However, it was a burning question in Palestine, and had been the cause of more than one rebellion. The tribute money was not regarded as a heavy imposition and, in fact, was no real burden at all. Dr. Barclay says the issue at stake was this: the fanatical Jews claimed that they had no king but God, and held that it was wrong to pay tribute to anyone other than God. Naturally, this also was a religious question for which many were willing to die. Jesus asked to be shown a denarius. In the ancient

world the sign of kingship was the issue of currency. It was universally admitted that to have the right to issue currency carried with it the right to impose taxation. So, the answer of Jesus was: "Render unto Caesar the things that are Caesar's, and unto God the things that are God's." In other words, "If you accept Caesar's currency and use it, you are bound to accept Caesar's right to impose taxes; but," he went on, "there is a domain in which Caesar's writ does not run and which belongs wholly to God." That is to say, if a man lives in a state, and enjoys all the privileges of a state, he cannot divorce himself from that state. The more righteous a person is, the better citizen he ought to make. Nonetheless, it remains true that in the life of a Christian, God has the last word and not the state. This answer of Jesus was not the clever footwork of a man in a corner, it rather depicts the two-fold relationship in which man was meant to live. The issue can never be God *or* government, but must always be a proper balance of God *and* government. The Christian gladly, joyfully pays his taxes and supports his government in this way. Since it is true that, "Where your treasure is, there your heart will be also," it should follow that he is vitally interested in the purposes or ends for which that tax money is used. This interest or concern he can express in a number of ways, but here I simply make the point that he is obligated to support his government.

(2) Loyalty. With the conscientious Christian it can never be, "My country, right or wrong!" His attitude must always be, "My country: if it is right, good, but if it is wrong, then I am obligated to do everything in my power to make it right. I owe it my loyalty." Blind adherence to party politics so often leaves one with a distorted moral vision. The passage of Scripture originally quoted from 1 Peter 2 instructs that the Christian must be a good and useful and faithful citizen of the country in which his life is cast. It seems to me that the New Testament is perfectly logical and just in holding that a man cannot accept the privileges with which the state provides him without also accepting the responsibilities and the duties which it demands of him. It seems to me that this implies that we, as Christians, have an obligation to participate in and serve in the affairs of our state. We are to render service to our government as demanded. We are to work for good legislation and serve in public office. By so doing, we can make our voice heard and our influence count in the state or economic order

where we live. "Loyalty" implies that we will be concerned about the best interests of the country and its citizens. We must prove this interest by exercising our right of franchise.

(3) Obedience. I refer again to 1 Peter 2:13, where Peter says, "Submit yourselves to every ordinance of man . . . whether it be to the king, as supreme; or unto governors." Submit means to be in subjection to. Even when you think it is unjust, or unfair, or even oppressive, the obligation of Christian citizenship is to be obedient to the authority of government. The Christian is to obey the laws of the land, even when he might not personally feel that the law is right or fair. He must not be a lawbreaker, or a law-violator. The only possible exception in his obedience to man's laws would be when they run counter to God's laws. Do not overlook the fact that Jesus commanded obedience to both. The Christian is free to exert his influence and vote to change laws, but not to break them. We might do well to learn the lesson involved in the action of Socrates. He lay in prison, unjustly condemned to death, and was offered a chance to escape through the help of some friends. This he refused. His explanation was that his conscience forbade him to violate the laws of his country.

(4) Prayer. This final point probably seems out of place in a discussion of stewardship, but in my opinion it is a very vital part. Each of us, as Christians, bears a tremendous responsibility of praying for those in authority—as Paul urged upon us. It appears to me that prayer is a very vital force in righting wrongs, solving problems, strengthening the hands of government officials, and especially in bringing to bear the will of God in the economic order to the end that the entire nation might recognize its solemn obligations under God, to discharge its stewardship responsibilities according to divine purpose and will.

BIBLIOGRAPHY

Byfield, Richard. *Your Money and Your Church,* New York: Doubleday, 1959.

Chappell, Clovis. *In Parables,* New York: Abingdon-Cokesbury Press, 1953.

Crawford, John. *A Christian and His Money,* New York: Abingdon-Cokesbury Press, 1963.

Dillard, J. E. *Bible Stewardship,* Nashville: Executive Committee, SBC, 1947.

Freeman, John D. *More Than Money,* Baptist Sunday School Board, 1935.

Hobbs, H. H. *The Gospel of Giving,* Nashville: Broadman Press, 1954.

MacIver, R. M. *Society: A Textbook of Sociology,* New York: Farrar, 1937; New York: Macmillan, 1938.

Maston, T. B. *Christianity and World Issues,* New York: Macmillan, 1957.

Moore, Merrill D. *Found Faithful,* Nashville: Broadman Press, 1953.

Powell, Luther. *Money and the Church,* New York: Association Press, 1963.

Simpson, John E. *This World's Goods,* New Jersey, Revell, 1939.

Christian Responsibility

Malcolm Tolbert

My topic raises the question about Christian attitudes and responsibilities in the matter of the acquisition, use, and disposition of possessions. This immediately presents the problem of determining the criteria on which my answers should be based. What is or is not a *Christian* attitude? How does one decide what *Christian* attitudes and responsibilities are?

When we deal with anything from the point of view of the Christian faith, we must necessarily take the Bible into consideration. Anything which deserves the title Christian presupposes the Bible, no matter what may be the perspective from which we view it. As the record of God's mighty redemptive acts, especially his saving deed in Jesus Christ, the Bible plays an influential role in determining Christian attitudes, decisions, and actions in every area of life.

But we must ask the question: What is the nature of that role? If we seek in the Bible a proof-text to give us infallible guidance for every decision or undertaking in our modern lives, we are confronted with a hopeless task. We can do justice neither to the nature of the Bible nor to the complexity of our modern situation. The truth of the matter is that the world of the Bible was vastly different from our multi-faceted, technological contemporary society. There is no area where this difference is greater than in the economic aspects of the Christian's life. In ancient times wealth was based largely on land and agriculture. Such manufacturing as existed was very primitive indeed. Wage earners were an unimportant class of society, much of the manual labor being performed by slaves. Only a privileged few possessed more than the absolute minimum for existence. There were evidently a few Christians of affluence during the first years of Christian history, but they were certainly a minority. What Paul wrote to the Christians in Corinth could just as well have been written to any church: "Few of you were wise, or powerful, or of high social status, from the human point of view" (1 Cor. 1:26 TEV). Consequently, they did not have to face the questions that modern affluent Christians must confront today.

In the ancient world there were no large factories, no assembly lines, no labor unions, no complex machinery, no wage and hour laws, no stock market, no social security, no pensions, no health insurance. We could go on ad infinitum with this list of factors that affect Christian decisions and activities in the economic sphere of life that were lacking entirely 1900 years ago.

The result is that we must face innumerable situations and questions for which there are not, neither could there be, concrete examples in the Bible. Therefore, we raise the question: Precisely what is the role that the Bible should play in Christian decision-making about financial matters?

The Solution

To begin with, we should recognize that the proof-text approach is a perversion of the Bible in any circumstance. It is a mistake to view the Bible as a "how-to-do-it" manual, containing a complete set of rules to govern Christian conduct in every area of life.

The Bible records how people responded to God in the concrete situations of their own lives. The books of the New Testament, for example, were all occasional. This means that they were written to meet actual needs and face genuine problems that existed in the first generations of Christian history. They do not even cover all of the situations that Christians faced at that time. Nor do they attempt to anticipate the new problems that might arise for their recipients at some future time.

Men like the apostle Paul did not even believe that they had to tell Christians what to do in every conceivable set of circumstances which they might confront. The reason for this is very clear. They believed in the illuminating, guiding presence of the Spirit of God in the life of the church. They did not believe that God ever left Christians without resources to make decisions, solve problems, and undertake efforts in new, unanticipated situations. There is, therefore, an emphasis in the Bible on the individual's need for "wisdom" and "knowledge," capacities that would not be necessary if the gospel presented concrete answers to every conceivable question. In James 1:5 we find this injunction: "If any of you lack wisdom, let him ask of God." Paul writes to the Colossians (1:9-10 RSV): "We have not ceased to pray for you, asking that you be filled with the knowledge of his will in all spiritual wisdom and understanding, to lead a life worthy of the Lord, fully pleasing to him." Wisdom and knowledge describe God-given insight into the will of God and the capacity to interpret it with reference to life's needs and questions. It is that sensitivity that the Christian needs in order to make the right decisions and do the right things, that is, "to lead a life worthy of the Lord."

We should believe in the Bible, but we should also believe in the Holy Spirit. Although the Bible does not deal with all the specific problems that we face, it does afford guiding principles for us to use in solving them. Furthermore, God still gives to his children the wisdom and knowledge essential for them to make the right decisions in terms of the concrete situations of the modern world.

The legalist who demands clear laws, a set of "do's and don't's" to cover every circumstance will hardly be Christian anyway. What he wants to know is what he must do to satisfy God and pass the religious test. If it takes ten percent of his income to do this, he will tithe. But he does so for the wrong reasons. His giving does not really express a Christian attitude toward possessions. On the other hand, if a Christian genuinely desires to give a testimony of his faith and devotion to God in every area of his life, there are divine resources made available in the Bible and in the presence of God that will help him to make the right decisions about possessions as well as about other matters.

General Biblical Principles

Next we turn to a consideration of general biblical principles that can be used to guide us in our decisions about the acquisition, use, and disposition of possessions.

1. The Christian's attitude toward goods is conditioned first of all by the conviction that God is the Creator of both the world and man. The world belongs to God and man is responsible to him. This means that we never really own anything. We talk about "my land," "my house," etc. But our titles are not worth anything. The proof of this is that fifty years from now somebody else will probably be saying "my land" while talking about the same piece of property. Whatever we acquire is for our temporary use, but it ultimately belongs to God. The phrase so popularly used, "God's tithes and our offerings," is, therefore, theologically unsound. We have no basis for dividing our possessions between what belongs to God and what belongs to us.

There are two characteristic aspects of a genuinely Christian attitude toward material possessions. First, we should be aware of the sacredness of God's creation and our responsibility to him for its use. Second, we are to be grateful to God for the gracious provisions that he has made for our material welfare.

2. God is sovereign Lord over all of life. This means that every decision is basically a religious decision, because all of life is lived before God. The child of God should think, speak, and act in every moment so as to honor his Father. This means that the decision about how one is going to spend money to support his family is just as religious as is the one about what he is going to give to support the preaching of the gospel. The division of life into sacred and secular is unbiblical. This is expressed in the Old Testament by the fact that one law governs all of life. There is no civil law as opposed to religious law for the Jewish people. In the New Testament the life of the Christian is brought under the all-embracing claim of the kingdom of God.

3. The greatest danger posed by possessions is idolatry. The man who has possessions is tempted to break the first commandment. And having placed his trust in things, he becomes the victim of constant, life-destroying anxiety. He is condemned to worry about what the morrow will bring, because he is aware that his gods are not capable of coping with all the contingencies and possibilities of the future. This was Jesus' primary concern in his teachings about attitudes toward material wealth. It is expressed in many places but especially in Matthew 6:19-34. In his teaching about man's relation to wealth, Jesus was moved by theological and not pragmatic concerns. He did not attempt to raise money to build buildings, fund programs, etc. He did, of course, underline his disciples' responsibility for the hungry, naked, sick, and imprisoned. But his primary attention was not even focused on the alleviation of human misery by the right use of wealth. His basic concern was the person who had wealth. He wanted to liberate him from the tyranny of things. He viewed material possessions as a rival to the place of God in human life. This is the key to understanding his teaching on wealth.

4. The Christian is a member of a community of believers. One New Testament word for this community is *koinonia*. Basically, *koinonia* is used to describe the shared life of Christians who participate together in the grace of God and who, therefore, can no longer talk about "I," "me," or "mine," but must think "we," "us," and "our." The classic text which illustrates the meaning of koinonia is Philippians 4:16 where Paul speaks of the partnership of giving and receiving. What the Christian has, whether it be in the nature of talents, energy, and knowledge or material possessions, no longer belongs to him alone. His attitude toward his possessions is conditioned

by his partnership with other believers in the shared life. Acts 2:44-45 shows just how clearly and concretely the earliest Christians grasped and interpreted this aspect of the Christian life.

5. What it means to be a Christian is to love. Jesus taught this and his followers echoed it (especially in 1 Cor. 13 and 1 John). But love is not a superficial, sweet sentiment. It is expressed in hard-headed, practical, concrete ways that are designed to meet human need. Jesus illustrated this clearly in the parable of the Good Samaritan (Luke 10:30 ff.). In 1 John 3:17 (TEV) this question is asked: "If a man is rich and sees his brother in need, yet closes his heart against his brother, how can he claim that he has love for God in his heart?"

As we indicated before enumerating these five principles, we cannot find from the Bible explicit rules and concrete illustrations that will indicate what a modern Christian should do with reference to acquiring, using, and disposing of material possessions. But the five principles discussed should be taken into consideration as he seeks God's leadership for the decisions that he will make in these matters.

With this background in mind we now turn to look in a somewhat more detailed fashion at some of the specific areas of the Christian's financial life comprehended in our topic to see what can be added to that which has already been said.

The Acquisition of Possessions

There is no blanket condemnation of the acquisition of possessions in either the Old or New Testament. Indeed, possessions are interpreted as a blessing from God in certain Old Testament passages (e.g., Gen. 26:12; 39:2 ff.). This, however, is not carried through in the New Testament where renunciation for the sake of the kingdom of God is a prominent theme and where the inherent danger of possessions is emphasized. In the light of the experience of Jesus, early Christians understood that complete commitment to God did not result in increased wealth, prestige, and power, but exactly the opposite.

Insofar as can be determined, some of the early followers of Jesus continued to own property, while for others the demand of discipleship involved giving up all material wealth. Some like James, John, Andrew, Peter, and Matthew left property and profession to follow Jesus. On the other hand, we read that some women ministered to Jesus and the disciples "out of their means" (Luke 8:3). Jesus required the ruler to give all that he had to the poor (Luke 18:22).

Zacchaeus, however, decided to give half to the poor and in addition to make amends to those whom he had wronged (Luke 19:8).

Not only do Christians raise questions about the validity of actually owning property, but they also face questions related to the methods by which one acquired possessions. In many places in the Bible we find warnings against gaining wealth in a way that violates the principles of morality, justice, and love. The law condemned charging interest to the poor (Ex. 22:25) or making a profit off a poor brother (Lev. 25:35 ff.). Also it enjoined Israelites to use consistent, full weights and measures in their transactions (Deut. 25:13-14). The prophets condemned those who sold the "needy for a pair of shoes" (Amos 2:6 RSV). Many other similar Old Testament texts could be cited that similarly condemn the unjust and dishonest acquisition of possessions.

The major danger in possessions is that they will become an end in themselves or a god. "The man greedy for gain curses and renounces the Lord," writes the psalmist (Ps. 10:3). In Deuteronomy 8:11 ff. the Israelites are exhorted not to forget God when they have good houses, large herds, and increased wealth. In the Old Testament, therefore, it is recognized that wealth can be a rival to God for man's loyalty and love.

This, we have pointed out, is the central concern in Jesus' teachings about possessions. "How hard it is for those who have riches to enter the kingdom of God!" (Luke 18:24 and par.) points up the conflict between God and wealth in the life of the person who has possessions. To possess just for the sake of possessing, or the unbridled accumulation of things because of the drive to feel superior, powerful, or secure is a common expression of this idolatrous relationship to wealth. Jesus was intensely interested above all else in the way that an individual related to his possessions. It seems to me in the light of this that our own primary interest in stewardship has been misplaced. We have directed our efforts primarily toward separating people from their money because of what can be done with it. We have failed to deal adequately with the basic human problem of idolatry. The truth of the matter is that a man can tithe and still be an idolater. In fact his tithing can deepen his idolatry, if it relieves him of a sense of responsibility to God for the rest of his possessions.

It seems to me that the primary pastoral concern should be with the spiritual welfare of the individuals to whom we minister. If we could come to grips with the basic problems that people have with reference to wealth, with their anxieties and fears arising out of a lack of trust in and dependence upon God who alone guarantees their future,

147

we probably could dispense with many of our gimmicks and pressure tactics. This point of view, admittedly, will be criticized as idealistic, unrealistic, and unworkable. So we shall probably go on with our pragmatic programs until finally they yield results no longer. Then we shall be left with nothing, because we have neglected the weightier matters of the gospel's teaching about possessions.

Naturally, the attitude of a person toward possessions will condition the methods and scope of acquiring them. The individual who is oriented by a Christian perspective about things will be Christian in his acquisition of them. The five biblical principles enumerated in an earlier section of this chapter will serve as a basis for this Christian attitude.

The Use of Possessions

What is the Christian to do with what he acquires? There are at least three specific ways mentioned in the Bible in which things can be used legitimately.

First of all, the Christian may provide for the necessities of his own life and for those who are dependent on him. Jesus himself taught us to pray for "our daily bread," that is, for the daily, physical necessities of life. When some people in Thessalonica used their expectation of the imminent return of Christ as an excuse to quit work, Paul issued this severe injunction: "If any one will not work, let him not eat" (2 Thess. 3:10 RSV). In 1 Timothy 5:8 (RSV) we read: "If any one does not provide for his relatives, and especially for his own family, he has disowned the faith and is worse than an unbeliever." Such a rule of conduct was made even more necessary in ancient times by the lack of any program of old age assistance, retirement, or welfare. The godly man was responsible not only for his children, but also parents, grandparents, aunts, or anyone of his family who was unable to earn a living.

In our modern world "daily bread" would certainly be interpreted in a broader sense than it was in the first century. Then it referred to the basic essentials to maintain physical existence. But the modern American father would rightly interpret providing the necessities of life for his children as including not only food and shelter but certainly also education. There is nothing at all wrong with using money to provide for the needs of people who depend on us. Many modern parents probably cripple their children, however, by giving them much more than they need.

In the second place, the Bible certainly commends the use of possessions to help unfortunate people who do not have the necessities of life. "The righteous (man) is generous," declared the biblical writer of old (Psalm 37:21). Not only were Israelites prohibited by law from defrauding the poor, from exploiting or oppressing them, or making a profit off money lent to them. Specific provisions were also made to care for the needs of the poor, a sort of rudimentary social welfare program. The poor were to be allowed to glean in the fields (Lev. 19:9-10, etc.). They had first right to sabbatical fruits (Ex. 23: 11; Lev. 25:6). The tithe of the third year was for the benefit of the poor and needy (Deut. 14:28-29; 26:14). This concern for the poor is also reflected in the teaching of Jesus (Matt. 19:21; John 13:29). The early church cared for its poor (Acts 2:45; 4:34; Gal. 2:10, etc.). A callous attitude toward the poor on the part of Christian or church constitutes a disregard for one of the basic teachings of Scripture.

In the third place, the Bible supports the use of money to share with those whose ministry involves the surrender of secular professions and the ownership of property. In Israel provision was made for the subsistence of the Levites by the people's tithe (Lev. 27:32-33; Num. 18:21, 24 ff.), a tenth of which was to be given to the priests (Num. 18:26-28).

In the New Testament the support of the preaching ministry has its roots in the teaching and preaching of Jesus. He sent out his apostolic emissaries with the provision that they were to receive food and lodging from people who were beneficiaries of their ministry (Mark 6:8-11 and par.). Although Paul himself worked for his own support, he defended the principle of koinonia, or sharing, as the basis for the support of preachers of the gospel. The preacher shared the gospel with others who in turn shared their material possessions with him. In 1 Corinthians 9:4-18 we find the fullest exposition of Paul's point of view on this subject. In 1 Corinthians 9:14 (RSV) he claims the authority of a word of Jesus for his position: "In the same way, the Lord commanded that those who proclaim the gospel should get their living by the gospel."

Support of one's self and one's dependents, aid to the less fortunate, and support for the ministry are three uses of money clearly founded on biblical practice and teaching.

The Problem of Surplus

One of the most important questions about possessions that can confront a person arises when he has more than he actually needs. So long as the individual has only that which is required for his subsistence and that of his family, he is not confronted with a problem about its use. The problem is in effect solved for him by the demands made upon him by his situation.

But once his income or possessions exceed the level of providing for necessities, the individual is confronted with the responsibility of making a decision. This is the dilemma faced by the rich farmer in the parable told by Jesus (Luke 12:66 ff.). His was the dilemma of surplus. It is the dilemma faced by every person who has more than he needs. "What shall I do?" he queried as he considered the problem of his abundance (Luke 12:17). Conceivably there were many options. No doubt there were people who had not been so fortunate —farmers who because of illness were unable to make a crop, widows who were unable to cope with the economic demands of life, little children without a father or uncared for by their parents.

There is probably no area in which a person's genuine Christian commitment is tested more severely than in his disposition of surplus. There are few things that will reveal more clearly what kind of person he is.

It seems to me that it is probably Christian in our modern society to devote some surplus to savings. As we have pointed out, our situation is vastly different from that in the ancient world. Then opportunities and methods for saving were very limited. People's needs were simple. There was nothing, for example, comparable to high-priced medical care. Under modern circumstances people who have no provision for illness, either in the form of insurance or savings, have often found themselves burdened for life because of a protracted treatment in a hospital.

Furthermore, in our society we place the burden of providing for old age on the person himself rather than on his children. In other days a large family, especially of sons, was a man's guarantee that he would be cared for when he grew old and buried when he died. In modern life, however, most of us would choose not to place this kind of burden on our children.

So the Christian must now raise these kinds of questions: Am I being a responsible person if I do not put some of my income in savings? Am I showing love for others if I do not attempt to provide resources for use in illness and old age so that I shall not create problems for them?

On the other hand, the Christian *must* be sensitive to the evil of unused wealth. In his indictment of the cruel and unfeeling rich people of his day, James declares: "Your gold and your silver have rusted, and their rust will be evidence against you and will eat your flesh like fire" (James 5:3 RSV). Rusty (unused) gold and silver cannot be justified in a world where so many people are hungry, ill, illiterate, and in need of the gospel. The building of more barns to harvest the fruit of prosperity is not the Christian answer to the problem of surplus.

I do not believe that there is any specific guidance that we can give to the individual Christian so that he will know just how much he should put into insurance, retirement, etc., and just how much he should use to meet the need of others. This is a decision that each one must make for himself in the light of his own circumstances and responsibilities. In the last analysis, this is the kind of personal burden that each one must bear, for every person is ultimately responsible to God for what he does with his surplus.

The Problem of Owing

In the Old Testament there are regulations to govern the payment of debts. These are primarily designed to protect the debtor rather than to define his responsibilities as such. A dim view is taken of charging interest (Lev. 25:36-37; Deut. 23:19-20), especially to the poor and to fellow clansmen (Ex. 22:25). Pledges of movable goods were given to creditors to assure repayment of loans. But objects that were indispensable to daily living could not be taken as pledges (Deut. 24:6). Provision was made for the periodic liberation of Hebrew slaves and all who were held on account of unsettled debts. From the pertinent references in the Old Testament we deduce that borrowing was taken for granted, while steps were taken to prevent abuses, especially of exploited people.

In the New Testament Jesus used situations of owing as illustrations in some of his parables (Matt. 18:23-35; 5:25-26 and par.). But we cannot conclude that he approved or disapproved of the practice of borrowing on this basis. He does enjoin his followers not to "refuse him who would borrow" from them (Matt. 5:42). In Luke (6:35) we find these words: "Lend, expecting nothing in return." In these cases Jesus is talking of his disciples as lenders, encouraging a generous spirit in them. There is, however, an implied approval of lending and borrowing.

The only clear statement about the Christian's obligation with reference to owing is found in Romans 13:8 (RSV) where Paul wrote: "Owe no one anything, except to love one another." A literalistic, rigid interpretation of Scripture could force us to conclude, as some groups have, that a Christian should never incur debts to anyone.

Once again, however, we must recognize the vast difference be-

151

tween the economy of the ancient world and our present system. Paul believed that Christians in his day should not owe money to others. There were very good reasons to avoid debt in those times, including the fact that a person was subject to imprisonment or slavery if he did not pay his debts. I refer, of course, to poor people, not to kings and other powerful men. Men who constitute the power structure have been exempt from the laws that the poor have to obey in almost every society.

But a money economy such as ours can hardly operate without some degree of lending and borrowing. Few people could ever own a home and many could never own an automobile if we were required to pay cash for everything. Many businesses could not expand to provide more goods and services and more jobs for people without borrowing.

It is almost impossible in our society for any person to avoid debts of some kind. Even people who "pay as they go" often use credit cards and so, at least for a brief period of time, owe sums of money. Furthermore, if everybody suddenly quit buying on credit, a terrible economic depression would be the result. People would lose their jobs, and children would go hungry. The point is that we must now ask: What is God's word to use in our situation? What would the gift of wisdom and knowledge lead us to decide in contemporary circumstances? It seems to me that it would be reckless, unwise, immoral, and, therefore, unchristian to conclude that no one should owe money today.

There are considerations that should govern the Christian in the matter of owing. I would like to suggest a few: (1) The Christian should not willingly and knowingly contract more obligations than he can meet. (2) If he can avoid it, his debts should not be of such a nature that they cause him undue preoccupation and sap his mental and spiritual strength. (3) Debts should not be incurred for unnecessary goods to such an extent that the Christian has no surplus to help those in need and to support the proclamation of the gospel. (4) His financial situation should not compromise his testimony as a Christian. He ought not to create a bad reputation for not paying his obligations.

Final Disposition

There was apparently no word for testament or will in the Hebrew language. The procedures that governed inheritances are not spelled out in detail in the law. Evidently they were determined by customary legal provisions of the day.

The eldest son received a double portion of the inheritance, while the other brothers received single portions (Deut. 21:17). In this, as in other matters in the ancient world, women fared poorly. However, a law was enacted to enable brotherless daughters to inherit their father's estate and so keep it within the family (Num. 27:1-11). This was in keeping with the idea that a family's portion in the land of promise was inalienable. Although the Old Testament does not give us a clear picture of the customs governing the final disposition of property, references like the above indicate that such customs did exist.

When we turn to the New Testament, we find that there are no specific teachings to guide the Christian in the making of wills. The fact of the matter is that the expectation of the imminent return of Christ characteristic of the early Christian community ruled out any preoccupation with such concerns.

However, the necessity for wills or of other methods to secure the transfer of properties upon the death of the owner is obvious. For the welfare of society there must be some procedure to ensure the orderly succession of property, unless drastic steps are to be taken to abolish the private ownership of all goods. In the absence of specific biblical teachings, the Christian once again must make his decision concerning this question on the basis of general Christian principles.

In the disposition of his property the Christian is confronted with two alternatives. One possible choice is to give everything away prior to his death. If he possesses the means to do so, he can give it away with provisions that will assure that his own physical needs are cared for during the rest of his life. The second possibility is to make provisions in a will for the disposition of property after death. The option exercised by the individual should be determined by what he concludes to be God's will in the circumstances of his own life. He can take either course and still be thoroughly Christian.

There is one important point that may sometimes escape people. The decision that we make about what we are going to do with our possessions after death is after all one that we make in life. The Christian is just as responsible to God for this decision about what is to be done with his goods after death as he is for the way that he spends money in his life.

Two major factors should be reflected in a Christian's will. They are responsibility and love. A Christian's will expresses mature and responsible Christian judgment. It reflects a concern for genuinely Christian causes and goals. It seems reasonable to assume that a Christian will indicate his commitment to Christian causes just as much in his will as he does in the way he gives his money in life.

If property is left for children and other heirs, love must be the guiding principle. Questions like these must be answered: How will the acquisition of property affect my loved ones? Am I helping or harming them through this bequest? Will they use the property received from me in a Christian way? Naturally these questions can only be answered by each individual as he faces his own peculiar situation. No one can give blanket, concrete rules to guide people in the making of their wills because individual circumstances vary so radically.

Conclusion

The way that a Christian relates to possessions is one of the most important aspects of his life. In fact, he reveals whether or not he is a Christian by his attitude toward possessions.

The Bible teaches us that we are to love God and people and that we are to use the things that God has placed in our charge wisely and responsibly. The common tendency, however, is to love possessions and to exploit God and people. Idolatry is not dead in our modern world. It simply expresses itself in more subtle and sophisticated ways.

It appears to me that one of the greatest ministries that the church can perform is precisely at this point. Our primary goal in stewardship should not be to build buildings and develop programs but to minister to people. We should adopt the same goal that motivated Jesus, that is, to free men from the tyranny of things so that they will direct their trust toward God and their love toward God and men. Only by so doing will they be liberated from anxiety and fear to live confidently and joyously in the present, knowing that the God they trust is more than adequate to deal with the problems and needs of the future.

The Practice of Stewardship

The first section of this book was concerned with the theological context of Christian stewardship. God's redemption of his creation was the context suggested. From this broad, theological focus, we sought a rationale for stewardship. That rationale, discussed in the second section, was the ultimate ownership of God of all that is and the trusteeship of man over the created order. Our discussion is cumulative. As the rationale of stewardship grew from the context, so the practice should be drawn from both. Our basic contribution of this work should be its insistence that theology, reason and purpose, and practice are inevitably related in the life of the redeemed community. Stewardship has been our particular focus for illustrating this basic procedure. It is to be desired that other segments of church and denominational life would articulate and apply these interlocking principles. Attention to theological context, adequate rationale, and appropriate practice is not enough. It must be asserted that the order in which attention is given to these elements is of great significance. Many of the problems of religious institutions and life today arise precisely because the proper order of these elements is not given adequate attention. It is contrived to seek reasons for our actions until we have expressed the theological context which alone can provide proper bases. It is catastrophic to begin with practice and method and subsequently try to bolster these with good reasons or theological sanction. It is for good reason, therefore, that we have placed the section on the practice of stewardship last.

In this division there is a particular and a general concern. The particular concern is tithing; the general concern is the broader motivation and implementation of stewardship.

Tithing: A Particular Method

Four chapters of this final section are devoted to tithing. Many of the previous chapters have allusions and references to the subject. That

the discussion is so heavily freighted on this one method of stewardship gives evidence of a historic and pragmatic concern of Baptists
with the practice of tithing. The four chapters were prepared in-
dependently and represent a variety of expressions and evaluations
concerning tithing. The original presentation of these chapters as
addresses provoked lively and energetic discussion on the part of those
attending the seminar. It is to be desired that this discussion be carried
on in a wider way by the readership of this book.

Common to the four discussions on this single method of stewardship, tithing, is an interest in the biblical and historical expressions on
the subject. Whatever the reader's personal preferences and convictions, he is given essentially all of the evidence about tithing on which
evidence he must reflect and by which facts he is confronted. The four
authors hold in common that tithing is, by no means, the whole of
Christian stewardship.

This second will provide a bonus for those who reflect on how varied
and multi-dimensional are Baptist views of interpreting Scripture. To
the editor, the section on tithing, aside from its direct information
about the subject, is prized as a hermeneutical study. Hermeneutics is
the science of interpreting documents. Christian theological hermeneutics has to do with the way in which one brings the Bible into
practical exhortations for the Christian community. The four challenging and quite diverse chapters are examples of how Baptists use
the Bible in addition to being good resources for information about
tithing.

Motivation and Application

The two concluding chapters of this section move once more from
the particular to the general. Author Ray explores carefully the biblical
basis for motives in giving. Professor Cunningham concludes the volume with an encyclopedic listing of the involvements and dimensions
which must be considered in the fuller dimensions of Christian stewardship.

Attention is long overdue for a consideration of the corporate aspects of stewardship. Churches, associations, agencies, boards and
institutions, which are themselves recipients of the stewardship of
countless individuals, must reflect on their corporate stewardship of
that which they hold under the ownership of God and on behalf of
mankind.

So we have moved from context, to rationale, to practice. What is
lacking is specific implementation of stewardship in methods, pro-

grams, and strategies. This lack may well provide the substance of a subsequent volume of stewardship studies. Preferable, is the idea that individuals, and the groups they comprise, who read this book will find both the dynamic and the motivation to perfect adequate and appropriate methodologies of stewardship.

The Christian and the Tithe

Brooks H. Wester

The first recorded instance of payment of a tithe is the offering of Abraham to Melchizedek in Genesis 14:20. Abraham had defeated an alliance of kings who had looted Sodom and had taken captive Abraham's nephew, Lot, and his family. As they returned from the victorious battle with all the loot and the people, he was met by the king of Sodom, and Melchizedek, King of Salem who was a priest of God Most High, who blessed Abraham. Abraham then gave Melchizedek a tenth of everything.

The late Professor D. M. Welton, writing in the *American Commentary on Genesis,* said of this event: "Hereby he practically acknowledged the divine priesthood of Melchizedek, and set an example of honor and support which should be given to those who minister to men in spiritual things. His act became an authoritative historical precedent among his descendants ever after. Jacob remembered it at Bethel (Gen. 28:22), and Moses incorporated it among his statutes (Lev. 27:30-33; Num. 18:21-32)." [1]

The second mention of the tithe is the promise of Jacob made to God in the light of his realization of God's presence at Bethel, that if God remained in his life, he would give God a tenth of all the increase he would experience because of God's blessing in his life. Dr. Welton wrote of this incident: "From this allusion to tithes, it is clear that the giving of the tenth to God was recognized before the giving of the law. Jacob fulfilled this vow on his return from Padan-aram (Gen. 35:6-7)." [2]

The Mosaic code as recorded in Leviticus 27:30-33 and reiterated in Numbers 18:21-32, lay claim in God's name to the tenth of the products of the land and cattle. An enlargement, and perhaps fuller interpretation of the law, fixed that the tithes were to be paid to the Levites for their services and they in turn were to give a tithe of what they received to the priests (Num. 18:21-28). Then sacred festivals were later made occasion for a further tithe which was allowed to come in money value (Deut. 12:5,6,11,17 and 14:24-26).

In the time of Hezekiah's reformation the people in eagerness presented their tithes (2 Chron. 31:5-6).

When the Jewish people were returning from the Babylonian captivity and rebuilding Jerusalem, Nehemiah made emphatic arrangements concerning the tithe (Neh. 10:37 and 12:44).

The prophetic preaching on the subject of the tithe is in the form of severe rebuke of the nation for their neglect in presenting the tithe unto the Lord. Both Amos and Malachi have harsh words for the people. Malachi accused them of robbing God. Amos reveals their lack of sincerity in their worship and bringing of tithes (Amos 4:4 and Mal. 3:10).

Through this review of Old Testament references to the tithe we can recognize the principle of giving a tenth of possessions to God was practiced before the Mosaic law and is therefore of ancient origin, probably predating Abraham.

The giving of one-tenth of one's income to the Lord's work is not explicitly mentioned in the New Testament, but the principle of systematic and proportionate giving is made quite clear. Dr. Goodspeed has a helpful article in *Dictionary of Christ and the Gospels*. He says: "Our Lord makes but three references to the tithes, and they are all of the observance of them by the Pharisees (Matt. 23:23, Lk. 11:42; 18:12). In the first two passages he contrasts the minute exactness with which the Pharisees observe their less important and external laws of tithe with their careless disregard of the inner and more important virtues of justice, mercy, faith, and the love of God. In Luke 18:12, he illustrates how compliance with external requirements, especially when these are exceeded, as in the case of the Pharisees, and disassociated from the corresponding state of heart, breeds a culpable and overwhelming self-righteousness. Our Lord in these references, as also in Matthew 5:19, recognizes degrees of importance in the Law's demands. Minute observance of the less important does not excuse from attending to the greater, but neither does compliance with the greater absolve from the obligation to observe the lesser. 'This ought ye to have done, and not leave the other undone.' Our Lord evidently thought the tithe, as well as other Old Testament institutions, of divine origin, and binding upon the Jews of his day. At the same time, he foresaw a period when outward observances should give place to the more purely inward, as men should worship the Father in spirit and in truth (John 4:21-24)." [3]

The only specific mention of tithes in the Epistles is in the Hebrews.

This section in the seventh chapter deals with the experience of Abraham offering a tenth of everything to Melchizedek and the Levites taking tithes from the people. The line of reasoning can be well presented that since Abraham offered tithes to Melchizedek as he exercised his priestly office for the God Most High, then we should not do less as we make our offerings to Christ who is a priest forever after the order of Melchizedek.

While the Epistles do not specifically mention tithes, they abound with illustrations and exhortations to giving of material blessings to the work of the Lord.

When one views the tithe from the historical view, he discovers that the tithe was not limited to the Jewish people in their observance of religious laws. John Henry Blunt in an article in a *Dictionary of Doctrinal and Historical Theology* published by Rivingtons of London, Oxford and Cambridge in 1870, wrote: "We find also abundant proof of heathen nations recognizing the duty of devoting a tenth to religious ends. Croesus advised Cyrus to station guards at the gates so as to secure the payment of tithes to Jupiter. (Herodotus i:89 also IX 81). Xenophon instances payment of tithes to Diana (Xen Cyropold V3,9). The Carthaginians are said to have paid tithes of all their profits (Hutchinsons' Xenophen—p. 248). The Roman generals used to devote tenths of the spoils to Hercules. Camillus, before the assault on Veii, vowed a tenth part of the spoil to the Pythian Apollo (Livy V21-23)." [4]

There are reliable records of the practice of tithing as early as 2100 B.C. in Babylon and also very early in Chaldea. Mythology locates it in Greece as far back as 1300 B.C. We are told in other recorded works of the practice by the Romans, Pelasgians, Samothracians, Silicians, Gauls, Britons, and Saxons.

In the first four centuries of the Christian age, not a great deal was written about the money matters of the church. It seems the enthusiasm of the believers, and their devotion to Christ, led them to give most liberally to the spread of the gospel in their own communities and to the other parts of the earth. The writings we do have from the early church fathers are exhortations to pay the tithes, and always presented them as due, not merely offered to God. Clement, Cyprian, Ambrose, Chrysostom, and Augustine laid stress upon the tithe. The writings of these men abound with allusions to this duty, and the response was made, not in enforced tithing but by voluntary offerings. Professor Selden is possibly right in maintaining that the custom of paying tithe cannot be traced before the fourth century. At the end of the fourth century the evidence is overwhelming that the moral and religious duty of paying tithes was recognized and had acquired the force of custom.

As a moral and religious custom the payment of tithes was enjoined by the public acts of Councils and Churches, and enforced by moral and religious sanctions: the Councils of Tours, A.D. 567; the second Council of Macon, A.D. 585; the Council of Rouen, A.D. 650; of Nantes, A.D. 660; and of Metz, A.D. 756.

The next step taken to insure the paying of tithes was by imperial decree by the state. This added civil sanction to religious custom. Charlemagne (King of the Franks, A.D. 768-814, and Roman Emperor, A.D. 800-814) originated the enactment of tithes as a public law and established the practice over the Roman Empire over which he ruled. From this start it extended itself over Western Christendom; and it became general for a tenth to be paid to the church.

In an article written by a W. H. Jellie in *The Biblical Illustrator*, he writes of the introduction of tithes into England. He said, "Offa, King of Mercia, is credited with its assertion here, at the close of the eighth century. It spread over other divisions of Saxon England, until Ethelwulf made it a law for the whole English realm. It remained optional with those who were compelled to pay tithes to determine to what church they should be devoted, until Innocent III addressed to the Archbishop of Canterbury, A.D. 1200, a decretal requiring tithes to be paid to the clergy of the parish to which payees belong. About this time also, tithes, which had originally been confined to those called praedial, or the fruits of the earth, was extended to every species of profit and to wages of every kind of labor, the great and small tithe. The great tithe was made upon the main products of the soil, corn, hay, wood, etc., the small on less important growths. To the rector the great tithes of a parish are assigned, and to the vicar the small." [5] The *World Book Encyclopedia* says Pope Adrian, as early at A.D. 786, demanded tithes from all lands except those belonging to the church and the crown. It further states, "A tithe rent charge is still used to support parishes of the Church of England, but it is no longer a tenth." [6]

The Reformation shook that part of the church that had to do with financial support as it did all the rest of the ecclesiastical structure. Soon after the Reformation began, a growing number of people revolted against compulsory tithing. Some protested on religious grounds, others on more mundane grounds.

History records that the Anabaptists, and later the Quakers, earnestly desired to return to a church more in conformity to the pattern in the New Testament. They opposed tithing on the basis that it violated Christian principles. Several church historians have declared,

"By and large, the Baptists—although inconsistent at times—remained true to the principles of separation of church and state and voluntary support of the ministry. They, more than any other group, are the representatives of the philosophy of church support which emphasizes voluntary support on the congregational level."

Some Englishmen opposed enforced tithing because it imposed financial hardship on them when they bought or inherited lands with a tithe lien against it. Regardless of the reasons for protesting against tithing, the system estranged many people from the Church of England.

These views that shook the established churches in Europe and in England were held by the Pilgrims who settled Plymouth in New England in 1620, consequently their views had some effect on the early church in America. Here, as in England and on the Continent, the Baptists were insistent on voluntary support of the clergy and church.

Roger Williams stood so firmly for the principle of voluntary support that he declined a call to the Boston Church because it paid a stated salary. He expressed his views very clearly when he wrote, "As to the laborer worthy of his reward, I answer, we find no other patterne in the Testament of Christ Jesus, but that both the converting (or apostolical ministry) and the feeding (or pastoral ministry) did freely serve or minister; and yet were freely supported by the Saints and the Churches, and that not in stinted wages, tithes, stipends, salaries, etc., but with larger or lesser supplies as the hand of the Lord was more or less extended in his weekly blessings on them." [7]

In spite of these noble sentiments expressed by Williams, David Benedict in his volume *Fifty Years Among the Baptists,* published in 1860, decried the lack of church support of the early Baptist ministers. He alleged that the majority of them had no settled income but were forced to provide for themselves and charged that "the Baptists were more parsimonious in their doings in this line than almost any other party in the country." He further maintained that in cases where moderate sums were pledged, "in too many they were slowly paid, if paid at all." [8]

Up through the Revolutionary War in America the practice of levying tithes was followed to a degree but never with the same ecclesiastical and civil force as in many places in Europe. Following the war, the voluntary support of the clergy and church was the rule. To a large degree emphasis on the tithe was not heard with any regularity in the work of the churches of all denominations. It is true that there was some emphasis on stewardship even though not on tithing as such.

Some church historians speak of the period between the close of the Revolutionary War, and the War of 1812, as a time of low spiritual fervor in the United States. But events were taking place in Europe that would change all that. The well documented "Modern Movement of Missions" under William Carey of England began in 1792. The spirit of missions came to America and in 1796 the New York Missionary Society was formed. The Baptists became organized for foreign missions in 1814 when Adoniram Judson and Luther Rice offered themselves for service as missionaries for the Baptists. Along with this awakened mission consciousness had to come enlarged financial support for the missionaries and their work. This led to increased emphasis on money support, but there was no widespread emphasis on the tithe. This remained true even during the Civil War and the reconstruction period of American history.

Dr. Salstrand in his book *The Story of Stewardship* opens chapter 6 with these three sentences: "The period that marks the close of the nineteenth century and the opening of the twentieth century was one which emphasized the tithing phase of stewardship. Previously we find only casual references to the tithe. However, near the close of the nineteenth century, the tithe was unveiled and recognized as a vital means whereby Christians could perform their stewardship." [9]

There were several significant movements organized to promote tithing in the churches during this period. The original "Layman Company" that became "The Layman Foundation" in Chicago was one. The Churchman's Tithe Club was founded in Omaha under the auspices of the Protestant Episcopal Church in 1896. The "Tenth Legion" was organized in 1896 and taken over in 1897 by the "United Society of Christian Endeavor" and by 1902 reported they had enrolled 19,490 tithers. "The Twentieth Century Tither's Association of America" was organized during a tithers conference held at Winona Lake Bible Conference grounds on August 24, 1904. These early movements made lasting impressions on many churches. They effectively linked missions and stewardship and brought about renewal of interest and support for both.

Since those days our nation has experienced great growth and sore trials. Great population and economic growth has been a part of two world wars and their post war periods. Trials have come during the wars, and in their aftermath, that have tested the churches and the people of the country. To construct enough church building space has been a problem. To pay for the construction and continue to support mission and benevolent causes of the various denominations has been of challenge to all. Programs for enlisting tithers in the churches are very much a part of the story of the churches meeting these challenges.

The record of Southern Baptists following World War II will serve to illustrate the part a renewed emphasis on tithing played in advance.

Most of us remember the crusade for "A Million Southern Baptist Tithers for Christ" that was launched in 1947. Merrill D. Moore has said it was one of the most significant single steps Southern Baptists have ever taken in the direction of stewardship advance. We also know it was followed in 1948 by the movement to enlist every Baptist in tithing. Our slogan was "Every Baptist a Tither." That these movements brought about marked advance in missions, education, and benevolence at home and abroad is well documented history. What has been true for Southern Baptists has also been true of other religious groups in America. Consistently the church bodies stressing the tithe as a minimum gift for the Lord's work show the largest per capita gifts each year. It is also true that those same bodies give much more per capita to missions than do others.

At present, tithing is a controversial issue in religious circles. There are those who declare tithing to be an integral part of the Christian life and is required of every Christian. There are others who reject tithing as being Old Testament legalism that leads to a self-righteousness of spirit in the one practicing the tithe. One pastor, who insists that tithing promotes self-righteousness, has said, "I don't have a tither in my church who is not a Pharisee." In spite of it being a controversial subject, tithing is very much a part of the religious scene in America and will continue to be an integral part of most stewardship programs in the churches. Therefore, it behooves us to develop some dynamics in stewardship that will make full use of all values that have accrued from the emphasis on tithing, and at the same time will avoid the criticisms levelled against the practice.

As Southern Baptists, we should insist that any practice in our ranks find its dynamic in the revealing Word of God. When the passages that record the beginning of the tithe are earnestly examined, and fairly presented, it becomes clear that Abraham was expressing a devotion to God. This expression included the gifts of tithes to Melchizedek as an acknowledgement of God having provided the possessions and had also given the victory that placed those possessions in his care. That same spirit breathes through the experience of Jacob. The letter to the Hebrews referring to these Old Testament incidents also make it clear that they were out of gratitude to God for what he had done for them. It was this kind of spirit that was lacking in the Pharisees' giving of tithes that led the Lord to say to them they should tithe, alright, but they ought to do so in love as they also keep the other parts of the law.

We would also agree with Luther P. Powell when he says, "A wrong interpretation of tithing (today) could also give rise to the idea of keeping the law for the sake of merit, and this cannot be glossed over, since one of the most persistent heresies in the Christian church has been the notion that man attains salvation by keeping the law by performing acceptable acts. The message of nonevangelical religions centers in what man can do to reach God; but evangelical Christianity is a message of what God has done for man. Thus it is crucial that tithing, as a discipline, be presented only to those who are in Christ. It must be presented from this side of the cross." [9]

Tithing cannot stand up to the enquiring mind of the Christian if it is presented only as "good business," or the best means of financing the church machinery. Neither can it stand if it is presented only from the view of being adequate to meet the spiritual needs of humanity that has never heard the gospel of Jesus Christ.

Tithing can be presented from the biblical message as being a spiritual exercise that honors God in his ownership of all. God, by grace, has put in the worshipper's care the material goods of life. The tithe is set wholly apart for God. The worshipper in presenting his tithe is performing an act that God has honored through the ages and continues to bless when it is practiced today. Tithing is basically an act of worship that declares the greatness of God and the worth of man when he is obedient to God.

When we, as Southern Baptists, proclaim this message we will discover the truth that God's Word does not return unto him void. It will bear fruit in all the vineyards of the Lord.

FOOTNOTES

[1] *An American Commentary* (Philadelphia: The American Baptist Publication Society), Vol. I, p. 130.
[2] *Ibid.*, p. 185.
[3] *Dictionary of Christ and the Gospels* (T & T Clark), Vol. 2, p. 732.
[4] *Dictionary of Doctrinal and Historical Theology* (Rivingtons), p. 755.
[5] *The Biblical Illustrator* (Revell), Vol. 4, p. 349.
[6] *The World Book Encyclopedia* (Field Enterprises), Vol. 18, p. 237.
[7] Powell, Luther P., *Money and the Church* (Association Press), p. 91.
[8] Salstrand, George A. E. *The Story of Stewardship* (Baker Book House), p. 15.
[9] *Ibid.*, p. 41.

BIBLIOGRAPHY

Blunt, John Henry. *Dictionary of Doctrinal and Historical Theology,* London, Oxford and Cambridge: Rivingtons 1870.

Buswell, James Oliver, Jr. *A Systematic Theology of the Christian Religion,* Zondervan, 1962.

Hastings, Robert J. *My Money and God,* Nashville: Broadman, 1961.

Lansdell, Henry. *The Tithe in Scripture,* Baker Book House, 1963.

Latourette, Kenneth Scott. *A History of Christianity,* Harper & Bros., 1952.

Long, Roswell C. *More Stewardship Parables of Jesus,* Abingdon-Cokesbury Press, 1947.

Newman, A. H. *A Manual of Church History,* American Baptist Publication Society, 1899.

Powell, Luther P. *Money and the Church,* Association Press, 1962.

Salstrand, George A. E. *The Story of Stewardship,* Baker Book House, 1956.

Shedd, Charlie W. *How to Develop a Tithing Church,* Abingdon Press, 1961.

Tithing in the New Testament

H. Franklin Paschall

Henry Lansdell in his classic work, *The Sacred Tenth,* says he traced tithing into almost "every known country of importance in the ancient world." John M. Versteeg in his book, *The Deeper Meaning of Stewardship,* writes: "There was a widespread custom among ancient peoples of paying one-tenth to the king. This practice existed among Greeks and Romans, Babylonians and Egyptians as well as among the Hebrews."

The first mention of tithing in the Bible is Genesis 14:20. Here Abram is reported to have given the tithe to Melchizedek, king of Salem. So tithing did not begin with the Mosiac law. Keil and Delitzsch say: "All that was required was to incorporate this (tithing) in the covenant legislation, and bring it into harmony with the spirit of the law."

In the Old Testament there were at least three distinct tithes. The first tithe known also as the Lord's or the Levite's or the whole tithe consisted of one tenth annually, whether of the seed of the land, or of the fruit of the tree . . . the herd or of the flock (Lev. 27:30-32). The Levitical priesthood was supported by this tithe.

The second tithe was given to support three great feasts—Passover, Tabernacles, and Weeks. It took care of travel and other expenses during the pilgrims' stay in Jerusalem (note Deut. 12:5-19; 14:22-27).

The third tithe was given every three years. It was kept in local communities for distribution to the needy (Deut. 14:28-29). The two annual tithes and the third year tithe amounted to about one-fourth of one's income.

I. Christ's Attitude and Example as to Tithing

The Romans ruled Palestine during the ministry of our Lord. Many Gentiles were impressed with the Jewish religion and there are notable

167

examples of generous giving on their part. The centurion at Capernaum built a synagogue (Luke 7:5). Cornelius prayed and gave alms (Acts 10:31). Herod the Great, though an Idumean, rebuilt the temple of the Jews.

Included in the influence of Jewish religion was tithe paying. Both Samaritans and Jews recognized their obligation to pay the tithes. The general practice of tithe paying may be seen in the words of Josephus (born in A.D. 37): "As to what presents were offered me I despised them as not standing in need of them; nor indeed would I take those tithes which were due to me as a priest, from those that brought them." Again he writes of Ananias, the high priest: "He also had servants who were there with him, who joined themselves to the boldest sort of the people and went to the threshing floors and took away the tithes that belong to the priests."

The Jews as Roman subjects were not required by the law of the Empire to observe the ordinances of the Jewish religion as they were under Jewish monarchs. Undoubtedly there developed some laxness among the Jews in observing the regulations of Judaism and some evaded tithe paying. In response to this laxity, there developed great zeal for religion among other Jews. This zeal may be seen in three religious parties: the Essenes, the Sadducees, and the Pharisees. The Essenes appeared in the second century B.C., renounced worldly goods, retreated to the desert, and extolled the virtue of poverty. The Sadducees did not reject completely tradition and the unwritten law, but tested them by the Pentateuch which they accepted as authoritative. The Pharisees accepted all the Old Testament writings plus the rabbinical interpretations on these writings. And they were exceedingly zealous for the religion of their forefathers. The Pharisees appeared about 150 B.C. Josephus says they numbered approximately 6,000. The purpose of the fraternity of the Pharisees was twofold—first, to demonstrate extreme care and exactitude in the payment of the tithe and religious dues, and secondly, to promote the strict observance of traditional laws relating to Levitical purity. The Pharisee could not take the vow of purity without pledging to pay the tithe. A Pharisee of the lower degree (tithe paying) was looked upon as a person accredited with whom one might freely transact business, since he was assumed to have paid on his goods, all religious dues. A Pharisee of the higher vow undertook not to sell to an outsider any substance, whether fluid or solid, nor to buy from him any such, nor to be a guest with him, and not to entertain the outsider in his own clothes because of possible defilement.

The Pharisees were tithe payers par excellence as distinguished from the Amhaaretz "people of the land." The uninstructed ones who knew not or cared not for the oral or unwritten law were looked down upon by the learned as "accursed." A Pharisee was regarded as an aristocratic, punctilious religionist and an Amhaaretz as a "heathen man and a publican" (John 1:49; Matt. 18:17).

According to the Pharisee, tithing was a major doctrine and practice. What was the attitude of our Lord toward their tithe paying? It would have been impossible for him to remain neutral on this subject.

Was Christ regarded by his contemporaries as an Amhaaretz (that is, one uninstructed)? The answer is clear in the New Testament: "He taught them as one having authority" (Matt. 7:29). In the synagogue in Nazareth, though some asked for the source of his learning, he was regarded as a man of wisdom: "What wisdom is this which is given unto him?" (Mark 6:2). When only twelve years of age he astonished the doctors in the Temple by his remarkable understanding of religious things. Josephus says that when he was a youth scribes and Pharisees consulted him on matters of the law. On numerous occasions the Pharisees asked him questions of vital significance. Certainly they did not regard him as uninstructed.

It is interesting to note that the Pharisees expected our Lord to live up to their standards. They asked his disciples this question, "How is it that your master eats and drinks with publicans and sinners?" They would not have been surprised in his doing this if he had been an Amhaaretz or one of the uninstructed or common people. If they expected him to be committed to Levitical purity, then certainly it is to be assumed that they expected him to have taken the lower vow of tithe paying. Further proof of this point may be seen in the invitation to Jesus by one of the chief Pharisees to eat bread in his house on the Sabbath Day. Even the enemies of Jesus never accused him of not paying tithes or ecclesiastical dues. If he had been negligent at this point, surely they would have exulted in this obvious shortcoming.

In the life of Jesus there are many examples of his observance of the law of Moses. On the eighth day he was circumcised and when the days of Mary's purification were accomplished, the child Jesus was brought to Jerusalem and presented to the Lord. They came to Jerusalem "to offer a sacrifice according to that which was said in the law of the Lord" (Luke 2:21-24). His parents went to Jerusalem every year to observe the Passover Feast, taking their son with them when he was twelve years of age (Luke 2:39). Jesus insisted that John baptize him, saying, "Thus it becometh us to fulfill all righteousness" (Matt. 3:15). When our Lord healed a leper, he said to him, "Shew thyself to the priest, and offer the gift that Moses commanded" (Matt. 8:4).

169

In the New Testament there is only one request of our Lord for money. This request was not for the compulsory tax imposed by the Romans but for the support of the Temple services. According to Moses everyone of the congregation was responsible for contributing a half-shekel for this purpose. After the people returned from captivity the contribution or fee was a third-part of a shekel yearly (Neh. 10:32). Peter was directed to find a stater or the equivalent of two half-shekels in the fish's mouth in order to pay this fee for himself and his master (Matt. 27:24:27). (See Edersheim, page 47.)

Jesus was a poor man financially and yet he made contributions to the poor (John 13:29). He and his disciples had a treasury or a purse and Judas was the treasurer. From this treasury they bought such things as they needed (John 4:8). It seems that these expenditures were made on a tripartite basis, daily needs, religious services and charity. It is a safe inference that Jesus not only paid the tithe and all religious dues but in all probability exceeded what the law required.

II. Christ's Teaching on Tithing and Beneficence

Jesus said that he came not to destroy the law but to fulfill it. Concerning respect for the law and obedience to it, Jesus was altogether righteous. Once a lawyer stood up and said, "Master, what shall I do to inherit eternal life?" Jesus replied, "What is written in the law?" Here Jesus is not saying that eternal life comes by obeying the law. But he is setting forth the importance of the law as the divine standard of living, and if of living, certainly of giving.

The following Scriptures will give the broad base and guiding principles for alms giving and religious beneficence of Jesus: "Give to him that asketh thee, and from him that would borrow of thee turn not thou away" (Matt. 5:42); "He that hath two coats, let him impart to him that hath none; and he that hath meat, let him do likewise" (Luke 3:11); "Give, and it shall be given to you; good measure, pressed down, shaken together, and running over, shall men give into your bosom" (Luke 6:38). When the apostles were ready to go on their first preaching mission Jesus admonished them, "Freely ye have received, freely give" (Matt. 10:8). Paul said to the elders of the church at Ephesus, "Remember the words of the Lord Jesus, how he said, It is more blessed to give than to receive" (Acts 20:35). Our Lord taught his followers to give as a part of their religious responsibility . . . "Sell what ye have, and give alms" (Luke 12:33).

The giving which our Lord did and that which he enjoined upon

170

his disciples was not a mere "perfunctory distribution of money." He was concerned with motives. He taught that giving was not to be done ostentatiously, so as to be seen of men, but rather unobtrusively, so that one's left hand was not to know what the right was doing (Matt. 6:1-4). Also he required that one be right with his brother before offering a gift at the altar (Matt. 5:23). Furthermore, he lifted giving above the expectation of recompense: Jesus said, "When thou makest a feast, call the poor, the maimed, the lame, the blind: and thou shalt be blessed; for they cannot recompense thee: for thou shalt be recompensed at the resurrection of the just" (Luke 14:3-14). Alms giving was done as unto the Lord. Jesus said, "Verily I say unto you, Inasmuch as ye have done it unto one of the least of these my brethren, ye have done it unto me" (Matt. 25:40). The giving which Jesus practiced and taught was free, generous, and even lavish.

The giving of Jesus was in bold contrast to the legalistic tithe paying of the Pharisees. The giving of the Pharisees was not wrong in a measure but in motive. Once a Pharisee, when he went up to the Temple to pray, said, "I give tithes of all that I possess" (Luke 18:12). Jesus did not condemn him for tithe paying but for trusting in himself as a righteous one and for holding others in contempt. On another occasion Jesus said, "Woe unto you, scribes and Pharisees, hypocrites! for ye pay tithe of mint and anise and cummin, and have neglected the weightier matters of the law, judgment, mercy, and faith: these ought ye to have done, and not to leave the other un-done" (Matt. 23:23). It is true that Jesus is not discussing the subject of tithe paying in this context. But he could have condemned it if the practice had been displeasing to him. The fault of the Pharisees was not in their practice of tithe paying but in their neglect of the weightier matters—judgment, mercy, and faith. The Pharisee in whose house Jesus was a dinner guest was surprised that Jesus did not first wash. Then our Lord replied, "Rather give alms of such things as ye have; and, behold all things are clean unto you" (Luke 11:41). Zaccheus, an Amhaaretz, gave half of his income to the poor. Jesus called him "a son of Abraham" and visited in his home. Also he com-mended the poor widow who gave two mites and said she had given more than all the others.

Jesus recognized tithe paying as God's law to the Jews. He kept the law to the letter and it may be confidently inferred that Jesus himself paid the tithe. The Pharisee was required to give about one fourth of his income for religious and charitable purposes. Jesus expected his followers to exceed the righteousness of the scribes and Pharisees.

III. Early Christian Giving

The Holy Spirit on the day of Pentecost took charge of the church. Almost immediately the Christians, members of the church, began to consider their responsibility with reference to properties. Luke wrote: "All that believed were together, and had all things common: and sold their possessions and goods, and parted them to all men, as every man had need" (Acts 2:44-45). Peter recognized the importance of helping the poor when he said, "Silver and gold have I none: but such as I have give I thee: In the name of Jesus Christ of Nazareth rise up and walk" (Acts 3:6). Barnabas, a man of considerable holdings, sold a field and brought the money and laid it at the apostles' feet (Acts 4: 36-37). Ananias and Sapphira sold a possession and brought part of the money to the apostles, claiming that it was the whole price of the possession. They were judged on the spot for their lies before God and man. This incident shows that the wholesale giving up of property by the early believers was not compulsory, for the land that they had was their own and their sharing it was to have been on a voluntary basis (Acts 5).

A dispute arose in the church because of some inequity in the distribution of church money or other provisions to the widows. There seems to have been a discrimination against the Gentile widows by the Jewish Christians. This cleavage between Gentile Christians and Jewish Christians occasioned the election of deacons to serve tables which undoubtedly included the distribution of alms (Acts 6:1-3).

The early church, though very interested in and committed to ministry to persons of need, refused to receive money from every source. Simon Magus offered money to Peter and John for the gift of the Holy Spirit. Peter said unto him, "Thy money perish with thee" (Acts 8:20).

When Peter went to Jerusalem following his visit in the house of Cornelius and the conversion of Cornelius, the Jewish Christians contended with him claiming that he ate with the uncircumcised and unclean. Peter justified his conduct by repeating his response to the divine message, "Not so, Lord: for nothing common or unclean hath at any time entered into my mouth" (Acts 11:8). Peter may not have been a Pharisee but here he talks as if he were one. He had been very careful at the point of Levitical purity which would presuppose that he had been a strict tithe-payer all his life.

The disciples were called Christians first at Antioch. One of the practical features of the Christianity practice in this church and community concerned their gifts to the poor. "The disciples, every man according to his ability, determined to send relief unto the brethren that dwelt in Judea: which also they did, and sent it to the elders by the hand of Barnabas and Saul" (Acts 11:29-30).

Certain men came from Judea to Antioch and taught that the Gentiles who had become Christians should be circumcised. This teaching caused such a stir that a delegation was sent to Jerusalem for a conference with the apostles and elders on this matter. The Jewish Christians, especially those who had been Pharisees, thought that the Gentile converts should be circumcised and that they should be charged to obey or keep the law of Moses, which of course would include spending a considerable portion of their income for religious purposes. Later, Christians at Jerusalem expressed the same point of view to Paul, "Thou seest, brother, how many thousands of Jews there are which believe; and they are all zealous of the law" (Acts 21:20). This zeal for the law undoubtedly included payment of tithes.

John and James in the letters or epistles that bear their names urge giving to meet human needs: "Whoso hath this world's good, and seeth his brother have need, and shutteth up his bowels of compassion from him, how dwelleth the love of God in him?" (1 John 3:17). "If a brother or sister be naked, and destitute of daily food, and one of you say unto them, Depart in peace, be ye warmed and filled; notwithstanding ye give them not those things which are needful for the body; what doth it profit?" (James 2:15-16).

IV. Paul's Teaching and Personal Example

The apostle Paul was interested in the poor. He was a part of a great movement to raise funds for the poor of the church in Jerusalem. With reference to this particular movement and somewhat as general instruction, he said, "Upon the first day of the week let every one of you lay by him in store, as God has prospered him" (1 Cor. 16:2). Four things stand out in this instruction: (1) everyone was to give; (2) the gifts were to be stored beforehand, that is, before the needs of the poor had been met; (3) the giving was according to prosperity; (4) the giving was to be done every Lord's day. The apostle gave directions for the support of the ministry: "Let him that is taught in the word communicate unto him that teacheth in all good things. Be not deceived; God is not mocked: for whatsoever a man soweth, that shall he also reap" (Gal. 6:6-7). On certain occasions Paul for personal reasons chose not to receive support but he did not disregard or think lightly of the responsibility of Christians to support their leaders. He pointed out that the priests who preached and ministered in the Temple were supported by the things of the Temple. They lived on the tithes of the people. "Even so hath the Lord ordained that they which preach the gospel should live of the gospel" (1 Cor. 9:14).

The church at Philippi seemed to be especially dear to Paul because of their love for him and their liberality in ministering to his needs. The apostle wrote: "In the beginning of the gospel, . . . no church communicated with me as concerning giving and receiving, but ye only. For even in Thessalonica ye sent once and again unto my necessity" (Phil. 4:15-17).

Paul was burdened for the poor and he put forth much energy to raise funds to meet their needs: "But now I go unto Jerusalem to minister unto the saints. For it hath pleased them of Macedonia and Achaia to make a certain contribution for the poor saints which are at Jerusalem" (Rom. 15:25). Again he wrote, "Distributing to the necessities of saints; given to hospitality" (Rom. 12:13). To the Christians in Ephesus he gave a practical exhortation: "Let him that stole steal no more: but rather let him labour, working with his hands the thing which is good, that he may have to give to him that needeth" (Eph. 4:28).

Paul praises the churches of Macedonia which in their deep poverty gave liberally to minister to the needs of the saints (2 Cor. 8:1-2). He appeals to the Corinthian Christians to pay their pledges and to have their gifts for the poor ready not as a matter of compulsion but of bounty (2 Cor. 9:1-5). The apostle seems to give priority to the needs of the saints: "Let us do good unto all men especially unto them who are of the household of faith" (Gal. 6:10). But others are certainly to share in the gifts. He gave instruction for hospitality to strangers (Rom. 12:13); for helping poor relatives (1 Tim. 5:8-16). John appeals for assistance to foreign missionaries . . . "Because that for his name sake they went forth taking nothing of the Gentiles. We therefore ought to receive such that we might be fellow helpers to the truth" (3 John 7:8).

Paul was a Pharisee and the son of a Pharisee. As such he was accustomed to giving about one-fourth of his income to religious and charitable causes. Tithe paying was a principal factor in his former righteousness which was under the law. Like Jesus, Paul makes love the motive for giving. The most impressive gifts are nothing without love (1 Cor. 13).

Let us give attention to a summary and conclusion:

1. Jesus was a tithe payer. He was part of a deeply religious family

who practiced tithing. He was never condemned even by his enemies for not paying the tithe or tithes.

2. Jesus never repealed or abridged the law. Rather he fulfilled it. Certainly the divine word on tithing was included.

3. Jesus recognized tithe paying but he did not emphasize it. The Pharisees were right in their meticulous tithing and wrong in the neglect of judgment, mercy, and faith.

4. Jesus emphasized stewardship of life which included far more than tithing. Tithing may be a part of Christian stewardship but it is not the whole of it. Christians are responsible for commiting all of life to the Lord Jesus Christ. Tithe paying is dangerous if it becomes the end of stewardship. It may be an expression or repression of stewardship.

5. "At least the tithe," "more than the tithe," "giving according to prosperity and needs," seems to be the New Testament standard of giving.

BIBLIOGRAPHY

Edersheim, Alfred. *The Life and Times of Jesus the Messiah.* Volume I. Grand Rapids, Michigan: William B. Eerdmans Publishing Company, 1943.

Hastings, Robert J. *My Money and God.* Nashville, Tennessee: Broadman Press, 1961.

Lansdell, Henry. *The Sacred Tenth.* Two Volumes. London: Society for Promoting Christian Knowledge, 1906.

Rolston, Holmes. *Stewardship in the New Testament Church.* Richmond, Virginia: John Knox Press, 1956.

Thompson, P. W. *The Whole Tithe.* London and Edinburgh: Marshall, Morgan and Scott, LTD, n.d.

Versteeg, John M. *The Deeper Meaning of Stewardship.* New York: The Abingdon Press, 1923.

Ward, Hiley H. *Creative Giving.* New York: The Macmillan Company, 1958.

Church History, Volume XXXVI, Published by The American Society of Church History, 1916, Editorial office Swift Hall, University of Chicago, Chicago, Illinois, March 1967.

The Life and Works of Josephus. Translated by Whiston. "Antiquities of the Jews," Philadelphia, Pennsylvania: The John C. Winston Company.

The Christian and the Tithe

Jerry Horner

Throughout Christian history churches have faced two perplexing and sensitive questions concerning the practical means by which they are to receive financial support. The first is the extent to which churches should concern themselves with material things, and within what limits. The second is how far the churches should seek to influence the decision of the individual as to what he is to do with his money, not to mention the wider decisions involving his time and his talents and, indeed, the whole of his life. For many years the trend among many Christian groups concerning this subject was to regard every man as a law unto himself, leaving him to reach his own conclusions in deciding how much money to give. The general consensus was that an insistence that the individual give according to some kind of plan would stifle the desired impetus towards spontaneous generosity.

However, the material response of Christians to the work of the churches was often disappointing. As a result, the churches gave renewed emphasis to Christian stewardship, seeking scriptural authority in imposing standards of giving upon their members which would compensate for their lack of generosity. Unfortunately, many such well-intended efforts took a legalistic turn which distorted the true meaning of stewardship. In addition to forcing into a Christian context a foreign sense of legal obligation, some ecclesiastical pronouncements concerning the subject of stewardship have led to the damaging implication that one has fulfilled his total responsibility to God in the disposition of personal possessions when he has met the financial demands of the church.

As men searched the Scriptures for some principle to guide them in determining how much Christians ought to give to God, they quite naturally turned to the Old Testament law of the tithe. Since the system of contributing a tenth of one's income supposedly is sanctioned in the Bible as the only means of satisfying one's financial responsibilities to God, and is therefore unrivalled by any other system, it is understandable why the law of the tithe has been the most widely employed law of stewardship throughout church history. Particularly has this emphasis been obvious in more recent years, when tithing has been preached as the solution of all the problems of Christian giving. Nearly all the major denominations are pouring out pamphlets on tithing. Some of them declare unequivocally that tithing "is the only way to finance God's program," and that it is a sure "evidence of one's faith." Because of its apparent scriptural warrants, most of the publications have little difficulty in justifying tithing, especially since they view Christian stewardship as an obligation, the nature and extent of which God himself has determined.

There are unquestionably many practical values to the individual in tithing, some of which we will examine later. Furthermore, tithing is obviously a boon to churches. It rescues faltering budgets and injects additional impetus even into financial programs which are already streamlined. But in the midst of all the hullabaloo very few people seem to be raising seriously the question, "Is tithing Christian?" Before any official pronouncement is made concerning the subject, we need to consider whether this system of church support is fundamental to our Christian faith. To state the issue simply, has God actually decreed that our stewardship responsibilities be discharged by giving a fixed portion of our material resources to the church?

The question demands that we know not so much the secular history of the custom of tithing, but its alleged scriptural foundations, particularly in the New Testament. It is also essential that we be aware of the historical interpretation of the scriptural evidence concerning tithing. Is it not possible that much of the modern view of the subject is in fact based on tradition itself rather than on Scripture? At least let us be willing to concede, whatever our own position may be, that the *Christian* position is to be found in the New Testament. With these thoughts in mind, perhaps several introductory statements are in order. These statements will both summarize my own position and determine the direction of the discussion which follows.

1. Tithing was a pre-Hebraic practice. However, this fact in no way suggests that tithing is an eternal universal law possessed intuitively by all men as a result of God's design. The Christian's authority and guide in all spiritual matters is the New Testament, not ancient history.

2. The Scriptures do not give the direct and unambiguous attestation to the tithe that many of its advocates have presupposed. A

close examination will reveal that the Old Testament practice of paying the tithe underwent many modifications and revisions, causing difficulty in making dogmatic statements concerning what the total scriptural practice was.[1] Even the Pharisees differed in their conclusions.

3. Regardless of what tithing meant in the Old Testament, as a binding obligation it was superseded by the higher demand of Jesus, who expected his followers to commit *all* their resources to the service of God, and not just a tenth.

4. It was in the early church that the tithe returned as a convenient method of fulfilling one's financial obligations. Thus, over a period of time a practical measurement obscured and replaced the higher call to total commitment.

Origin and Early History of the Tithe

The word "tithe" is an English word derived from the Anglo-Saxon *teothe* and meaning the tenth. As a religious practice, tithing may generally be defined as the giving of a tenth of the annual produce or other income for the support of a particular religious ministry. The idea finds roots far back into antiquity. It is not particularly a biblical nor a Jewish idea, but seems to be an outgrowth of man's reflection concerning his responsibility to deity. Centuries before the Hebrews existed as a separate people, the Chaldeans and the Egyptians were offering to their gods a tenth of the increase of their lands in the rich valleys of the Euphrates and the Nile. When the idea was first conceived, and how the ratio was fixed at one-tenth, remains an insoluble puzzle. However, the mystery begins to unravel somewhat when we realize that primitive man was basically religious, recognizing a supreme being, or group of beings, who gave increase to his fields and flocks. Therefore, as an expression of his dependence and gratitude he brought an offering from his produce.

Other ancient nations also practiced the tithe. There is evidence that the custom was not unknown to the Phoenicians, Arabians, Chinese, Carthaginians, Greeks, and Romans. Even then the fourth century B.C. Aristotle could refer to the tithe as "an ancient law." Other ancient writers, such as the Greek historians Herodotus and Xenophon and the Romans Pliny and Cicero, also mention the tithe.

The basic idea of the tithe underwent several changes during its long history, not the least of which was the motivation behind it. Originally, it appeared to be essentially a spontaneous act of worship, a token of dependence and thankfulness. However, the practice was

178

corrupted in two directions, both of which find modern parallels when the tithe is reduced to a legalistic obligation. First, the tithe came to be regarded as an appeasement of deity, for fear that failure to pay would result in a curse. Another motive which developed was a desire to bargain, whereby the worshipper sought to influence his god and thus purchase certain material advantages or forgiveness.

Interesting though a historical survey of tithing may be, it is not to determine the means of fulfilling our own stewardship responsibilities. It is the desire and duty of Christians to enter into the full purpose of God, and this divine purpose is to be discerned in Scripture, not in the experience of particular individuals or groups, however valid and rewarding those experiences may be. What we ourselves do and what we teach to others must be governed by the Scriptures. This is certainly not to minimize the importance of a historical study. We can at least profit from the knowledge that primitive man, in his vague and imperfect concept of deity, recognized a divine ownership of all things and searched for an appropriate manner in which to meet his obligations to his gods.

The Tithe in the Old Testament

The Pre-Mosaic Period.—The law of the tithe is the focal point of the Old Testament teaching concerning stewardship. In the pre-Mosaic period the primary thought in the payment of the tithe was an acknowledgment of God's ownership of life and property and that man is responsible to God for all the possessions received from him.

Many scholars see a reference to the tithe in the offering of Cain and Abel and feel that Cain's "offering was rejected because he did not bring the whole tithe of his increase as an offering to the Lord, basing their conclusions largely on the Septuagint version of the incident in the Greek text." [2] However, a close examination of Gen. 4:6-7 in the Septuagint makes such a conclusion untenable.

The earliest definite reference to tithing in the Old Testament is in the experience of Abraham with Melchizedek (Gen. 14:18-20). The latter was king of Salem and priest of the Most High God. We are told nothing of his antecedents, but only learn that he appeared mysteriously on the scene of history and just as abruptly disappeared from the story. The author of Hebrews interprets this obscurity as the purposeful design of God so that Melchizedek could be a type, or divinely appointed prophetic symbol, of Christ, who has an eternal priesthood (Heb. 7:3). Abraham recognized the office of Melchizedek and gave him a tenth of the spoils regained from those who had captured

Sodom and other cities of the plain. However, we must understand that Abraham gave tithes to Melchizedek not because of Melchizedek's ownership, but because he served as the priest of God, the true owner of man's possessions.

The only other pre-Mosaic reference to tithing is in connection with Jacob's dream at Bethel (Gen. 28:10-22). After he had heard the voice of God blessing him in the dream, Jacob promised God, "Of all that thou shalt give me I will surely give the tenth unto thee" (Gen. 28:22). It is apparent that Jacob regarded the tithe as an acknowledgment of God's ownership and God's rightful claim on all. We can infer from this and the earlier incident that tithing was a common practice among godly men of the Patriarchal Age.

The Tithe and the Law.—Under the influence and leadership of Moses, the tithe, which began as a spontaneous act of worship, was made a legal requirement. It was not an offering in the strict sense of the word, but a compulsory obligation placed upon every man under the law. Thus, the Israelite, if he were to keep the law, was left no option in the matter of paying tithes. He either paid the tithe or was considered a lawbreaker.

The law of the tithe is found at various places in the Mosaic legislation. The earliest statement of it records explicit instructions which the Hebrews received concerning the tithing of the produce of their fields, their livestock, and their other possessions:

And all the tithe of the land, whether of the seed of the land, or of the fruit of the tree, is the Lord's: it is holy unto the Lord. And if a man will at all redeem aught of his tithes, he shall add thereto the fifth part thereof. And concerning the tithe of the herd, or the flock, even of whatsoever passeth under the rod, the tenth shall be holy unto the Lord (Lev. 27:30-32).

In addition to the command itself, the law stipulated various kinds of tithes. The Levites received tithes from the people for their services on behalf of God and the sanctuary (Num. 18:21), and they in turn were to tithe their tithe (Num. 18:26). There was also a tithe for the feasts and sacrifices of the Lord, of which the offerer himself and his family partook (Deut. 14:22-26). A tithe for benevolent aid to the poor was prescribed every third year (Deut. 14:28,29). We are not to understand that tithing was the complete program of giving under the law. The tithe was an obligation upon every Hebrew, but godly Israelites gave offerings to God above and beyond the tithes (Deut. 12:11).

The Old Testament indicates that many Israelites disobeyed God in their failure to bring the tithe as he had commanded. Of particular interest at this point is Malachi's solemn accusation that the people of his day were guilty of robbing God by their refusal to pay tithes and give offerings (Mal. 3:8-10). Many serious Christians assert without reservation that Malachi's words apply directly to the practice of stewardship today, thus making the requirement of the tithe unconditionally binding. However, as we shall see, there is no commandment in the New Testament which demands that the Christian must tithe. There are definite principles of stewardship to be found in the teachings of Malachi and other Old Testament passages, but the matter of giving for the Christian is not based on legal obligation. The person who thinks that the whole of Christian stewardship is tithing lacks an understanding of the complexity of the legal system. A Christian may tithe if he chooses to do so, but if he holds to the tithe as a legal duty, he misunderstands the teaching of Scripture about grace. He would have to *pay* the tithe before he could claim to *give* anything to God.

The Tithe in the New Testament

Specific References.—The argument for the tithe in the New Testament is very weak. It is estimated that one-sixth of Jesus' sayings deal with money, but he never mentioned the tithe in his teachings concerning the attitude of a person toward his possessions. In fact, Jesus mentioned tithing only twice, and in both instances in negative pronouncements pertaining to Jewish legalistic piety. In Luke 18:12 he described a Pharisee as boasting, "I give tithes of all that I get." Jesus contrasted the Pharisee with a publican, considered a "sinner," and declared that the sinner "went down to his house justified rather than the other," that is, the tithing Pharisee. In his denunciation of the Pharisees in Matt. 23:23 (RSV) Jesus said: "Woe to you, scribes and Pharisees, hypocrites! for you tithe mint and dill and cummin, and have neglected the weightier matters of the law, justice and mercy and faith; these you ought to have done, without neglecting the others." The question of the tithe is not at all the issue in this verse. The context demands that we understand the statement as a censure upon the scribes and Pharisees, and its application is to them, not to Christians. To interpret it otherwise is improper exegesis which violates the context and disregards the point of the verse. Jesus was speaking directly to those who were under the law. He rebuked the Pharisees for their undue concern for trivial matters, such as the tithing of herbs, while at the same time failing to give enough attention to the things which are really vital. Since they were bound by the law, the Pharisees should have observed all its other requirements, as well as the tithe. The phrase "these you ought to have done" refers to the demand of the law for justice, mercy, and faith. Actually, it is an impersonal construction, and literally says, "These things it was necessary to have done." The most that can be gleaned from the words "without neglecting the others" is that the concern with the minute details of the law by those under the law was not condemned by Jesus as long as it was not separated from a profound concern with the purusit of the more important moral obligations prescribed by the law. It is difficult to interpret this casual reference by Jesus to tithing, occurring as part of a stringent and sarcastic condemnation of the formal legalism of the Pharisees, as expressing either approval or disapproval of the tithe as a principle of Christian stewardship.

The only other references in the New Testament to tithing are in the seventh chapter of Hebrews. However, those references are merely a part of the larger argument for the pre-eminence of Christ, and have no bearing whatever on the question of stewardship in the early church.

Arguments from Silence.—Since the New Testament nowhere explicitly demands that a tithe is to be paid, those who feel that the tithe as an obligatory principle is upheld by the New Testament are forced to search for implications and arguments from silence. Many people point out that Jesus himself was a tither. He was reared in a pious Jewish home where he evidently saw tithing in continual practice, and it is reasonable to believe that he met this demand of the law as well as others. Furthermore, the hawk-eyed Pharisees searched constantly for wrong in the Lord, but never once criticized him for failure to tithe, though this was an immensely important affair to them. Yet it is a very poor argument to bind the tithe on the basis of Jesus' practice, for he kept all the other ordinances of the law as well, including circumcision, animal sacrifice, paying the Temple tax, etc. If the fact that Jesus tithed is a basis for requiring Christians to tithe, then why not require them to observe the other practices?

It is significant that Jesus did not ask for a tithe or a proportion; he asks only that we give "freely" (Matt. 10:8). If Jesus had established definite rules requiring a tenth or any other proportion of our income, the force of his teachings about possessing and giving would be enervated. He showed that riches pose a danger to faith and alienate men from each other (cf. Mark 10:21-27; Luke 12:13 ff., etc.). Furthermore, he taught that God judges our gifts not by *how much we give,* but by *how much we have left* after we give (cf. Mark 12:41-44). One should not feel that in the payment of the tithe he has fulfilled the obligations of Christian stewardship.

But this does not mean that Jesus expressly rejected and opposed the commandment of the tithe as it was applied in his time. He could allow it to continue in the same way that he did not abrogate the connection to the temple in spite of all his criticism of it. There is, therefore, no reason to assume that he hindered anyone in the payment of the tithe. We may only conclude that Jesus so deepened the problem of having possessions that a positive adoption of the Old Testament commandment of the tithe could not be considered; for the will of God is not fulfilled through the payment of the tithe.[3]

Another argument from silence involves the apostle Paul. Many who advocate that the New Testament teaches the tithe as an obligation assert that Paul, as a strict Pharisee, was a tither, and that nowhere in his writings did he condemn tithing. It is true that he practiced tithing as a Pharisee and that he did not condemn it as a legal requirement, but it is also true that there is no reference at all to the tithe in Paul's writings. All the apostles were Jews, reared in tithing but not one of them spoke a single word which would intimate that in the new covenant Christians might regulate their practice of stewardship by the law of the tithe. This strong negative is immensely reinforced by Paul in the many passages which deal directly or indirectly with the matter of stewardship. In such passages as 2 Cor. 3:1-15 he appealed to diverse motives which would stimulate Christian giving. But he never mentioned the tithe. Exegetically and thus dogmatically the New Testament does not recognize tithing as a regulation in the new covenant. In fact, the main point lacking in all the arguments for the law of the tithe is New Testament authority.

The Termination of the Law.—The teaching of such passages as Rom. 6:14 that the believer in Christ is not under the law is sorely neglected. Paul's assertion that the Christian is "not under the law, but under grace" does not mean that the believer is lawless, but it does denote that the Mosaic system has no direct claim upon him. To try to separate the law into parts, declaring that one part belongs to the Christian while another part does not, is to do violence to Scripture, which always recognizes the law as a unity (James 2:10; cf. Gal. 3:10; 5:3). The Christian, since he is not under the law, is not under obligation to tithe, precisely as he is not under obligation to observe the Jewish feasts or to offer Levitical sacrifices. Therefore, to enforce the tithe on Christians as a biblical command involves a misunderstanding

183

of the relationship between the Old Covenant and the New. That which was required of the Hebrews was for the support of a local, temporary ministry, while those under the New Covenant give for an eternal and unshakable kingdom. Only in shadow and promise did those of the Old Testament know the unutterable blessings we possess in Christ.

However, many insist that tithing is binding upon the Christian because it did not originate with the law, but was given as God's plan before the law. The same could be said of circumcision, which God gave to Abraham before the law. Like tithing, it was later incorporated into the law. But surely, in view of the clear teachings of Acts 15 and the Epistle to the Galatians, no one can legitimately claim that Christians must keep the rite of circumcision simply because it is older than the law.

In declaring that the believer is not under the law, the New Testament does not allow for antinomianism, or completely lawless behavior. Paul showed that the Christian is neither under the law, as the Jews were, nor lawless, as the Gentiles were, but in an entirely new relationship, which he referred to as "under the law (literally, in-lawed) to Christ" (1 Cor. 9:20,21). The believer is not under an external code, but enjoys a new position under grace which is neither legalistic nor antinomian. This relationship of grace affects our stewardship. While a formal observance of the tithe as law entails something of the bondage of legalism which Paul rebelled against, grace provokes a response of love. Although the demands made upon us by grace move in different realms than the demands of law, they are even more exacting.

The Principle of Grace.—We have noted that the Christian, in his new relationship to Christ, is not subject to the Mosaic law, nor is he lawless in his behavior, but is subject to Christ. This fact does not forbid Christians to tithe, but we must understand that the New Testament does not command them to tithe. If a Christian decides in his own heart out of love that he will give a tenth of his income to the Lord, he is free to do so and will find the practice highly rewarding. But he must not tithe from a sense of legal obligation, and must not do it with the idea that the tithe is the full measure of his response to the call of Christian stewardship, or that the other nine-tenths are his own to do with as he pleases without consulting God. Many Christians sincerely use the tithe as a convenient measuring tool in the matter of giving. But should the tithe be the measure of the obligation of all Christians, regardless of their income? If a man having a limited income with heavy responsibilities is bound by the tithe, does this mean that the tithe is also to measure the obligation of a man having a greater income with comparatively fewer responsibilities? A sound principle of taxation is to increase the percentage as the taxable income increases. Our response to God in the Christian dispensation is a concern of grace, not law; but if that response is to be as God has prospered us, it should involve a larger percentage of the income of the rich than of the poor (cf. 2 Cor. 16:2).

However, the fact that the tithe is not binding upon Christians does not at all mean that they are to be careless or random givers. Obligatory tithing is a form of legalism, especially if one tries to lay the obligation upon another. But random, cursory, occasional giving is a form of antinomianism. We should bear in mind that the New Testament nowhere tells us to give less than a tenth, and while taking care to avoid a legalistic system we should beware lest we fall into a reckless and haphazard system. Some are so fearful of establishing a definite amount and a fine point that they wind up with no point at all. They speak of our stewardship under grace as though being under grace means we can give more cheaply than those under law. Christ did not die on the cross to enable us to give two percent instead of ten percent, and the word grace is not a cloak of covetousness to do less instead of more. The man who argues for less than a tenth may be saying more about his depth of dedication than he intends to say. At least his argument indicates that he himself plans to do as little as he can.

What then is to be the standard for a Christian under grace? Christian giving is based not on certain Old Testament passages or on the Mosaic legislation, but on the supreme self-giving of God himself through Jesus Christ. Just as the believer has been saved by grace, so he is to live by God's grace. His stewardship of money is to be in the sphere of grace. Christian stewardship must flow from our understanding of what God has done for us in Christ and his sacrifice. We give out of the spontaneous promptings of our hearts, in thanksgiving and love. When Christians recognize in any measure the height and depth of God's love which has made them partakers of the redemption wrought by the cross, there is no need to make rules about giving. No giving can be called too much in the light of this love. No percentage can be considered impoverishing in comparision with Christ's hundred percent giving of himself (cf. 2 Cor. 8:9). Had God prescribed a definite amount for us to give, most of us would probably do no more than that. However, the compelling rule of love allows for the development of a larger spiritual life bounded only by our deepest longings. An amount set for us would name the limits, but on our honor and love we are free to soar to the heights in going beyond the requirements of law.

The Tithe in the Early Church

The primitive church held tenaciously to the radical perspective of Christ concerning possessions and giving. Christians of the first century were repeatedly exhorted not only to refuse to permit earthly possessions to hinder their discipleship, but to renounce their material possessions completely and to make sacrifices out of their income according to the need. It is inconceivable that the Christians at Jerusalem, recently converted from Judaism, could give less to Christ as Christians than they had formerly given without him as Jews. Theirs was a background of liberality, and in Christ it did not become less but more, for in their new joy, "No one said that any of the things which he possessed was his own" (Acts 4:32 RSV). Theirs was an attitude which viewed all of the Christian's resources as being at God's and his brother's disposal. They often gave a hundred percent that their brethren might be fed and clothed, being always ready to "contribute to the needs of the saints" (Rom. 12:13). In the first church no man considered anything his own until the need was met.

However, this attitude began to be displaced by a legalistic spirit when the Christian's total commitment was more and more conceived of as an obligation commanded by Christ. Many of the Lord's statements were interpreted in such a way that their original significance faded into the background. In addition, a pattern of thought developed in the post-apostolic period which reasoned that if even the Israelites were commanded to tithe, Christians are much more obligated to bring offerings out of their income. This reasoning was usually followed by the accusation that Christians were guilty of not matching the Jews in generosity, even though the Jews did not know Christ. From this kind of argumentation, it was only a short step to the reintroduction of the Old Testament law of the tithe. The church fathers almost unanimously agreed that the law of the tithe fell short of Christ's teachings concerning the necessity of forsaking all worldly possessions, but that nevertheless it was a divinely ordained law. This line of thought remains to this day.

Conclusion

Tithing has been preached as the solution of all the problems of Christian giving. There are definite values in tithing. It has a distinct practical value as a systematic means of providing support for the financial needs of the church. It has a spiritual value as a definite and constant reminder of God's ownership and man's stewardship. When the tithe is viewed in such a manner, and not as a religious obligation laid upon us to meet God's demands, its practice may both be defended and commended.

However, churches must avoid presenting a program of stewardship that is not squarely based on convictions that are distinctively Christian. We must not allow the reintroduction of the commandment to tithe to weaken the challenge of Christ. "Christ's challenge was diminished as soon as nothing more than the tithe was required; and its evangelical character was obscured when the amount of that which Christ challenges us to do was fixed a priori." [4]

New Testament stewardship is not a bookkeeping matter; it is all-inclusive. There is no room here for a ten or even a fifty percent standard. A Christian has no need to invoke old laws. He is under a new law—the love of Christ. Tithing is good business and does bring returns, but it is incorrect to classify it as a Christian standard.

FOOTNOTES

[1] Compare, for instance, Deut. 14:22-23 with Num. 18:24-28.
[2] George A. E. Salstrand, *The Tithe* (Grand Rapids: Baker Book House, 1952), p. 19.
[3] Lukas Vischer, *Tithing in the Early Church* (Philadelphia: Fortress Press, 1966), p. 11.
[4] Vischer, p. 30.

SUGGESTED READINGS ON STEWARDSHIP

Aycock, Jarrette. *Tithing: Your Questions Answered.* Kansas City: Beacon Hill Press, 1955. Leaves many questions unanswered and others answered inadequately.

Costen, James Hutten. *The Stewardship of Possessions in Pauline Thought.* Unpublished Th.M. thesis, Southeastern Baptist Theological Seminary, 1963.

Currier, Bruce. *The Development of Stewardship in the Priesthood of Christ.* Unpublished Th.M. thesis, Central Baptist Theological Seminary, 1946.

Edwards, Walter Ross. *The Doctrine of Stewardship in the Synoptic Gospels.* Unpublished Th.D. thesis, Central Baptist Theological Seminary, 1945.

Fletcher, Joseph F., ed. *Christianity and Property*. Philadelphia: The Westminster Press, 1947. A study of the history of Christian thinking about property and its bearing upon present-day problems of ownership.

Fuller, Reginald H. and Brian K. Rice. *Christianity and the Affluent Society*. Grand Rapids: Eerdmans, 1966. A consideration of the biblical attitude to wealth and prosperity and a critique of the affluent society based on biblical insights.

Harrell, Costen J. *Stewardship and the Tithe*. Nashville: Abingdon Press, 1953. More helpful on the subject of stewardship in general than with the tithe.

Hatch, C. W. *Stewardship Enriches Life*. Anderson, Indiana: Warner Press, 1952. A study of the spiritual values in stewardship practice. Written on the premise that stewardship is basic and lies at the very heart of Christian living.

Havlik, John Franklin. *A Stewardship Commentary on the Greek Text of II Cor. 8 and 9*. Unpublished, 1955.

Henderson, Edwin Harold. *Old Testament Doctrine of the Tithe*. Unpublished Th.D. thesis, Southwestern Baptist Theological Seminary, 1963.

Kantonen, T. A. *A Theology for Christian Stewardship*. Philadelphia: Muhlenberg Press, 1956. An excellent treatment of the subject from an evangelical point of view. Helpful particularly to pastors.

Kauffman, Milo. *The Challenge of Christian Stewardship*. Scottdale, Pa.: Herald Press, 1955. A serious discussion of philosophy and practice.

Lansdell, Henry. *The Sacred Tenth*. Grand Rapids: Baker Book House, 1955. An exhaustive study of the tithe in Scripture and in history. This reprint of the 1908 edition serves as a valuable source and reference book on the principles and practice of tithing.

McClure, Cicero H. *Study of the Old Testament Teachings on Stewardship*. Unpublished Th.D. thesis, Southwestern Baptist Theological Seminary, 1954.

McRae, Glenn. *Teaching Christian Stewardship*. St. Louis: Bethany Press, 1954. A text for leadership training in stewardship.

Mark, James. *The Question of Christian Stewardship*. London: SCM Press, 1964. A study of the concept of stewardship in the Old and New Testaments and an application to Christians in an affluent society.

Rolston, Holmes. *Stewardship in the New Testament Church*. Richmond: John Knox Press, 1959. A superb discussion of proportionate giving. Extremely helpful in the subject of giving for Christian missions.

Salstrand, George A. E. *The Tithe.* Grand Rapids: Baker Book House, 1952. A concise treatment of the exhaustive study by Lansdell.

Shedd, Charlie W. *How to Develop a Tithing Church.* Nashville: Abingdon Press, 1961. A description of the program, materials, and resources to encourage church-wide tithing.

Smith, Roy L. *Stewardship Studies.* Nashville: Abingdon Press, 1954. A commentary on several hundred key stewardship passages in the Bible.

Sutton, Jack A. *Witness Beyond Barriers.* St. Louis: Bethany Press, 1968. A readable study of the role of stewardship in a Christian's discipleship and testimony.

Thompson, T. K., ed. *Stewardship in Contemporary Theology.* New York: Association Press, 1960. A broad survey of stewardship in the Old Testament, in the teachings of Christ, in church history, and in Christian doctrine. Offers insights on contemporary problems of the individual Christian, the church, and society.

Thomason, George D. *The Doctrine of Property in the Teaching of Jesus.* Unpublished Th.D. thesis, Southern Baptist Theological Seminary, 1953.

Vischer, Lukas. *Tithing in the Early Church.* Philadelphia: Fortress Press. A conclusion, based on an examination of the scriptural evidence and its interpretation by the early church, that the tithe is not the rule and norm of Christian stewardship.

Ward, Hiley H. *Creative Giving.* New York: Macmillan, 1958. Forceful discussion of proportionate giving.

Werning, W. J. *Investing Your Life.* Grand Rapids: Zondervan, 1956. Brief and readable stewardship planning guide for young adults.

The Christian and the Tithe

William L. Hendricks

In recent stewardship as promoted and practiced by Southern Baptists, tithing has been the central emphasis. This emphasis is overdue close scrutiny in the light of the biblical materials.

The appropriate posture for the people of God is always forward, never backward. In submitting the idea of the tithe to a rigorous examination of the biblical bases for tithing the forward look is the only adequate one.

Many have forced Scripture to say things about tithing it does not really say. Others, eager to be relieved of even minimal obligation in giving, have sought exegetically or hermeneutically to remove tithing from the roster of biblical teachings. Both positions are unfortunate and should give way to a rigorous, descriptive study of what the biblical materials say about tithing. Then, the discussions about contemporary applications are appropriate. In moving toward this ideal this paper will follow a twofold format: first, a biblical and historical study; second, questions theological and practical.

I. A Biblical and Historical Study

A. The Old Testament

1. *A descriptive account.* The Hebrew word for tithe *maaser* means a tenth. The fascination of ancient man with the religious significance of numbers is a well-known but little-explored subject. Was ten significant because of the digits on a man's own hands and feet? Surely the *deka* (Greek for ten) has a place in the religious life of Israel. The symbolism is so extensive as to apply to the measurements in the temple and ark, the prescribed number of plagues, and the complete number of God's commandments.[1]

The origins of the notion of the tenth of one's substance offered to the deity out of gratitude or obligation are lost in antiquity.[2]

In the Old Testament the patriarchal figures are represented as being familiar with the tithe. Abram gives a tenth of his war booty to Melchisedek (Gen. 14:20). Jacob, awaking from his dream, builds an altar and makes a vow to give a tenth of his possessions to God (Gen. 28:22). Amos 4:4 evidences that tithes were paid at the ancient shrine of Bethel.

The first instructions prescribing the use of the tithe (Deut. 14:22-29) assume its legitimacy. The tithe is primarily of the agricultural products and along with the offerings is to be used once a year in a celebration meal at one of Israel's cultic shrines. The celebration includes the Levites and the possibility that a portion of this tithe was for the Levites cannot be ruled out (Deut. 14:27; cf. Deut. 12:5-19). Every third year the agricultural tithe was to be kept in the town of the individual Israelite and used for the support of the Levites and the relief of the poor (Deut. 14:28-29). Upon the fulfillment of this obligation of the third year tithe for the Levites and the poor, the Israelite was to make a solemn declaration before God that his tithe was paid (Deut. 26:12-15).

Cultic acts grew in ancient Israel even as they do in modern times. Numbers 18:20-32 reflects a diverse insight about tithing. A tithe of agricultural products (the meat was provided from offerings, Num. 18:8-20) was set aside for the Levites because they had no part in the inheritance of the land. In turn the Levites paid a tithe of the tithe to the priests. Nehemiah (10:37-38; 12:44; 13:5, 12) gives evidence that the tithe for the Levite was primarily an agricultural tithe.

However, in Lev. 27:32-33 it is recognized that animals are included in the tithe. Every tenth animal was sacred to God. The animals could not be sold for money, then different animals be purchased for giving at the shrine, as was the case with grain. Rather the animal must be driven to the shrine or the temple and there offered to God. If a man sought on the sly to sell the animal and purchase another when he arrived at the place of celebration, he owed both the originally-sold animal and the newly-purchased animal to God. Grain and produce could be sold and the money used to purchase new celebration-produce at the site of the shrine or temple. Twenty percent additional purchase price was required in such transactions (Lev. 27:30-33; cf. Jer. 33:13). Animals are also included in 2 Chron. 31:5-12 when Hezekiah gathered the unpaid tithes into the temples. In later days Israel counted three tithes: the tithe of produce and cattle; the tithe for the Levites; and the tithe for the poor (the third year tithe). It is apparent that Israelites were not always faithful in their tithing as evidenced by such admonitory passages as Neh. 13:10-12 and Mal. 3:8-10.

2. *An assessment.* The beginning of tithing as a religious act and obligation is lost in the antiquity of semitic and near eastern religious customs. Israel's origins, in the patriarchal period, assume tithing as a religious rite. The shrines of Israel and her temple were the places where Israel celebrated her ritual tithing meals and paid her tithes in keeping with Mosaic law and requirements.

There are diverse customs and prescriptions concerning the payment of the tithe in ancient Israel. In the times of the later prophets possibly three tithes were exacted from each Israelite. Whereas this paper is limited to tithing *per se* any full discussion of the Old Testament insights concerning worship and giving would have to include materials on offerings and sacrifices. The relation of the tithe to the offering of the first fruits is a particularly involved problem.[3]

B. The Tithe in Late Judaism and the Intertestamental Period

1. *A descriptive account.* The protestant often supposes that in those centuries between the testaments things stood still and all was quiet. Nothing could be further from the truth. There is a climate of growing awareness that the times between the testaments shaped the world in which Jesus was born and the church was begun. Sources for a study of this period are: the Talmud (at least the mishna of the Tannaitic period);[4] the Apocrypha;[5] and the works of Josephus.[6]

The rabbinic teachings on tithing may be found in fullest detail in the Zer'aim "Seeds," the first order of the tractate of the Mishna.[7] It is here that the regulations of seeds and plants to be tithed are given (cf. Matt. 23:23; Luke 11:42, 18:12). Space prohibits the full chronicling of the teachings. Topics included for discussion are: rules concerning the first and second tithe and the regulations of tithes to the poor. Specific problems involve: when does a fruit or grain become "tithable" (Masaroth VII, 1.5-7); whether one may eat his neighbor's figs if it is suspected he has not tithed them (Masaroth VII, 2.1-3); if one must tithe produce placed on sheds and summer houses—he does not (Masaroth VII, 3.1-3).

References on tithing from the Apocrypha yield the following information. Tobit went faithfully to Jerusalem to pay tithes. He gave his produce tithes to the Levites ministering at Jerusalem. He took the proceeds of a second tithe to spend in Jerusalem, and he gave the third tithe to those whom his grandmother specified for charity (Tobit

1:6-8).[8] Judith misinforms Holofernes, as part of her deceptive plot, that the Jews in beseiged Jerusalem are planning to eat the items dedicated as tithes and in such an instance God will let Jerusalem fall to Nebuchadnezzar's forces (Judith 11:11-15). In 1 Maccabees 3:49 the armies of Judas Maccabees camped at Mizpah opposite Jerusalem had brought religious relics and the tithe to their camp to countermand the divination of Ptolmey's army and win the favor of God. It worked.

Josephus remarks that under Herod Agrippa the followers of the High Priest Ismael created great civil disturbances and sent brigands to the threshing floors to steal the portions of grain due the priests with the resulting that many of the lower groups of priests died from want (*Antiquities* XX. 8,8).[9] When Josephus is telling of the famous Greeks who were aware of Jews and Jewish customs, he mentions that Theophrastus was aware of Corban, a custom related to the giving of a tithe or offering (cf. Mark 7:11).[10] In his autobiography Josephus mentions that seven of his friends were Jewish priests who had become rich from the tithes due them (*Life*, 12), but with typical "humility" denies that he took tithes due him as a priest (*Life*, 15).

2. *An assessment.* These references from the intertestamental period bear witness to the fact that tithing was an integral part of Jewish life. The elaborate rabbinic rules regulating tithing were not so much intended to bind burdens on the Jews as to provide them with custom-made regulations which would help them acknowledge the ownership of God over all things. The intention became lost in a maze of rules.

The few references from the Apocrypha illustrate how tithing was held as a virtuous custom of godly men (Tobit) and how its practice promised the favor and protection of God (1 Maccabees). The threat of its discontinuation or abuse was enough to place Israel in dire peril (Judith).

Josephus makes reference to the abuse of the tithes by the temple officials and provides a glimpse of what a burden the paying of tithes to absentee priests must have been. The practice must have been quite comparable to the later church custom of benefices in Western European ecclesiastical customs.

C. The Tithe in the New Testament

1. *A descriptive account.* There are three passages in the New Testament which mention tithing. Matthew 23:23 and its parallel in Luke 11:42 are by far the most significant references Luke 18:12— the publican and the Pharisee—is the second reference. Hebrews 7:1-

10 with its theological use of the Abraham and Melchisedek event is the third reference.

Matthew 23:23 and Luke 11:42 occur incidentally in a rebuke of the scribes and Pharisees. The specific regulations mentioned here may be found in the Talmud (Masaroth 4:5 and Demai 2:1).[11] The direct meaning of the passage is clear. The scribes and Pharisees have paid minute attention to the rabbinic requirements of the agricultural tithe, but they have neglected the weightier matters of the law such as justice, mercy, and faith (cf. Micah 6:8). Some ancient manuscripts of Luke (Beza and Marcion) omit the phrase "these you ought to have done, without neglecting the others." The strongest textual evidence supports the phrase). Grammatically it is probable that the phrase "these you ought to have done" refers to the weightier matters of the law, justice, mercy, and faith. The phrase "and not to leave the other undone" refers to the tithing.

In Luke 18:12 the Pharisee exceeds the law in giving tithes of all that he possesses. He thereby transcends the requirements of tithing agricultural products only. The meaning is obvious. The Pharisee justifies himself because of his deeds. The deeds are neither approved or disapproved. What is criticized is the proud attitude of the Pharisee and his theological supposition that his actions make him just.

In Heb. 7:1-10 the point of the passage is to illustrate the superiority of Christ to the Levitical priesthood. In the author's argument Melchisedek is a prototype of Christ. If Abraham paid tithes to the greater Melchisedek then Jews should recognize that Jesus as priest "after the order of Melchizedek" (7:17) is a superior priest deserving their allegiance. It is a strained exegesis which goes further and indicates that Jews also must pay their tithes to Christ as Abraham did to Melchisedek. The passage is christological, not liturgical; that is, the author is speaking about Christ, not about Christian worship.

The introduction of the tithe in this passage permits the author to play on three themes: the Levites, the law, and the descendants of Abraham.[12]

2. *An assessment.* The sparse New Testament references to the tithe *per se* show that Jesus and the early church were well aware of the custom in Judaism. The references in the Gospels occur in passages condemning legalism and self-righteousness. Jesus' acceptance of the tithe by the affirmation that it should not be left undone is not a direct or intentional "teaching" about tithing. Likewise he did not disallow the custom; his only word was a positive one of acceptance.

The author of Hebrews takes occasion to use the event of Abraham paying tithes to Melchisedek to illustrate the precedence of the

Melchisedekian priesthood, which is like that of Christ, to the Levitical priesthood. The argument is based on the premise that the one paying thus recognizes the greater position of the one to whom he pays the tithes. It should be understood the position is that which arises from the divine call and commission and not from the person of the priest.

The above section has presented the biblical materials on tithing. It is now needful to explore certain crucial questions and implications that help to explain the wide disparity between the sparsity of the biblical materials and the stress given that subject in the contemporary religious context.

II. Questions Theological and Practical

A. The Relation of Law and Grace

The fundamental religious question always deals with God. Who is God? How does man know him? What are his purposes for the created order? Failure to give attention to these questions is to abort a meaningful understanding of tithing in particular and stewardship in its broader implications. Classically stated the problem has to do with law and grace. Christians have always affirmed that God is one God (in three persons); there are not two Gods. Therefore the Old and New Covenants must have some continuity. Morcion, the second century writer, spoke of the God of the Old Testament as the creator God who was wrathful, and he posited the New Testament redeemer God of love as a second God. Marcion was rightly declared a heretic, and many Christians have veered toward his heresy from then to the present.

Normative Christianity has always felt obliged to hold together the Creator and the Redeemer; the Old Testament and the New Testament; wrath and love; law and grace. The catholic perspectives of Christianity (Roman and Greek) have stressed this unity much more than Protestants. And within Protestantism various positions have been held. The Reformed (Calvinist) churches have stressed the positive relation of law and grace whereas the Lutheran churches have tended more to place law and grace in antithesis. The radical reformers tended to disjoin law and grace, the Old Testament and the New Testament even more completely than the Lutherans.

The consensus of contemporary Christian theology is toward meaningful ways of relating law and grace, the creator and redeemer, the Old and New Covenants. It is highly desirable that Baptists should concur in this stress on the continuity of creation and redemption.

Practically speaking, what this would mean for stewardship is to find the larger categories in which the God of Scripture seeks to redeem his creation. Physical substance and all other created things must find their meaningful place within this broader theological understanding of God's purpose.

B. The Relation of the Biblical Materials

The resolution of the question of law and grace will lead logically to another question. What is the relation of Israel to the church, of the Old Testament to the New Testament? Various answers have been given to this question paralleling the answers concerning law and grace. A narrowing of this question would ask: Does the church teach tithing because the Old Testament commands it or because Christ approves it or both? The Roman communion has established both the priesthood and tithing from Old Testament insights and the approval of Christ, working forward with the approach of tradition.[13]

Most Protestant groups, however, have tended to argue from the slender New Testament expression about tithing and to extract the Old Testament expressions about tithing as a suggested model for Christian practice. It might be argued that Christians are bound literally by all of the Bible; therefore they are literally bound to perform the tithing requirements of the Old Testament. Only the most unreflective and uncritical persons would seek to establish tithing from the Old Testament in such a way as to observe the literal Old Testament customs. The historical context of Israel's practice of tithing involved only an agricultural society. Therefore only an agricultural (grain, wine, and fruits) type of tithe would be a literal Old Testament tithe.

Such a view should be criticized primarily because it fails to acknowledge that Christ has deepened and transcended the law and that he expressed disapproval specifically at the legalism involving matters of the tithe.

Protestants would do well to strengthen their perspective that the tithe is given tacit approval by Jesus and in retrospect we adopt the Old Testament idea of a tenth of the income as a viable model for a practical and partial understanding of stewardship. The Catholic way of bringing the tradition forward and the literal and unreflective way of taking all biblical customs, however historically impossible, as equal are not appropriate ways for the modern evangelical to establish his insights about tithing.

Practically speaking, this means that if Christians speak about the tithe they should begin with Christ's tacit approval of it in Matt. 23:23. Then in this context we may use Mal. 3:8-10 as an Old Testament rhetorical reminder of the relation between the necessity of man's remembering God's ownership of all things and God's pleasure in man's practical acting upon such awareness. The community of grace (the church) should not be motivated by law. Rather the church should speak out of a gracious redemptive experience to accomplish more than the law required.

This leads to a third and vital question.

C. What Is the Theological Basis for Stewardship?

Stewardship is not to be equated with tithing. Such an equation would yield wrong answers every time. Tithing is only one small specie (and in the New Testament exceedingly small) of the larger genus, stewardship.

The New Testament concept of stewardship is based on God's redemptive plan (*oikonimia*) itself.[14] It involves the body of Christ as composed of Christians who become a living temple in which God dwells through his Spirit (Eph. 2:20-22). The upbuilding (*oikodomeoo, oikodomein*) or edification of fellow believers is an intrinsic part of stewardship as is being a steward of the mysteries of the gospel (*oikonomos*). This means Christian stewardship is involved with evangelism and Christian growth.

Only when this wider basis for stewardship is recognized may one speak about the stewardship of substance. The biblical premise is that life and all of its substance and experiences belong to God because he has made, sustained, and permitted them. It is at this point that tithing should be placed as a practical biblical model for partially discharging the stewardship of substance. T. A. Kantonen has aptly said, "Theology thus has the same relation to stewardship that a philosophy of life has to life itself. And a theology of stewardship can be nothing less than an interpretation of the Christian meaning of life as a whole." [15]

Since stewardship is the larger category and tithing only one possibility of its expression, we must ask the further question: How did tithing come to assume such a large and disproportionate part in some Christians' understanding of stewardship?

D. Factors Effecting the Formation of Doctrine and Church Polity

It is naive to assume that any church anywhere does everything just as things were done in biblical days. And if there were such a church, it would be in error—in the grave error of pretending that God does not take history seriously and does not continually lead his people in the setting and circumstances in which his providence has placed them.

It was amply illustrated in the first section of this paper how the customs of tithing in biblical times changed, grew, and took on different forms. This has continued in the history of the church.[16]

What we must acknowledge is that tradition, expediency, and success have shaped many of the customs of our churches. It must also be candidly acknowledged that every church program based on tradition or expediency or blessed with success has felt it was based on biblical insights. Much of what is traditional is not necessarily biblical. It is honest motivation and a desire to "live from the Scriptures" that has led many Christian groups to document their practices from the Bible, however strained the exegesis.

Tithing has had an interesting career in the twisting currents of church history. It was not a formal requirement in the Roman church until A.D. 585, but once established it became firmly entrenched in all of western Europe not being seriously questioned by anyone except the Swiss Anabaptists until the Enlightenment.[17]

In the last quarter of the nineteenth century a powerful tithing movement began in America initiated by laymen and enjoying marked success.[18] A work by James A. Hensey entitled *Storehouse Tithing* was enormously influential in spreading the concept of tithing among evangelicals in America. Southern Baptists were influenced indirectly by this movement in the early part of the twentieth century. In addition to the general evangelical stress on tithing Southern Baptists have pioneered in various types of stewardship programs such as: the Cooperative Program, budget subscription campaigns, every member canvass programs, and various forms of financial pledging and fiscal policies.

These have been enormously successful.[19] And when coupled with fervent preaching on stewardship and testimonies about the joys of tithing have produced astonishing financial results in the life of America's largest denomination.

Nothing succeeds like success, and it is fervently to be hoped that the enlarged vision of stewardship being promoted by the Southern Baptist Stewardship Commission will produce even greater practical results.

In the midst of these programs of expediency and success we must be extremely cautious that we do not posit specific biblical sanction for what are obviously contemporary financial programs. It is even more important that our stewardship be based on legitimate biblical insights and not on forced exegetical conclusions. This warning leads to our final question: How should we teach, preach about, and regard tithing in our contemporary church practice?

E. Practical Implications in Preaching and Teaching About Tithing

1. *Ways of presenting the tithe.* In the earlier section "The Relation of the Biblical Materials," approval was given to the general Protestant approach to the tithe. That is, begin with Jesus' tacit approval and use the Old Testament idea of a tenth as one practical way of effecting stewardship. This is preferable to beginning our biblical insights by working from the obscure and diverse applications of the tithing laws expressed in the Old Testament. In addition to this suggestion, several other practical and ideological insights have already been suggested from the very structure of this article. Rephrased in brief, suggestive form they are:

    a. Let all implications of stewardship grow from adequate answers to the larger theological questions about who God is; what he requires; and what he is doing for his creation.

    b. Let biblical interpretation about tithing be historically based and have theological integrity. For example, let us actually know what the specific biblical materials about tithing are, and let us not apply Scriptures that have nothing to do with tithing to the specific teaching about tithing.

    c. Let tithing be a small part of the larger doctrine of stewardship. It is unwarranted to identify the part (tithing) with the whole (stewardship).

    d. Do not apologize for good and workable stewardship programs in our congregations. But do not feel obliged to proof-text these from Scripture.

    e. Recognize that the original principle behind tithing, namely the recognition of God's ownership of all of life and its experience, is still applicable to the church.

2. *Dangers in stressing the tithe.* Every negative possibility is the backside of a positive implication. And as one has said the backside will show through if you push the front too hard. There are both practical and theological dangers to be avoided in the churches' presentation of tithing. In brief form they are:

    a. If the implication is left that by tithing one has paid his full obligation to God, distortion of the biblical meaning of stewardship results.

b. If tithing is presented as a legal requirement for being Christian (a good Christian or a dedicated Christian) such an assertion cannot be proved from Scripture. Moreover, spiritual pride is a temptation for the tither, and bitter resentment is the crippling response of the non-tither. In both instances the grace of God is frustrated.

c. If tithing is presented as a commercial venture (if you give God a tithe he will always bless you financially and physically) the ways of God with men are misrepresented and the problem of the physical privations of countless godly people goes unanswered. This commercialization of tithing is perhaps the most theologically grave mistake made in many presentations of tithing.

d. If the motivation for giving anything to God is less than willing love, it is inadequate. People should tithe only if convinced it is an adequate and appropriate way of recognizing the claim of God on one's life.

e. Under no conditions should the withholding of or the promise of giving a tithe be used as an economic pressure in the church. Such pressure has often been used to control the pulpit, prevent adequate presentation and implementations of the social implications of the gospel, and to promote the will of dominate wealthy persons in the congregation. It is better that the church be impoverished than that she be bought. It is better to proclaim the "full counsel of God" with integrity than to silence genuine conviction for reasons of economic expediency.

Conclusion

The length of this paper about tithing is several times greater than the actual biblical materials on tithing. That is parabolic of our approach to the subject in current church life. We say considerably more than the Bible says on many subjects, and considerably less than it says on certain others. It is hoped that this imbalance may be corrected. In the final analysis the Christian's relation to tithing can be proper only if his understanding and experience of God and the redemptive action of God is right. From a true knowledge of God grows an adequate concept of stewardship, and only in this broader view can tithing be meaningful for the Christian.

FOOTNOTES

[1] See *Theological Dictionary of the New Testament,* ed. by Gerhard Kittel, trans. by Geoffrey W. Bromiley (Grand Rapids: Wm. B. Eerdmans Publishing Co., 1964), II, 36-37.

[2] *The International Standard Bible Encyclopedia,* ed. by James Orr (Grand Rapids: Wm. B. Eerdmans Publishing Co., 1947), V, 2987-88; *The New Westminster Dictionary of the Bible,* ed. by Henry S. Gehman (Philadelphia: Westminster Press, 1970), pp. 952-53; *The Interpreters Dictionary of the Bible,* ed. by George A. Buttrick (4 vols.; New York: Abingdon Press, 1962), IV, 654-55. Hereinafter cited as *IDB;* Henry Lansdell, *The Tithe in Scripture* (Reprinted from the 1908 edition; Grand Rapids: Baker Book House, 1963), pp. 7ff.

[3] See Lukas Vischer, *Tithing in the Early Church,* Facet Books, Historical Series, trans. by R. C. Schultz (Philadelphia: Fortress Press, 1966), pp. 2-3.

[4] For good introductions to the Talmud see Hermann L. Strack, *Introduction to the Talmud and Midrash.* Authorized translation of the fifth German edition (New York: Meridian Books, Inc., 1959).

[5] See Bruce Metzger, *An Introduction to the Apocrypha* (New York: Oxford University Press, 1957).

[6] See *The Life and Works of Flavius Josephus,* trans. by William Whiston (Philadelphia: The John C. Winston Company, n.d.).

[7] Cf. Strack, pp. 3-8, 26, 29-34; see also Lansdell's two chapters on the Talmudic teachings about tithing, pp. 87-104; see especially the general rule in Masaroth, I, 1.

[8] *The Apocrypha of the Old Testament.* R.S.V. (New York: Thomas Nelson & Sons, 1957).

[9] *The Life and Works of Flavius Josephus, op cit.*

[10] *Against Apion,* I, 22; on Corban see *IDB in loco,* and Matthew Black, *An Aramaic Approach to the Gospels and Acts* (Oxford: Clarendon Press, 1959), p. 101.

[11] See *The Interpreters Bible,* ed. by George A. Buttrick (12 vols.; New York: Abingdon Press, 1951), VII, 535 f.; VIII, 216 f.

[12] *Interpreters Bible,* XI, 663 ff. Note, in passing, the illuminating discussion of Melchisedek.

[13] For the earliest beginnings of this approach to tradition see Lukas Vischer's *Tithing in the Early Church.*

[14] For complete discussions of the wider context of stewardship in the New Testament see "The New Testament Idea of Stewardship," *Southwestern Journal of Theology* (April, 1971).

[15] A *Theology for Christian Stewardship* (Philadelphia: Muhlenberg Press, 1956), p. 2.

[16] For the earliest chapters of this change see Vischer's *Tithing in the Early Church;* for a contemporary expression of tithing see *Stewardship in Contemporary Theology*, ed. by T. K. Thompson (New York: Association Press, 1960), especially R. P. Roth's chapter "A Twentieth Century Conception of Christian Tithing," pp. 132-155 which provides an excellent historical synopsis of the practice of tithing from biblical times to the present.

[17] Thompson, *Stewardship in Contemporary Theology*, pp. 136-139.

[18] Cf. George A. Salstrand, *The Story of Stewardship* (Grand Rapids: Baker Book House, 1956).

[19] See Merrill Moore, "Southern Baptists and Stewardship: Retrospect and Prospect," *Southwestern Journal of Theology* (April, 1971).

The Christian and His Giving

Cecil Ray

Twentieth-century Christianity needs the explosive impact of an awakening to greatness in Christian giving. Only an awakening in giving that is solidly Christo-centric in its nature can be equal to the giant task confronting today's believer and also be equal to the new and unprecedented financial capabilities he possesses. Neither mere tokenism in giving nor rigid legalism will capture the commitment of Christ's followers; likewise these attitudes will not flame the fires of missionary and evangelistic passion.

The matter of Christian giving has been approached by most churches and denominational leaders as an economic necessity. Unfortunately, little attention has been given to the more basic spiritual, and distinctively Christian, imperatives. To succeed, the development of Christian giving must be put in its rightful place—at the very heart of the Christian life. To do this will be to declare that the true Christian giver is one who has first found Jesus Christ as the real Lord of life and then has sought to make both his words and his deeds bear witness to this lordship.

Christian giving, when approached on this plane, finds its motives, its objectives, and its dimensions in the individual's personal relationship to Jesus Christ. It functions within the recognized truth that the final and supreme purpose for material things is spiritual and that they exist primarily for the achievements of God's purposes. The Christian giver, understanding this, finds excitement not only in how much he gives but also in that he is linked with God's great purposes in dealing with sin, in meeting human needs, in proclaiming forgiveness, and in redeeming the world.

If Christianity is to experience a great awakening in giving, it must be convinced of the urgency of *now*—of *today*. Christians must be impelled by the crying needs of the lost, the hungry, the sick, and the lonely. Yet, too, giving must be guided by the unerring hand of God's eternal purposes. The Christian giver must act as one who is in the world and part of the world; yet he must never lose sight of the fact that he, too, is a pilgrim here with a transforming message for this world.

The tidal wave of a moving revival of Christian giving cannot merely ride the crest of an affluent age. The two do not tend to flow together. Instead, the call for Christian giving must confront prosperity, challenge it, and, if successful, redirect it. To date, in the era of affluency, the cause of Christian giving has fared poorly. Even though its quantity has increased, its quality has diminished. To an alarming degree, the giving of Christians has been based on sheer abundance. Many now find they have the capacity to act with a seeming flare of generosity. They may give a sizable amount, but, compared to their whole income, it may be only 1%, 2%, or 3%. This is then only the casting of the crumbs of their abundance towards the Lord—not real, meaningful giving.

It is interesting that wealth, not poverty, has brought Christian giving into a crisis. This should not be surprising, however, to any student of the Scriptures. For example, the apostle Paul in writing to Timothy (1 Tim. 6:9-11) clearly warns that money is the source of all kinds of evil. He asserts that those who would be rich endanger their lives with all kinds of hurt and, more seriously, expose themselves to a way of life that pulls them away from the faith. How true this is proving to be in today's prosperity crisis! Therefore the call for a revival in giving is urgent, not only to meet the pressing need to spread the gospel, but also to reclaim the Christian for his God-given life and task. The truth is that only when prosperity is controlled by one who is controlled by Jesus Christ can it be used as a means of doing good.

This introduction is, in brief, the summation of the biblical study that this paper undertakes. The study is an effort to probe the issues of Christian giving in light of the place and purpose assigned to it in the Scriptures. The inquiry must confront the basic questions about giving such as—

Is giving really a part of the Christian way of life?

Is giving inherently involved in the Christian experience of salvation?

What motivations for giving are found in the Scriptures?

How are these motives to be evaluated in light of the distinctly Christ-centered purpose of the New Testament?

What is meant by sacrificial giving?

Is sacrificial giving important to Christian living in times of prosperity?

I. Is Giving an Inherent Expression of the Christian Experience?

1. The Christian Experience Makes Giving a Natural Response.

(1) *Giving is inherent in the Christian experience and is thus a very natural believer's response.* "Let Jesus happen to a man and something happens to his money." This quotation declares that there is an instinctive or spontaneous response in the life of one who has been redeemed by Jesus that makes him want to share his money with Christ and his work.

One of the questions proposed for this study asks "Is this really true?" It was obviously true with the woman who anointed Jesus with the costly perfume in the house of Mary and Martha in Bethany (Luke 7:37). For her this was a spontaneous act of loving gratitude. The fact that it was a costly perfume made her response more purposeful. Christ's gift to her had meant so much that the response was one of deep gratitude.

The same was true with Zacchaeus (Luke 19:1-9). Immediately upon his acceptance of Christ as Saviour and Lord, he responded with a declaration of bold giving. His commitment involved more than one half of all that he possessed.

To declare that Christian giving is inherent in the new-life experience of the believer is not to say that giving is always instantaneous or automatic. To assume this is a tragic mistake evidenced by the lives of many Christians. Rather, the emphasis is that this "inherentness" becomes the basis for expecting a response. Because one is in-Christ he has in him the new nature that prepares him to be responsive to true Christian giving. The author of 1 John (1:8-14; 5:13) bases his appeals on this "inherentness." He states, "I write to you . . . because ye have known . . . ."

(2) *Natural and responsive giving is linked to believers' understanding of what is meant by the Christian experience.* The way he responds through acts of giving is inevitably rooted to the Christian's understanding of what God has done for him in Christ. In like manner, it shows how seriously he believes that Christ is really "the way, the truth, and the life." Coming to know Jesus Christ as personal Saviour begins new things—(2 Cor. 5:17)—a new life, a new strength for facing life, and a new purpose. It begins a new purpose in the believer for the use of his material resources. This is true because Christian giving, like all aspects of Christian stewardship, is basically a matter of a personal relationship to Christ. A major characteristic of the new life is the transfer of the dominant control of life from a self-centered operation to a Christ-centered one. In other words, the new

life strikes at the very heart of selfishness. This move toward selfless-ness is a move forward in the grace of giving, for giving is basically an unselfish act.

2. The Christian Experience Establishes a Relationship That Ma-tures the Giver.

(1) *Christ becomes the Lord of one's life in the Christian experi-ence.* This experience of grace is more than a temporary stirring of the emotions of generosity. It is, instead, the beginning of a relation-ship in which Christ is Lord. Christ enters the believer's life to be en-throned as Lord and, with this, the whole meaning of life begins to revolve around this sovereignty of Christ. Maturing in the Christian grace of giving comes with the acceptance of this rule of Christ.

(2) *To be "in Christ" is to become a partner with Christ in his ministry.* This partnership role with his new-found Lord is actually a family affair. It is a family partnership in which the believer sees his new role as an adopted "son." It is a relationship destined to mature the believer in the grace of giving. He shares his Lord's purpose and is trusted with responsibilities. The impact of this sense of divine ministry plus the scope of Christian missions becomes for the believer a major incentive for growing in the grace of giving. To lose this sense of purpose has a negative effect on giving. This is demonstrated in the ministry of William Carey. God used Carey to awaken this passion for the souls of people through missions and set in motion what has come to be known as the modern missionary movement.

Paul appealed to the Christians of Macedonia and was used of God to awaken in them this moving sense of partnership in service. The miracle of great giving happened as these people gave themselves in fresh commitment to God (2 Cor. 8). This voluntary and responsive quality of Christian giving played an important part in the history of the early church.

(3) *The Christian experience brings the indwelling of the Holy Spirit.* This becomes still another of the established relationships for the new believer which are destined to affect his entire life—including giving. The indwelling Spirit works to give understanding of the mean-ing of the lordship of Christ and of the partnership ministry. The spirit-filled life evidences itself most notably in the believer's relationship to material possessions. This is characterized not by an attempt to draw a line of distinction between the spiritual and the material, but rather by a grasp of the right and wrong use of material things. Christians have tended to be more spiritual about the non-tangible things of life —as if to·say that the material is basically evil. Yet the work of the Holy Spirit touches both alike. The account of the early Jerusalem

Christians (Acts 2, 4) shows the people moving under the glow of the Spirit and responding with unusual love, matching this love with a joyful sharing of their possessions.

II. What Motivates Giving?

1. The Place of Motives in Christian Giving

(1) *The motives that prompt people to give are varied and numerous.* A study of the Scriptures quickly verifies this fact. It becomes evident that the biblical givers were motivated by a wide range of reasons. Their motives included those that were intensely self-centered and appealed to selfish ambitions while other motives were completely opposite—opposite in that they were Christ-centered and produced acts of devoted love. The study of those motives points up a very important consideration for all Christian leaders. It stresses the great importance of how leaders use the various motives that can prompt giving.

(2) *There is danger of being sub-Christian and acting simply to exploit the giving potential without regard to the development of the individual.* It is altogether possible for the well-meaning leader to chart a course that has worthy ends but unworthy means. If "getting money for the church" is to be the only concern, then the exploitation of almost any or all the known motives will seem justified. But if achieving divine purposes, including the maturing of the follower of Christ into his true role as a Christian giver, is to govern the approach, then only distinctly Christ-centered motives will be used. This emphasis on Christian motivation (on the part of leaders) does not mean that all giving by Christians will automatically be done from the right motives. But it will result in a new quality of Christians.

2. The Biblical Issues of Motives

(1) *The law versus the gospel is the basic issue discovered in the study of biblical motives in giving.* This issue of the Old Testament law and the New Testament gospel comes into clear focus when viewed in light of the study of motives. The sharp contrast between legalism in giving and love for Christ in giving quickly appears. With this comes the realization of the danger of compromising the gospel through rigid legalism as well as the danger in completely abandoning the value and guidance of the Old Testament law. This raises the basic question—just what is the role of the law in developing Christian giving?

The law established a very real stewardship concept. It is important to remember that this stewardship existed prior to the historical coming of Christ. That is to say that there existed an emphasis on giving that is "pre-Christian" or, perhaps more accurately defined as sub-Christian. Much can be said for this sub-Christian stewardship. It had meaning and impact but lacked the distinctly Christ-centered meaning and purpose. Its role can thus be seen as preparatory for Christ's approach.

(2) *Christ came to fulfill the law.* He declared that he did not come to destroy but to fulfill. As in the other aspects of the law, Christ did not destroy this law-centered stewardship. Instead he took it and set it into a whole new scheme of things. He exploded it into new meaning and purpose. But, most of all, he moved the spotlight from the law to himself. In doing this he built a whole new meaning of stewardship, including the meaning of giving, that revolves around himself as the central point. In doing this he made the supreme motive for giving to be love for him. Christ's new approach to giving is very lofty in its ideals, very visionary in its purpose, and very demanding in its scope. Yet it is to be love that motivates it.

3. The Use of Motives

(1) *The temptation to appeal to sub-Christian motives confronts many church leaders.* Perhaps the temptation is greater because employing these lesser motives seems to promise quicker results. Also they seem to be simpler to program and to promote. The fact is, it is easier to declare the explicit "thou shalt" of the law than to present the meaning of the lordship of Christ. It is easier simply to demand the tithe. Carl Bates has stated that Southern Baptists are now suffering from the error of simply settling for the tithe. In doing this, he states, Baptists have neglected the development of the higher "trustee witness" approach given by Christ. Christ's meaning of trusteeship and of giving is both exciting and great!

(2) *Shallowness in Christian giving is now evident.* Christ's exciting approach to giving has been missed by many of his followers. Instead, there is much evidence of shallowness in today's attitudes toward Christian giving. The bashful and apologetic voice, that indicates an embarrassment in having to talk of money when spiritual things are preferred, speaks loudly of a serious theological void. The same is true when church leaders boast that money is never mentioned in "our" church. Shallowness, however, is not limited to cases involving bashfulness. For example, there is the appeal to give that feeds only the self-interest of the giver. This is done by the promise of prosperity in exchange for giving. In addition, alarmingly shallow motives are fostered by leaders who preach an aggressively selfish purpose for money. Whatever the scheme, the end result is not desirable.

(3) *Love is the Christian motive and the one motive worthy of limitless use.* This overflowing joy and gratitude of the Christian for what Christ has done for him is the keynote for Christian giving. True Christian giving must be motivated by Christ himself. It must stem from an awareness of his sovereignty and blossom into actions based on a conscious loyalty to him. This love-tie relates the Christian giver to the great purpose of God in dealing with sin, in loving people, and in a redemptive mission. Christ's passion for people gives his follower a missionary passion that opens him to great generosity in giving. Church leaders are wise to remember this fact and to balance their appeals for generosity between the church "sent" and the church "gathered." Christians giving prompted by love for Christ is not less than law-giving, instead it is giving at its greatest.

4. Motives for Giving in the Old Testament

(1) *In order to prosper.* This is one of the dominant motivations to giving found in the Old Testament. The Old Testament approach to giving is dominated by the idea that riches are a sign of God's blessing and come as a reward for faithfulness and obedience.

Deuteronomy 8:18, "But thou shalt remember the Lord thy God: for it is he that giveth thee power to get wealth."

Deuteronomy 28:9-11, "The Lord shall establish thee an holy people unto himself, as he hath sworn unto thee, if thou shall keep the commandments of the Lord thy God, and walk in his ways. And all people of the earth shall see that thou art called by the name of the Lord; and they shall be afraid of thee. And the Lord shall make thee plenteous in goods, in the fruit of thy body, in the fruit of thy cattle, in the fruit of thy ground, in the land which the Lord sware unto thy fathers to give thee." (Also in Deut. 39:9)

Proverbs 3:9-10, "Honour the Lord with thy substance, and with the firstfruits of all thine increase: so shall thy barns be filled with plenty, and thy presses shall burst out with new wine."

Malachi 3:10, "Bring ye all the tithes into the storehouse, that there may be meat in mine house, and prove me now herewith, saith the Lord of hosts, if I will not open you the windows of heaven, and pour you out a blessing, that there shall not be room enough to receive it." It is important to observe that this promise is preceded by instructions on how the gifts to God are to be made—"in righteousness."

(2) *To gain God's favor.* This is a second motive evident in the giving practices of the Old Testament.

Genesis 28:20-22, "And Jacob vowed a vow, saying, If God will be with me, and will keep me in this way that I go, and will give me bread to eat, and raiment to put on . . . I will surely give the tenth unto thee." This act of Jacob was an attempt to gain God's favor through bargaining about the tenth.

In Isaiah 1:11 the prophet decries the idea of man trying to buy God's favor. "I am full of the burnt offerings . . . I delight not in the blood of bullocks. . . ." Neither the forgiveness of sin nor the favor of God can be purchased with man's gift, however he may try.

In Psalm 50 man is reminded that if God were hungry he would not need their offerings. He declares, "The fowls of the mountains: and the wild beast of the field are mine."

(3) *To build a place of worship.* This motivation is illustrated in the building of the Temple and in the building of the Tabernacle. (Ex. 25-28—25:2) "Speak unto the children of Israel, that they bring me an offering: of every man that giveth it willingly with his heart ye shall take my offering. And this is the offering which ye shall take of them; gold, and silver, and brass . . . . And let them make me a sanctuary that I may dwell among them." This is followed by detailed instructions for the building of the tabernacle.

Exodus 35:21 is a beautiful example of the generosity of a people giving in the glow of God's spirit with the commitment to achieve a God-given task. "And they came, every one whose heart stirred him up, and every one whom his spirit made willing, and they brought the Lord's offering to the work of the tabernacle . . . ."

(4) *To fulfill the requirement of the law* is found as a giving motivation in much of the Old Testament.

Leviticus 27:30, "And all the tithe of the land, whether of the seed of the land, or of the fruit of the tree, is the Lord's: it is holy unto the Lord."

Exodus 34:26, "The first of the first fruits of thy land thou shalt bring unto the house of the Lord thy God."

Full instruction is given to Israel regarding the offerings. They are instructed to observe the sin offering for ignorance, the trespass offering, the thanksgiving offering, and the sin offering, involving the scape goat.

(5) *To pay a vow* is a reason for giving followed in the Old Testament.

Deuteronomy 23:21-23, "When thou shalt vow a vow unto the Lord thy God, thou shalt not slack to pay it: for the Lord thy God will surely require it of thee; and it would be sin in thee . . . . That which is gone out of thy lips thou shalt keep and perform; even a free will offering."

5. Motives for Giving in the New Testament

The Scriptures used in this selective study of giving in the New

Testament are divided into sections as follows: the Gospels, Acts, Paul's letters, and the General Epistles. The study follows the same procedure as that used in the Old Testament. The selections of Scripture studies reveal motives evident in accounts of gifts made as well as in the appeals for gifts to be made.

(1) *In the Gospels*

a. *To fulfill the requirements of the law,* many Jews in Jesus' day placed a rigid emphasis on the tithe. While the New Testament refers only briefly to the tithe, it leaves no question as to its existence as a giving practice. Matthew 23:23 (TEV), "Impostors! you give to God one tenth even of the seasoning herbs, such as mint, dill, and cumin, but you neglect to obey the really important teachings of the Law, such as justice and mercy and honesty. These you should practice, without neglecting the others." Although Jesus is not primarily dealing with the tithe in this reference, it gives insight into the rigid legalistic motivation being used for giving.

b. *To remove a spiritual barrier,* Jesus challenged the rich young man to give. Matthew 19:16-22 (TEV), (also Mark 10:17-31; Luke 18:18-30): "If you want to be perfect, go and sell all you have and give to the poor, and you will have riches in heaven; then come and follow me." This is clearly an appeal for the rich young man to give in order to remove the very things that were preventing him from turning to Jesus.

c. *To right wrongs,* Zacchaeus made a declaration of gifts to the poor and restoration of funds. Luke 19:1-10 (TEV), "Zacchaeus stood up and said to the Lord, 'Listen sir! I will give half my belongings to the poor; and if I have cheated anyone, I will pay him back four times as much.'" Zacchaeus is motivated by the warm glow of a genuine commitment to Jesus and by the evident wishes of his new Lord. The account shows Jesus' attitude to wealth accumulated by unrighteous means and reflects his dual concern for a man's soul and then for his ministry to others.

d. *To express love and gratitude* is the highest Christian motive for giving. In reality this is the one truly Christian motive, and it is to this supreme motive that the other worthy motives relate.

Luke 8:3. This love is seen in the account of Mary, Joanna, and other women who helped Jesus and his disciples with their "belongings" or possessions.

Matthew 26:6-13 (also Mark 14:3-9; John 12:1-8). The woman's anointing Jesus with the expensive perfume from the alabaster box is a beautiful expression of grateful love. She was obviously prompted by her love to show gratitude for what Jesus had done for her. Jesus responded by commending her gracious gift.

Mark 12:41-44 (also Luke 21:1-4). The widow's mite brought forth from Jesus the highest praise. He commended her sacrificial gift and indicated she gave all she had to live on. Her gift was noble because of the magnitude of its expression. Jesus compared her sacrifice with the gifts of others whose gifts were larger but represented only a small part of their abundance.

e. *To receive recognition* prompted many of the gifts of the Sadducees and Pharisees. Matthew 6:1, "Take heed that ye do not your alms before men to be seen of them." Jesus labeled as hyprocrites those who stand in public places to make their gifts to the needy. He ascribed to them the motive of "giving to be seen of men" and then added, "They have their reward."

f. *To help the needy* is a worthy motive and grows out of a love for Jesus. Matthew 25:40 (TEV), "Whenever you did this for one of the least important of these brothers of mine, you did it for me." Jesus is talking of their visiting the sick and prisoners, and of giving food and water.

Luke 10:25-37 records the beautiful account of the good Samaritan. Christ relates the story to show the real meaning of love for people and to commend a worthy use of possessions. The good Samaritan demonstrated how possessions can be given to express genuine love.

g. *To gain spiritual achievement*—is another motive linked to the basic motive of love for Christ. In Matthew 6:19-20, the appeal to store up "riches in heaven" is an attempt to put material things in their proper relationship to things eternal. This same prompting is given to the rich young man that he may find "riches in heaven." Matthew 6:33-34 describes Jesus talking to people who are worried about food, clothes, and wealth. He admonishes them to seek first the kingdom of heaven. This point of motivation helps place all of man's relationships to material possessions, including giving, into a proper relationship to eternal realities.

(2) *Motives for Giving in the Acts*

a. *To express their love for each other,* the Jerusalem Christians demonstrated a warm and exciting motivation for giving. The accounts of Acts 4:32-37 and Acts 2:45 tell of a voluntary and spontaneous sharing of wealth among the fellowship of believers. This high expression of brotherhood was achieved in the spiritual fervor of an experience with Christ and the knowledge of his resurrection. It was a profound kind of fellowship which gave witness to the great meaning of the resurrection and to the transformed life of the community created by it. It was truly a remarkable demonstration of brotherhood based on love.

b. *To receive recognition* is a motive for giving in the Acts just as in the Gospels. Acts 5:1-11 tells of Ananias and Sapphira who observed the esteem given to Barnabas and others who sold their property and gave their money. They, too, wanted this praise. They were prompted by a very sub-Christian motivation. Their sin was the attempt to gain prestige by getting credit for a more generous gift than they were willing to make.

c. *For the joy of giving.* This is a worthy reason and comes as an inherent expression of the Christian faith. Acts 20:35 declares, "It is more blessed to give than to receive." This beautiful principle of Christian living came in the account of Paul's commendation for the support given to his ministry.

d. *For selfish gain.* This is a very wrong and distinctly unchristian motive for giving. An example is seen in Acts 8:18-24. Here Simon offered to give money in exchange for the power of the Holy Spirit. He had witnessed the evidence of this power in the apostles and he wanted it, too. His mistake was not in wanting spiritual power but in desiring it for selfish purposes. The apostles rebuked him with the declaration that God's gift cannot be bought with money.

(3) *Motives for Giving in Paul's writings*

a. *To share in furthering the gospel.* Philippians 1:3-5 (TEV), "I thank my God for you . . . because of the way in which you have helped me in the work of the gospel." Paul's reference included their support through material gifts.

b. *To minister to the needs of the saints.* Much of Paul's effort dealt with the securing of financial support for the needy Christians of Jerusalem. (See 2 Cor. 8-9 and Gal. 6:10.) This effort brought about the first joint missionary enterprise of the churches. In turn, this served to set the pattern for churches, as well as individuals, to work together in a common Christian cause. It established the voluntary and responsive approach to giving as the pattern for the New Testament church.

c. *To prove the quality of love.* Paul referred to the beautiful example set by the Macedonian Christians as an occasion to challenge the Corinthians. He called on them to show their love with their gifts in the same way (2 Cor. 8:1-8). In 1 Corinthians 16:1-2 the apostle further appealed to them to follow a systematic and regular plan of giving each week.

(4) *Motives for Giving in the General Epistles*

The major appeal for giving made in the General Epistles was to meet human needs. 1 John 3:17 (TEV), "If a man is rich and sees his brother in need, yet closes his heart against his brother, how can he claim that he has love for God in his heart?" Love that is simply a matter of words and declarations is empty. Love to be real must express itself. It will express itself in giving and will find a way to serve the needs of others.

The message of James 2:14-16 is similar. James labels the faith that is not matched by works as dead. He asked, "What good is faith if it does not prompt actions of love toward the hungry or the cold?"

This brief look at motives for giving in both the Old Testament and the New Testament indicates that a sharp contrast exists between the worthy and unworthy motives. In the New Testament there is really only one distinctly Christian motive—that is as a response to one's love for Christ and others. This is the keynote for Christian giving and the basis of all the worthy motives found in the New Testament.

III. How Is Sacrificial Giving Applied to the Affluent Christian?

1. The Christian's Problem with Affluence

(1) *Affluence confronts stewardship* with its most severe test. At the same time it offers the Christian steward his best opportunity to exercise the grace of great giving. However, the experience of the past is that giving and great abundance have seldom been compatible. Affluence tends to create an attachment to things. It makes one forget his ideals and his commitment to Christ. The rich fool of the New Testament was a fool, not because of his abundance, but because of his reaction to economic plenty. Like this rich fool it is possible for a Christian steward to so desire wealth that he becomes mastered by this passion. Then to all practical effects he denies the lordship of Christ in his life.

(2) *Affluence endangers Christian commitment!* Unless riches are subjected to the control of Christ in the believer's life, they constitute a major threat. So grave is this threat that the Christian faces the danger of missing the very direction and purpose of life meant for him. Instead of experiencing spiritual maturity he is in danger of facing spiritual bankruptcy. Equally as great as the danger to the individual Christian is prosperity's menace to society. The dangers are so acute that it appears doubtful whether society can survive. The only hope is for Christians to gain a spiritual insight which cannot be found in man but must be derived from a point of view outside man. It must be a view from heaven—a view that makes the Christian an example of

victory over materialism. This provides the strength for a great ministry made possible by prosperity.

(3) *Affluence tends to confuse the purpose of wealth.* There are many spin-offs from the dangers of prosperity. One of these is the notion that riches are an evidence of God's favor. This notion prompts the attitude that God is pleased or he would not have given prosperity. With this tends to come a smugness and a selfishness in the use of wealth—the idea that "God meant it for me."

This notion is fostered by numerous promoters who say that God wants his people to have wealth. All one has to do, they promise, is to obey God's commandments with the gift of their "first fruits." In turn, God will bless them with a "full barn" (Prov. 3:9-10).

This point of view raises the basic question about God's intent for prosperity. Is it God's desire for all his people to have prosperity? Will he always reward faithfulness with riches?

It is obvious that God has blessed man with material plenty on many occasions. In the Old Testament there are frequent promises of material reward for faithful giving. By contrast, it is striking to note that these promises are not found in the New Testament, thus provoking deeper consideration of how these Old Testament promises of plenty are to be interpreted and applied. This sharp contrast is not surprising when viewed in light of the totally new relationship of life established by Jesus Christ. With this new scheme of things comes a shifting from lesser to higher sets of values. Characteristic of these new values is Christ's explanation that "life does not consist in the abundance of one's possessions" (Luke 12:15). Instead, he makes the spiritual life and its application in the lives of men the supreme purpose of God. It becomes clear that the abundant spiritual life is his interest and desire much more than the abundant material life. It is also clear that Christ makes the achievement of the purposes of the kingdom of heaven central for both himself and his followers.

It seems valid to conclude that the New Testament does not deny that God will bless man with material plenty as a reward for faithfulness. However, it must also be concluded that this is not the emphasis of Christ and therefore should not be the emphasis of his followers. It is simply not in harmony with the Christ-centered approach to motivate giving by the promise of economic reward.

(4) *Affluence threatens the Christian's witness!* This is another of the ill-effects of prosperity. What happens is that the Christian becomes so involved in the struggle to acquire things that he is emptied of a clear and effective witness for Christ. He becomes so much a part of the problem that he is incapable of being part of the solution. Add

to this the fact that nonbelievers caught up in the vain race for materialistic success are unable to see a clear example in the Christian's life. As a result they are neither helped nor challenged by Christians in their struggle with this great problem.

(5) *Affluence is deceptive!* It is so easy for the Christian to deceive himself about seeking God's kingdom. In truth he may be only casually involved in kingdom affairs but quite anxious about accumulating worldly goods. Further evidence of its deception is seen in the large number who enjoy the abundance of material things but still call themselves "poor." They cite the absence of a large bank account as evidence of their poverty, but neglect to count the almost numberless material items accumulated and paid for by increased earnings. It is easy for the Christian caught up in this materialistic-minded age to deceive himself about his involvement with things as well as about his new financial abilities to serve God.

What affluence has done is to give better wages, better homes, more luxuries, and much more time to be used in doing what the person himself decides. This is time beyond that which is required to earn the necessities of life. All of this gives the Christian the choice of what to do with more hours and more material resources. Yet the deceptive force of prosperity makes the right decision difficult. However, prosperity does not have to be bad; it can be the opportunity for Christian triumph. The problem is great, but equally great is the new potential for service to God.

2. Sacrificial Giving—the Answer to Affluence

(1) *The place of sacrificial giving* in the life of the Christian is that of a depth response that renews his commitment to the lordship of Christ. The willingness to understand the important place of sacrificial giving and, in turn, to respond with such giving becomes the big task for the affluent Christian. It is actually a test of his acceptance of his place of service under Christ. It tests him to see if he is willing—

—to allow his standard of living to be determined by the will of God and not solely by the size of his income
—to accept the role of a trustee and recognize that he has no right to indulge himself
—to fulfill the enlarged trust offered to him with the coming of prosperity
—to see the needs of others and accept responsibility to help care for them in the name of Christ
—to share in the urgency of the gospel.

(2) *Sacrificial giving is a lost grace for most Christians*—so much

so that it is now hard even to define or illustrate what sacrificial giving is. The dictionary states that "to sacrifice is to surrender something prized or desirable for the sake of something having a higher or more pressing claim." This definition leaves the Christian with many unanswered questions. The major point it singles out, however, is the "higher claim." The keynote to be sounded in the search for a rediscovery of the grace of sacrificial giving is the higher claim of Jesus Christ.

(3) *Biblical examples of sacrificial giving* help to determine its true meaning. While the New Testament does not use the term "sacrificial giving," it does give some notable examples and does set out principles for living that call for sacrificial action. For example, the "widow's mite" (Mark 12:41-44) is clearly an example of such giving. Jesus' words about the widow provide insight into the distinction between giving which is sacrificial and that which is not. Of the widow he said that she gave all she had to live on, while the others gave from abundance and took nothing from their living. Another example is found in 2 Corinthians 8, in the case of the Macedonian churches. According to Paul, they gave beyond their ability. A similar case may be discovered in Acts 4:32-37 when Barnabas sold his estate and gave the money to be used among the brethren. The common factor is that the giving of each of these cost them something—it affected their very way of life.

These illustrations do not define completely the term "sacrificial giving" but they do help put the issues into perspective for twentieth-century Christians. It becomes clear that the Christian is expected to be willing to forego material things that he greatly desires. The unique problem for the affluent is that he can give a sizable gift without altering his standard of life. The magnitude of the problem is best seen in light of the fact that most Christians are only giving token amounts, a much smaller number give well, while only a few have approached a level of giving that is sacrificial.

(4) *Sacrificial giving for today* holds the answer to an urgently-needed Christian triumph. Therefore a major challenge for church leadership is to develop this grace of great Christian giving in the lives of Christ's followers. To achieve this Christian maturity, extensive teaching and enlistment will be required. New insights will also be required into what sacrificial giving means and why it is necessary today.

A word of caution needs to be sounded—namely, that church leaders must not assume the role of manipulators. The appeal for great Christian giving must be Christ-centered and must major on the great purpose of Christ and his kingdom. Responses motivated in this way can be the beginning of a victory over the danger of affluence. They can initiate the birth of an urgently needed move toward greatness in giving for Christ.

(5) *The call for sacrificial giving* must be accompanied by help to the Christian in seeing how he can be a part of such a new awakening to the Christian grace of giving. This calls for lofty idealism properly mingled with practical actions. Many devoted followers of Christ have admired the "widow" and her gift but have seen little way to identify with her. More have been able to see themselves as the Macedonians in their response to Paul's appeals. A similar greatness in Christian giving can be realized in a growing number of today's Christians. Sacrificial giving for these Christians will find expressions much like those in New Testament days. For example:

a. Sacrificial giving may come as a spontaneous act motivated by the spiritual impulse to do something very meaningful. This is an act of Christian maturity and devotion that is desirable.

b. Sacrificial giving may be a response to a specific and urgent need. The need may be a disaster in the community, an unusual missionary opportunity, a major church task, or the hurt of people who are hungry and cold.

c. Sacrificial giving reaches its highest expression in the purposeful altering of one's standard of living or style of life in order to be involved regularly in a committed service to Christ. Examples of this kind of worthy sacrifice are found in the banker who leaves a lucrative position to accept an assignment on a mission field, in the doctor who turns from a promising practice to be a missionary, or in the family who stays in the same work in the same community but voluntarily adjusts their way of life to be able to give more for Christ's work.

The urgency of an awakening to true greatness in Christian giving makes it vital that church leaders actively cultivate the grace of sacrificial giving in Christ's followers. Much of the success or failure of the people of God in this day is linked to the coming of such an awakening. Only this quality of response can avert the disaster of prosperity and convert it into a time of Christian victory.

Principles and Procedures
of Responsible Giving

Richard B. Cunningham

Jesus said, "It is more blessed to give than to receive" (Acts 20:35). A simple affirmation! Yet its implementation is not so simple, because giving touches virtually every facet of life. How, when, and where do we give? Of what and to what do we give? These are questions to be explored in this study of "Principles and Procedures of Responsible Giving." In order to give structure to a variety of questions in this complex subject, the paper will deal with five major areas: (1) The Giver and His Treasure; (2) Objects and Concerns of Giving; (3) Channels of Giving; (4) Occasions for Giving in the Church; and (5) Corporate Stewardship.

Numerous problems are involved in developing giving procedures. One is the nature of the biblical materials. Old Testament requirements are complicated and difficult to unravel with certainty.[1] The New Testament provides few specific giving procedures, so that principles must be extracted from limited contexts and passages. Even then, there is no direct parallel between Old and New Testament structures, nor between the loosely organized apostolic church and modern denominations. Further, New Testament grace has supplanted Old Testament legalism, a fact that demands discernment in interpretation. There are also important political and socio-economic differences between the biblical and modern settings. In the United States, church and state are separate. And other social and governmental agencies have preempted many traditional church ministries, such as aid to the poor, elderly, orphans, and sick. Consequently, when one applies biblical principles of giving to our modern situation, he must do it with humility, not pontifical absoluteness.

In trying to solve problems of modern giving, one must make an initial choice. Should we approach the subject from the perspective of securing financial support for the church? Or should we view giving within the larger biblical picture of the steward's responsibility before

God for all of life? Institutional needs determine many approaches to Christian giving. In a day of dwindling church finances, it is tempting to approach giving as a way to increase church income. All of us who love the church have a deep commitment to financial support of her mission. But the Bible begins with the stewardship responsibility of the individual and only in that light speaks of giving to the church and to other concerns. We must commit ourselves without hesitation to biblical authority on giving, and develop church stewardship programs within those principles.

I. The Giver and His Treasure

Stewardship and Giving

The Bible approaches giving within the more inclusive context of stewardship. As man's responsibility before God for all of life, stewardship includes the proper use of self, time, talent, and treasure. Christian giving is nothing less than the total giving of our human and material resources to serve God and man. Giving is only a part of stewardship, money giving a part of total giving, and proportionate giving a part of money giving. Proportionate money giving, our usual focus of attention, is only one aspect of the steward's overall giving in life.

Yet within his total dedication of life, the Christian is commanded to give a portion of his assets—including self, time, talent, and treasure —to God and other men. The giving of treasure can never substitute for the giving of self, time, talent, and treasure. But because of time limitations, we will assume the importance of giving self, time, and talent. The paper will limit itself to principles and procedures of financial giving.

The Purpose of Giving

What is the purpose of giving? In commending Corinthian liberality in the Jerusalem offering, Paul provides a succinct, inclusive statement: "Under the test of this service, you will glorify God by your obedience in acknowledging the gospel of Christ, and by the generosity of your contribution for them and for all others; . . ." (2 Cor. 9:13 RSV). Here the three purposes of giving are: (1) to glorify God, (2) to serve man, and (3) to discipline the self.

The first purpose of giving is to glorify God. It acknowledges that God is sovereign in the universe and the source of life's blessings. The Hebrew tithe partly taught man the fear of God (Deut. 14:23).

Paul speaks of the Jerusalem offering overflowing in many thanks-givings to God (2 Cor. 9:12).

The second purpose of giving is to serve the needs of man. The Hebrews gave part of their tithes and various charity gifts to serve the needs of people. A major purpose of giving in the New Testament is to alleviate different kinds of human problems. In fact, Jesus indicated that when we give to men in need, we give to the Lord himself (Matt. 25:31-46).

The third purpose of giving is to discipline the self. The foundation of stewardship is the affirmation that "the earth is the Lord's and the fulness thereof, the world and those who dwell therein" (Ps. 24:1). The gift reminds us that God is owner of our resources, and we are stewards who must give an accounting to him. It reminds us that we are to be open handed in sharing with others and are to lay up treasures in heaven. One's ease in giving is an accurate barometer of his sense of value and of his degree of self-discipline.

Motivation for Giving

Motives determine the spiritual value of giving. Among motivating factors in Christian giving, at least six are of great importance.

(1) Giving is a response to grace. Man gives because God first gives to him and then by grace enables him to give (2 Cor. 9:8). Paul repeatedly calls giving a "gracious work" (2 Cor. 8, 9).

(2) Giving is a response to the example of Christ who became poor that we might become rich (2 Cor. 8:9).

(3) Giving is a response to human need. Paul says that the believer out of his own abundance supplies the other person's want (2 Cor. 8:14). The good Samaritan embodies this motivation.

(4) Giving is an expression of thanks to God. The thank offering has ancient roots in Hebrew life. Paul speaks of the Jerusalem offering for the saints also overflowing in many thanksgivings to God (2 Cor. 9:12).

(5) Giving is concrete proof of love. According to Paul, the Jerusalem gift is a proof before the churches of genuine love (2 Cor. 8:8, 24).

(6) Giving is a form of sacrifice to God. In daring language, Paul describes the Philippians' gift to him as "a fragrant offering, a sacrifice acceptable and pleasing to God" (Phil. 4:18).

The Method of Giving

How should one give of his resources to God? On the basis of proof texts, one cannot set up any elaborate rules on the method of giving. Yet certain principles run throughout the Bible, despite differences in detailed application. Among those that should guide us are the following.

(1) Seek first the kingdom of God (Matt. 6:33). When the steward obeys life's first priority, everything else falls into its proper place, including responsible giving.

(2) First give the self. In biblical thought, the giver should be identified with his gift. The prophets condemned people who make the gift a substitute for dedication of the self to God. Paul claims that before contributing to the Jerusalem offering, the Macedonian Christians "first . . . gave themselves to the Lord and to us" (2 Cor. 8:5 RSV).

(3) Give as God prospers. Proportionate giving is the basis of Old Testament tithing. In removing giving from a legal basis, the New Testament retains the idea of the individual giving as God has prospered him. Paul writes, "It is acceptable according to what a man has, not according to what he has not" (2 Cor. 8:12 RSV).

(4) Give God the first and best. The Old Testament system requires the first fruits and the best of animals or harvest for God (Ex. 22:29ff.; Deut. 17:1; Mal. 1:6ff.). In giving God first priority, the giver dedicates the remainder of his resources to God's service.

(5) Give systematically. Giving is not a hit and miss affair. Although geared primarily to an agricultural economy and a particular theocratic culture, the Old Testament tithing system built in regular patterns that avoided spasmodic giving. In a similar way, Paul instructs the Corinthians to put something aside and store it up on the first day of the week (1 Cor. 16:2).

(6) Give generously. New Testament liberality of love supersedes Old Testament legalism. Generosity, not percentage rules, becomes the guiding principle. Paul says the generous Corinthian gift overflows in a wealth of liberality (2 Cor. 8:2, 9:11).

(7) Give voluntarily. Old Testament legal obligation is unworthy for the Christian. Paul insists that giving must not be an exaction but of one's own free will (2 Cor. 8:3, 9:5). The only gift that honors God is one that comes from a willing, loving heart. The only rule Paul sets is this: "Each one must do as he has made up his mind, not reluctantly or under compulsion, for God loves a cheerful giver" (2 Cor. 9:7 RSV).

(8) Give spontaneously. Immediate needs often require spontaneous response. Giving of alms was hallowed by Jewish tradition and emphasized by Jesus. The poor, hungry, sick, homeless, and others in

want must be served when and where encountered. No amount of systematic, proportionate giving can offset a neglect to give personal help as worthy needs arise.

The Treasure Man Gives

What are the resources out of which the Christian should give? The answer is: The whole wealth of life itself. Paul states: "You are not your own; you were bought with a price" (1 Cor. 6:19-20 RSV). Through creation and redemption, the Christian's total life belongs to God. Thus all our resources are the vault out of which specific gifts are drawn. When we give God ourselves, we give him all that we are and have—time, talent, and treasure.

Among life's resources, money has unusual potential for good or evil. The Bible warns that the craving for wealth can be the root of all kinds of evil. In a strange way, money is an extension of the self. It represents work, energy, and investment. Someone has called it "congealed sweat." For that reason, it is specially important how one handles his financial resources.[2]

The treasure house for our potential giving contains both total income and accumulated wealth—every penny we receive. In a capital investment economy, both the getting and giving of our treasure is complex. Income may come from salary, interest, capital gains, bonuses, rents, payments, royalties, honorariums, bequests, inheritances, judgments, rewards, and numerous other sources. All income is subject to proportionate giving.

Christian giving also involves the use of accumulated wealth and the disposal of estates at death. It is poor stewardship if one squanders his accumulated wealth in careless spending or in unplanned court probate at death. It is easier to suggest principles for giving weekly or other income than for giving accumulated wealth and estates. In a money economy where investment plays a major role, to give money away in the immediate situation may diminish its potential for good in the longer run. Consequently, a total approach to giving leads into such technical inquiry as wills, gift annuities, life income agreements, life insurance, trusts, endowments, and other estate plans.

The Responsible Steward

The Christian is responsible for the whole of life. Only the individual steward himself can determine when, where, what, and how he gives. The key principle to stewardship and giving can be stated like this: *The Christian steward will manage his resources and his giv-*

ing in responsible freedom. The principle of individual responsibility is rooted in the basic stewardship term *oikonomos*—house manager. It is at the heart of Jesus' major stewardship parables. The master of the house holds the steward responsible and accountable for all within his domain. The master will return and require a reckoning from the steward.[3]

The Christian steward exercises this responsibility in the freedom of grace. Christ has set us free from the letter of the Old Testament law, even in giving. Christian giving flows from gratitude and generosity, not from legal demand. But freedom does not mean lawlessness. The Christian lives in *responsible* freedom, bound by the demands of love. He will be intent upon glorifying God and serving man. He will seek the best biblical guidance he can get about God's expectations in giving. But the giver himself must be responsible for the use and giving of his resources, particularly in complex situations where there are no clear guidelines. This idea surely lies behind Paul's standard that each one must do as he has made up his own mind (2 Cor. 9:7).

II. Objects and Concerns of Giving

What are the objects and concerns of Christian giving? If we give to glorify God and serve the needs of man, then the objects and concerns of giving are as broad as life itself. God and man are bound together. Our gifts to God are to be used to serve the needs of man. The Bible gives some helpful guidelines to fill out this general principle.

Old Testament Concerns

The Old Testament tithing system demonstrates the general concerns of the Hebrews, although it is impossible to reconcile Deuteronomic, priestly, and rabbinic requirements. There were three tithes in the final rabbinic system. One tithe was given to the Levites for maintenance of the temple cultus (Numbers 18:21ff.). A second tithe was consumed by the worshiper and his family in a celebration at the temple or other chosen place (Deut. 12:5-19, 14:22-23). The third tithe, given in the third and sixth years of the sabbatical cycle, was for charity. It was stocked in the towns for the Levite, traveler, fatherless, and widow (Deut. 14:28-29). There were additional provisions for the poor. The Hebrew left the land fallow in the sabbatical year, and wild crops were gleaned by the poor (Lev. 25:1-7; Ex. 23:10-11). Also all debts were canceled in the sabbatical year. So Old Testament giving focused primarily on temple cultus and charity.[4]

The New Testament indicates similar concerns in giving. In the most general way, there were three: (1) support of the church, (2) provision for one's family, and (3) service to men in the world. Gifts to the church provided for the particular concerns of her official ministry, welfare needs within the church, and her missionary work in the world.[5]

In the apostolic period, several concerns were uppermost in giving to the church. (1) A first concern of church giving was the support of the ministry. Jesus sent his disciples on their mission with only life's bare necessities, requiring them to be supported by those to whom they ministered (Matt. 10:10). Paul taught that those who proclaim the gospel should get their living from the gospel (1 Cor. 9:14; 1 Tim. 5:17). (2) A second concern of church giving was the needs of church members. The Jerusalem church established a community of goods, and many Christians sold property and gave the proceeds to the apostles for distribution to the needy (Acts 2:44ff., 4:34ff.). Each church cared for her own widows, orphans, and poor (1 Tim. 5:17). (3) Concern for needy fellow Christians extended to those in other congregations, as in the Jerusalem relief offering (2 Cor. 8, 9). (4) Gifts to the church also supported the church's mission to the world. Traveling missionaries, evangelists, and others were financed by the church. Although Paul mainly supported himself, he also received gifts from some of the churches (Phil. 4:16-18).

A second major area of giving for New Testament Christians was to needs within their own families. This is an important dimension of giving often overlooked in modern stewardship teaching. In teaching that care of parents is a basic duty, Jesus severely rebuked Jews who avoided financial responsibility to needy parents by declaring their wealth "corban," reserved for God (Matt. 15:5). In the apostolic church, a first duty was the care of one's own family and parents. This relieved the church of unnecessary welfare burdens and allowed her to assist those who had no other source of help (1 Tim. 5:16). In his major passage on giving in 1 Timothy, Paul advocates that Christians must "first learn their religious duty to their own family and make some return to their parents" (1 Tim. 5:4). To dispel any further doubt about this aspect of giving, Paul goes on to say, "If any one does not provide for . . . his own family, he has disowned the faith and is worse than an unbeliever" (1 Tim. 5:8 RSV).

The New Testament underlines the needs of men in the world as a third major responsibility of Christian giving. Jesus regarded almsgiving as a chief duty of man (Matt. 6:2-4). He commends the good Samaritan for his spontaneous gift to a stranger in need (Luke 10:29-37). Zaccheus gives one half of his good to the poor (Luke 19:8). Jesus commands the rich young ruler to sell his property and give the money to the poor (Luke 18:22). Jesus taught that those who help the poor will be rewarded at the resurrection (Luke 14:14). In the parable of the sheep and goat judgment, Jesus makes service to the physical needs of men the test for entrance into eternal life. He teaches that giving to the hungry, thirsty, stranger, naked, and imprisoned is giving to the Lord himself (Matt. 25:31-46).

Modern Concerns

Modern Christians live in another time and setting than that of the Bible. There are few direct parallels between the Old Testament or apostolic settings and our own. And yet we still have many of the same objects and concerns in giving. These include support of the church's ministry and mission, care of fellow Christians, provision for our families, and service to human need outside the church. Specific areas of need may shift from one era to another. But the scope of our giving remains as close as our family and as wide as the family of man. However much life has changed, the responsible steward must assure that his gifts reach all these biblical objects and concerns—in whatever modern form they are found.

III. Channels of Giving

The Problem of Where to Give

It is one thing to determine the major concerns of Christian giving; it is another to find modern channels for giving to those concerns. Where and how much should we give to be faithful to the biblical pattern? For a number of reasons, it is impossible to establish ironclad rules for every detail of giving in each circumstance.

The complexity of the biblical situation.—The complexity of giving situations and practices in the Bible makes it difficult to draw up a precise formula for where and how much we give. In some stewardship literature, there is an unwarranted oversimplification of the Old Testament tithing system, which is then coated with Christian grace and imported into the New Testament. The logic usually follows that the Jew gave a tithe, so the Christian who is under grace should take the tithe as a minimal starting point for giving. The fact is that there were three major tithes that covered obligations far beyond support of the temple cultus. And by the time of Jesus, there were at least twelve regularly prescribed tithes and offerings, plus the spontaneous giving of alms to people in immediate need.[6]

The tithing system had several limitations. These were basically agricultural tithes. F. C. Grant contends that there was no tithe imposed upon artisans, tradesmen, fishermen, and others. Nor was a tithe paid to the temple by Diaspora Jews. There was no tithe in the sabbatical year since no crops were planted.[7] Consequently, it is impossible to calculate precisely how much was tithed by the average Jew and where it was given. In addition, the Old Testament tithing system had a theocratic basis. During the priestly period, civil, military, and religious needs alike were supported by the tithing system. Estimates of the amount of combined religious tithes plus the Roman tax in the time of Jesus run as high as forty percent.

This complexity indicates the impossibility of transplanting the Old Testament system into the apostolic church, much less into our modern situation. Inferences about the giving pattern in the New Testament church based upon Old Testament practices are tenuous at best. The major New Testament passages on giving do not provide many specifics on where and how much we are to give.

Total giving and church-giving.—Christian giving is far more than a restricted ecclesiastical obligation. Just as stewardship is more than giving, so giving is more than giving to the church. And that helps create the problem. Hundreds of good causes bid for the financial support of the Christian. The practical difficulty is to determine where and how we are to give financial resources in order to serve the biblical concerns in giving. The only adequate procedure is for the individual steward to exercise responsibility within the best possible biblical guidelines.

The solution is simple, of course, if one takes a legalistic or pragmatic view geared to secure support for the work of the church, and then ignores other dimensions of giving. This view would argue that a flat ten percent of one's untaxed income should be given to the local church, and that any money given elsewhere should be given apart from the church's ten percent. It would interpret Malachi's charge of robbing God to mean keeping a tenth from the church. But as we have seen, the Old Testament situation was not that simple. And there is no directive to that effect in the New Testament. A number of denominations which teach tithing with some enthusiasm do not hold this demand to be biblical, however desirable it might be from the standpoint of church finance.[8]

The changed church-state relationship.—Among several modern factors that might influence the pattern of Christian giving is the changed socioeconomic and political situation. The state has assumed certain traditional human concerns of the church, such as welfare assistance, old age security, medical care, and education, to name a few. The Christian citizen pays substantial taxes to support these services. In the apostolic church, the Christian's gifts to the church partly would have gone to the same needs. The church has educated the state to serve human need.

This may have several implications for the church. First, in estimating the level of the individual's financial stewardship, we might ask whether in God's eyes the portion of tax money that provides social services is part of the Christian's giving. Second, the changed situation should propel the Christian into active citizenship to assure that social needs will be met adequately, humanely, and constructively by the state. Third, the church might need to rethink her corporate stewardship. With the state having assumed many traditional social services of the church, can the church still justify using limited financial resources for numerous educational institutions, hospitals, children's homes, retirement homes, and other institutions? Should these historic services be expanded, frozen, or reduced? Or should they be delegated to the government? What principle should determine the nature of our contemporary institutional and service commitments? The scope of these questions takes us beyond the limits of this study. But in long range corporate stewardship, they must realistically be faced.

Awareness of the intricacy of the problems and questions we have noted should relieve us of a simple kind of legalism in our approach to giving. The individual steward must exercise informed responsibility as he determines where and how much to give to legitimate Christian concerns.

Giving to the Church

A biblical principle for church giving.—Although a Christian gives to more than strictly ecclesiastical concerns, a substantial portion of his proportionate giving is channeled through the church. If we are to avoid an arbitrary and unbiblical legalism in church giving, we must rediscover a biblical basis that allows the responsible Christian to experience the joy of generous giving in the freedom of faith. The New Testament picture of the church as a covenant community provides that basis. It can be put in a formula: *Responsible Steward in Covenant Community Equals Dynamic Fellowship and World Outreach.*

The Christian is a responsible steward for all of his life. But the individual does not exercise his responsibility for giving in splendid isolation. Individual responsibility is bound to corporate commitment. Lines of responsibility might be traced like this: (1) The individual is responsible for his own giving. (2) The congregation places a claim on the individual. (3) The church at large places a claim on the congregation. (4) The world places a claim on the whole church. In this sense, we are debtors to the world in and through the church. At every level of stewardship, responsibility must be exercised.

When a Christian joins a church, that church places a claim on his time, talent, and money. The individual surrenders his autonomy, though not his responsibility, to the congregation in whose life he shares. The church is a covenant community, a living organism, where men bind themselves together for internal life, worship, education, service, and proclamation in their own locale and to the ends of the earth. In describing this corporate commitment in the church, Paul writes: "This is how one should regard us, as servants of Christ and stewards of the mysteries of God. Moreover it is required of stewards that they be found trustworthy" (1 Cor. 4:1-2 RSV).

In light of the Christian's commitment to a covenant community, there is no necessity to establish a proof text that requires generous giving to the church. As a member of a covenant community, the Christian commits himself to support the church's internal life and worldwide mission. Thus he will joyfully share in this life and work by giving substantially of his time, talent, and money to his own congregation. Healthy individual stewardship is essential to the health of the whole organism, the body of Christ. In determining how much to give to the church, the individual might find ten percent a useful thumbnail guideline. But it cannot be made a biblical rule. In many cases, the Christian will give more than ten percent. In other cases, there could be justification for giving less.

Biblical stewardship requires that the individual give generously to the church. It also requires him to exercise strong leadership responsibility to insure that the congregation uses the money efficiently, directs it broadly to all biblical concerns, does not retain too high a percentage for local ministries, and exercises responsibility at state and national levels to guarantee its efficient and inclusive use. The responsible steward will not turn loose his gift at the altar and then ignore what it is used for. Within the priesthood of believers, he should participate in that determination.

Designated giving.—The question of designated giving inevitably arises in connection with giving to the church. As a general principle, within the covenant community the individual should avoid designated giving. He should seek to accept the will of the congregation in matters affecting the community's life and work, including the assessment of financial priorities. He should abide by the general consensus, unless he must do otherwise as a matter of conscience.

There could be particular exceptions to this general principle about designated giving. One exception might be that of large gifts that could be counterproductive in the congregation's life. Another might be when the church does not exercise good biblical stewardship in expending finances. What, for example, if the church is overly occupied with impressive buildings and facilities instead of with human concerns? Or what if it ignores clear biblical teachings about ministry to total human need? Or what if a denomination misappropriates substantial funds for questionable purposes (as has happened recently in a major denomination, according to the reaction of many lay members)?

When there is a breakdown of collective stewardship, should the individual then reassert his personal responsibility and channel his gifts to other church agencies or designate gifts within his own church? This is a difficult question. The best solution would be for him to lead the church to reorder priorities. Even then democracy is a protection, but not absolute insurance, against group irresponsibility. The problem of democratic rule is that the lowest common denominator of the group, rather than the high demands of the kingdom, can become the criterion for the congregation's use of money. When that is the case, then the principle of individual responsibility would seem primary. But designated giving should not be used capriciously or maliciously, as is demonstrably often the case. It is possible for designated giving to be abused. But that is part of the risk of the freedom of faith.

Giving to Church-Connected Ministries and Institutions

New Testament churches are to support other Christian ministries outside the immediate congregational environment. In the modern era, the church's varied ministry includes educational institutions, new mission work, hospitals, children's and retirement homes, Christian camps, Christian centers and other social ministries, plus many other types of ministry. These ministries often require substantial support from individual Christians to supplement denominational allocations.

Many Christians, particularly those with accumulated wealth, feel commitments and have resources that permit them to give directly to specific ministries throughout the spectrum of the church's work. Here again, personal responsibility is the key to how and where we give. There is a twofold benefit in direct giving to church-connected ministries and institutions. Financial gifts undergird the long range plans of the institutions. And direct giving, by involving the giver directly with his gift, offers a joy in giving that cannot be matched in less personal ways.

If the church seeks to follow biblical principles of giving, she ought to review one traditional practice of fund raising. Agencies, institutions, and sometimes individual congregations frequently solicit gifts with an appeal to erecting memorials. Jesus leveled a stern warning against sounding trumpets to draw attention to one's almsgiving. Could that have some implication for institutional giving as well?

Giving to Meet Family Needs

A first duty of the Christian is to care for the needs of his family. Both Jesus and Paul regard this as a religious duty in one's stewardship of giving (Matt. 15:5; 1 Tim. 5:4). This priority in giving cannot be ignored. Paul's warning stands, both for the individual and the church: "If any one does not provide for his own family, . . . he has disowned the faith and is worse than an unbeliever" (1 Tim. 5:8 RSV). Fortunately, in our day there are many provisions for the elderly and other financially insecure people, such as social security, retirement funds, insurance, medicare, old age assistance, and food stamps. But these do not relieve the Christian of this first obligation to care for his parents and relatives.

The nagging question is how this family responsibility relates to the giving of one's total resources to God and others. In some cases, it becomes a flimsy excuse for poor stewardship in giving outside of one's own family wants. But in other cases of unusual family financial obligation, it might be a substantial part of one's total giving. One example is that of a highly committed young deacon who assumed a substantial medical debt of his aged mother. When he was unable because of his limited income to tithe directly to the church, he was pressured by the church to resign as a deacon. In biblical terms, was this parental care a gift to God or not? Jesus condemned Jews who avoided responsibility to needy parents by declaring their wealth "corban," reserved for God. Is it any better for the church to declare the individual's wealth "corban," if the Christian would then be forced to neglect a more fundamental obligation—the care of his family. Only the principle of individual responsibility within the freedom of faith can remedy this type of legalistic either/or.

231

Direct Giving to Immediate Personal Need

The Old and New Testaments repeatedly underline the Christian's personal responsibility to people in need. Christians can so exclusively orient their giving to ecclesiastical concerns that they can become callous to serious human problems in their immediate communities. No amount of impersonal giving through the church or state taxation can compensate for our ignoring needs of persons face to face.

We should give directly to human need, but the gift must not be separated from genuine love or offered indiscriminately. Paul writes, "If I give away all I have, . . . but have not love, I gain nothing" (1 Cor. 13:3 RSV). Far too much loveless giving represents "conscience money" to cover guilt for social inequities that need to be corrected in our communities. Giving should also be discriminating. Immediate physical needs must be met. But at times there are long range needs that require continuing love, attention, and effort. When possible, our giving should help people toward self-realization and self-sufficiency. In this way the good steward makes investments that produce rich dividends in personhood.

Giving to Organized Secular Charities

Organized charities are a major factor in modern life. Many of them offer valuable and essential services to people that were once within the proper province of the church. Various communities make a concerted drive for numerous charities through the United Fund or Community Chest. As an expression of Christian citizenship, it is wise for Christians to contribute to these community services. This may be difficult for Christians who already give liberally of their income to the church. Yet many of these services are also a part of Christian concern. To neglect them is to force people outside the church to bear complete responsibility. For those who cannot conscientiously support all United Fund organizations, it is possible to designate to specific organizations.

Giving to Non-church Institutions and Needs

The Bible rejects our modern division of life into secular and sacred spheres. As a citizen of this world, the Christian man is responsible for many human endeavors—education, science, the arts, man's cultural and aesthetic needs. Many good causes require private financial support. As a good steward, the Christian can legitimately contribute to whatever enhances the beauty, enjoyment, and humanness of life.

In a time of emerging nations and of vast movements toward social justice and equality, the responsible Christian might assign part of his general giving to organizations that work in the social arena. War and disaster victims, refugees and poverty relief, food programs for undernourished children, and dozens of other programs are worthy of support. There are noble projects in the area of culture, the arts, education, scientific research, and ecology to which one can contribute. In this area of giving, the guiding principle would be to give to causes that alleviate human misery, or ennoble human life, or advance the frontiers of the human spirit. Surely these things honor God too.

IV. Occasions for Giving in the Church

The Christian gives to various good causes. But a substantial portion of his giving goes to the church. There are quite different occasions and ways for the Christian to give to the church. At a minimum, these would include one's systematic proportionate gift, the giving of wealth and accumulated income, and the giving of estates at the end of one's life. Gifts should be presented at times and in ways that best achieve biblical purposes of giving and high standards of stewardship.

Systematic Proportionate Giving in the Church

An act of worship.—The Christian's first responsibility is systematic, proportionate giving. The Bible teaches that the steward is to give the first fruits, proportionately, and systematically—and that this is to go to the church. To speak of first fruits, proportionate, systematic giving is only to speak of the mechanics of determining and setting aside the gift. The attitude and manner of giving are also important. The gift should be both an act of thanksgiving and a way of dedicating the self and one's total life to God. This means that proportionate giving is preeminently an act of worship. It ought then to be a focal point of thanksgiving and self-dedication in weekly worship.

Ideally, the first fruits of the preceding week's financial blessings should be brought to the altar within the congregation as an act of worship and thanksgiving. The proportionate weekly gift is impossible for many people who receive income semi-monthly, monthly, irregularly, or periodically in large sums from investment, commissions, farming, etc. They must exercise responsible freedom. The best guiding principle would be for them to give in a way that enhances weekly worship—perhaps a token or prorated offering—without violating good business sense.

Sunday School collections.—In the American church past, giving has not always been central in worship, nor worship in giving. Fortunately, the church has largely abandoned bazaars, rummage sales, pew rentals, collection boxes, and class and organizational collections. But there is one practice, with its own positive value, that nevertheless detracts from the worship phase of giving. It is possible that the widespread practice of giving in Sunday School, while promoting efficiency, may diminish important worship dimensions of proportionate giving. It is not realistic to assume that our entrenched practice of Sunday School collections will be abandoned. Perhaps there is another solution. When gifts are collected in the Sunday School hour, there may be symbolic value in bringing them to the altar along with gifts gathered in the worship service—so that the congregation in a specific act dedicates themselves and their resources to the service of God and man. Some churches fail to dedicate even the worship offering to God because they have their ushers immediately remove the money to the church safe. It is far more fitting to bring the gifts to the front of the sanctuary for a visible, concrete dedication as one essential part of worship. It is a way of saying, "We dare not come before the Lord with pious words and empty hands, any more than with elaborate offerings and tawdry lives."

Credit card giving.—The identification of the giver with his gift is an indispensable aspect of giving. Depersonalization in giving is a perpetual danger. A new mode of giving, made possible by computerized technology, seems to minimize the identification of giver and gift. Some churches are now experimenting with credit card giving. Dallas First Methodist Church has installed a credit card booth in the lobby. A writer in a recent issue of *Church Administration* magazine looks favorably upon the idea for Southern Baptists.[9]

A strong case can be made against credit card giving. There is a dangerous psychology about credit card buying that could infect its use in giving. Many people are attracted to credit card buying because of the illusion that the purchase actually does not cost them anything. In this sense, there could be an enormous identification difference in giving between writing a check and using a credit card. Regular proportionate giving must avoid the "it-doesn't-cost-me-anything" mentality. One's gift should be offered up to God as a symbol of his total dedication of life to God.

Responsible Giving of Wealth and Accumulated Income

Congregation or not?—Special problems arise with certain types of giving. Both the very wealthy and those who accumulate money over the years face problems about when and where to give large sums of money. Under some circumstances, it may not be best for the Christian to give all his regular proportionate gift or a large special gift to the church. For example, when a wealthy individual may tithe an amount equal to the normal budget of his congregation, the very size of his gift may have an unfortunate influence on the congregation's life. The average member then possibly could minimize his own responsibility and cease to be a good steward. Or the wealthy individual could assume a position of political power commensurate with the size of his financial gifts.

In these cases or with other large gifts, it might be better for one to designate his gift through his church to denominational causes. Or he might entirely bypass the congregation with part of his proportionate gift. Bequests, endowments, and memorials raise similar problems. Stewardship involves responsibility—even here. A good guide for large gifts might be: Give to the church for its capital needs, but not as an endowment gift that provides operating expenses which should be given by the whole church.

Delayed giving.—The large immediate gift does not necessarily always represent the best stewardship. The U. S. economy influences when we give. In a capital investment economy, the steward may benefit God and human need more by investing wisely and giving a larger sum later. The parable of the talents points to the value of multiplying one's treasure. Business requires investment capital. The businessman may err as steward either by investing so much capital that he cannot give proportionately and regularly, or by giving so much of his wealth that he cannot invest. The responsible steward is only required to use and give his wealth to the glory of God. He himself must decide whether sooner or later.

The Stewardship of Estates

The Scripture observes: "For we brought nothing into the world, and we cannot take anything out of the world" (1 Tim. 6:7 RSV). Most people leave some treasure behind. The good steward should deliberately determine that his estate will go to productive uses. Most people want to provide for their families. Many also wish to leave some wealth to a church institution or agency. One has a choice in how to do this.

The will.—A will is the legal way of disposing of one's estate at death. There are several disadvantages in the will as a way of giving to institutions. The will is often a cause of controversy and court litigation. Inheritance taxes usually diminish bequests in wills. The deceased giver does not receive the joy of seeing his gift do good for others. There are usually tax advantages in disposing of an estate while one is still alive.

Outright gifts.—While still alive, one can make outright gifts by several means. (1) The cash gift is possible for those who have adequate old age security. The gift is tax deductible. (2) Life insurance may list an institution or agency as beneficiary. (3) Trust funds allow the donor to invest his gift and designate the income to a specified cause for a stated length of time. (4) Endowment funds allow the donor to invest his gift and designate the income in perpetuity to his chosen cause.

Income gifts.—There are several ways one may give to an institution or other cause and still have income until his death. (1) The gift annuity arrangement allows one to consign his gift to a foundation that will then guarantee a specified income to the donor until his death, and also that at least fifty percent of the gift will go to his designated concern at death. (2) A life income agreement consigns an estate to a foundation for investment management. The donor then receives the dividends from the investment until death, at which time the entire estate goes to the designated concern.

Most major denominations have foundations that assist this dimension of stewardship. Southern Baptists, in addition, have established state foundations. Stewardship education in the churches should include this vital aspect of overall giving.[10]

V. Corporate Stewardship

Stewardship in giving requires corporate as well as individual responsibility. The Bible never views individual man in isolation. Man is man in the totality of his social relationships. That is a practical as well as a theological truth. We live in groups. The twentieth century is the age of mass man. The individual is a member of family, community, church, different social aggregations, nation, and worldwide humanity. Principles and procedures of giving must extend to our handling of resources at every corporate social level. Three groups are of special concern for the individual Christian: congregation, denomination, and nation.[11]

Congregational Stewardship

The Christian is a member of the church, the body of Christ. The congregation is the visible localized aspect of that universal body. Corporate stewardship requires that individual members recognize their essential spiritual unity within the body and commit themselves to the health and mission of the church. Corporate stewardship refers primarily to what the congregation does with its corporate treasure—its time, talent, and money—as stewards of the gospel. Quite as much as the individual's pattern of giving reflects his concerns and the ordering of his life, so the congregation's pattern of giving of its resources reflects its own spiritual health.

The priesthood of believers.—The priesthood of believers is the basis of congregational stewardship. In addition to meaning that we are priests to one another, it means that each believer participates in discerning the Lord's will for his church, including use of her resources. As fellow priests, believers bear equal responsibility for corporate stewardship. The responsible congregation will encourage good stewardship for each member and practice good stewardship as a body. Each believer is a participant in collecting, budgeting, and expending church funds. This brings personal responsibility into corporate relationships and binds us to God's will for his church. As the church seeks to implement God's will in the allocation of corporate funds, it should move with as much unanimity as possible to achieve the essential tasks of the church. The good steward cannot abandon responsibility for congregational stewardship to a small group within the church—or the denomination.

How are we to spend the church's money? The apostolic church funded welfare needs, her official ministry, and missionary work. Living with a sense of eschatological urgency, they had no need of church buildings or ongoing institutions. Under the Spirit's leadership, forms of ministry may shift because of changing circumstances in different eras. The governing principle that should determine spending priorities is the essential mission of the church, which is primarily a servant ministry to the world.

Stewardship program.—At this point the stewardship program of the congregation has authentication. It is a practical work of the priesthood of believers. The stewardship program is far more than raising money. It does educate and encourage individuals to achieve a high level giving and personal stewardship. But the budget and stewardship campaign are also a corporate way of finding and doing God's will. In planning a budget, a church not only handles finances in an orderly way, but also has a yearly opportunity to reexamine priorities in light of the gospel. The unified budget is the best way yet devised for the whole church to share organically in the corporate responsibility of stewardship.

World mission.—The world mission of the church should receive a sizeable portion of the congregation's budget. The principle of proportionate giving applies to the church as well as to the individual, in this case involving worldwide causes outside the immediate congregational context. It is incongruous for a church to teach proportionate first fruits giving for its members and yet retain a disproportionate percentage for its own local ministries. The percentage a church gives will vary with a number of factors. But massive support of community, home, and foreign missions, Christian education, mass communication of the gospel, theological education, and many other ministries is essential to the global impact of the gospel. Here the congregation can give proof of its love for all men.

Local ministry.—Local expenditures are basic. Priorities should flow out of the basic New Testament pattern. Care of ministers is as essential now as in the first century. It is still true that the worker is worthy of his hire. Many mission-oriented churches are guilty of bad stewardship in the salaries paid their staff members. Churches would enhance their overall ministry by providing adequately for the servants of the servants.

The internal life of the congregation demands large expenditures. In our commitment to ministry in the world, it is easy to forget that there is also an essential ministry within the church. Education, training, music, fellowship, worship and many other needs are not optional extras. They are at the heart of the church's life. On a recurring basis, the congregation should measure her own internal life by the standard of the biblical view of the nature and mission of the church. There is always the danger that organizations and structures originally designed for mission become self-perpetuating ends in themselves and continue long after they have outlived their usefulness. Institutional introversion is also a constant danger, so that we spend money keeping all the structural gears turning and forget the world they were conceived and built to reach.

Buildings and property.—Increasingly, numbers of people think that many churches have been poor stewards because of the disproportionate amount they have invested in church property and facilities. Biblical stewardship might demand that we seriously rethink our use of church facilities, and measure the mass capital investment against the few hours they are used per week. Churches may need to find new ministries that will make increased use of our buildings. They may need to cut some of the frills and ask whether proposed expenditures are really necessary to perform the church's mission. Far too often building obligations hamstring congregations and siphon off funds needed for more important ministries. What is important is for the church not to become so preoccupied with housekeeping chores that she forgets her mission to the world.

Agape giving.—For the church too, "it is more blessed to give than to receive." But we must be careful how we give. A church can give from *eros* love rather than from *agape* love. In contrast to *eros, agape* does not seek to get but to give. *Agape* giving means the church should avoid giving money only when she can receive a guaranteed return on the investment. Such a standard would eliminate many necessary service ministries. We urge the individual not to give on a *quid pro quo* basis, i.e., in order to receive back personal benefits. The church likewise will severely limit her ministry if she insists on reaping her own benefits from giving. Bonhoeffer helps us toward a proper role with his image of the "church for others." The church is called not to be served but to serve.

Denominational Stewardship

Apostolic and modern structures.—Corporate stewardship inevitably involves the denomination. The denomination is simply the contemporary structure through which individual churches accomplish the work of the whole church. Although the early churches knew nothing of modern divided denominations, they were bound together at many levels. The oneness of the church gave rise to structural interrelatedness as the church responded to needs inherent in her life and mission. Structures emerged in connection with a relief and welfare group in Jerusalem (Acts 6), a council on doctrine and practice (Acts 8, 16), the appointment and support of missionaries (Acts 13), and the collection and administration of the Jerusalem offering (2 Cor. 8, 9). The structures centered not on themselves but on needs to be met. In this sense much of what we call denominational structure is utilitarian. It is designed to help the churches more effectively be the church and accomplish her mission. It is subject to change as certain organizational structures outlive their functional purpose.

A number of American denominations originated in response to missionary needs. First came commitment to foreign and home mission work, followed generally by care of ministers, educational institutions, hospitals, homes for children and the aged, and other ministries. At the state and national levels, the denomination is one of God's instruments in mission. It plays an important role in education, planning and promotion, as well as in direct mission ministry.

Denominational responsibility.—Some kind of denominational structure is almost indispensable as the church engages in mission. The denomination has a number of values. It allows individual churches to accomplish tasks they could never do alone. It allows churches corporately to establish priorities for limited funds. It eliminates solicitation of funds by special interest groups. Most of us tend to see the world through the eyes of our own agency, so that foreign missions, home missions, or education, or something else becomes *the* most important work of the church. The executive board can balance requests by various boards, agencies, commissions, and institutions, and then recommend a budget to the denomination. Thus, reasoned decisions, not fund raising pressures, determine denominational expenditures.

Good denominational financial stewardship has several requirements. (1) It should require that all programs and ministries be designed to implement and further the life and mission of the church. (2) It should require efficient and controlled use of money, so that with a minimum of bureaucratic drainoff it gets the money to human need. (3) It should be continually reassessing expenditures and ministries in light of changing circumstances and need. It is not merely important that people give; it is also important what their gifts are used for.

Dangers in denominational stewardship.—Several dangers are inherent in the denominational structure. One is the corrupting effect of power, even ecclesiastical power. Power is intoxicating. Bureaucracy, wherever it exists, tends to be self-perpetuating. Agencies tend to entrench, expand, and then try to justify their continued existence. Anyone familiar with Reinhold Niebuhr's analysis of the power drive in all social institutions knows that the denomination is not immune. In fact, temptation is always more subtle and sinister when close to the altar. Another danger is that structures tend to rigidify and regard themselves as ends and not means. Thus they cease to be critical of themselves. Jesus charged, "Every one to whom much is given, of him will much be required; and of him to whom men commit much they will demand the more" (Luke 12:48 RSV). In a consummate way, that applies to denominations.

National Stewardship

The church-state context.—The Old Testament tithing system was forged in a theocratic state and was designed to cover a broad range of civil, human, and religious concerns. In our time, there are at least two important changes. First, there is a marked line between church and state. Second, the state has assumed many responsibilities formerly accomodated in the Old Testament tithing system and in the apostolic church. But the Christian remains responsible for human problems, whatever the means of dealing with them.

Christian citizenship.—Modern American Christians live in a secular state where money flows through various channels to help mankind. Vital Christian citizenship is imperative today. We must influence the government to use our vast tax resources for human priorities and values—e.g., in poverty, health, old age security, education, environment, and culture. Christians should welcome and help guide the caring state to deal creatively with human problems. Tender hearts are not enough. We should be "wise as serpents" so that welfare is not misused. Paul's injunction that if a man eats, he should work (2 Thess. 3:10), and his warning that the church should care only for genuine widows (1 Tim. 5:16), indicate that giving is not to be handled by soft headed people.

Changing factors.—Several new social factors should affect our corporate stewardship in larger social or economic groups and in the state. One is our affluent society. Most societies in history have known widespread poverty. That is not our problem in the United States today. The poor have not disappeared, to be sure. But rather than being among the masses, the poor are now locked into special poverty pockets and groups—racial minorities like Negroes, Indians, Mexican Americans, small farmers, the vocationally displaced, the aged, widows with children, and a few other groups. We must still provide for the poor. Living in an economy of abundance, Christians should encourage the state to do more by adopting policies that will progressively eradicate poverty and develop the poor into productive persons. Other human values—better health, education, public facilities, and ecological matters like clean air and open land—will profoundly affect the quality of human life in the years ahead. Christians should influence governmental priorities, so that human concerns take relative precedence over such things as military and space appropriations.

Another major factor is the organizational revolution in modern industrial-technological society. Modern man is mass man. Life and work increasingly involve us in complex kinds of associations. The days of independent farmers and small businessmen are yielding to giant corporations which employ thousands of individuals. Christian action is essential on many fronts in our economic structures, particularly in the state and in the business community. The Christian worker must help his company or industry collectively assume its stewardship obligation for a variety of human concerns. Bound up with diverse mass groups, modern man cannot restrict his stewardship and giving responsibilities to private sectors of life. His giving will partly correspond to his getting—in corporate or community giving and in social planning and public welfare.

Macrostructure responsibilities.—Macrostructures—the large social groupings of modern society—require corporate responsibility. The distribution of tax wealth is a matter of stewardship. In an affluent society, Christian stewardship should produce a concerted effort to eliminate poverty and provide basic human services for all citizens. Major corporations, along with the state, must accept a greater social role. Corporations must take new responsibility for vocational training of the unskilled and for vocational retraining of those whose skills are made obsolete by shifts in technological or economic needs. In labor-management relations, Christian stewardship would lead us to require equitable earnings for investor and worker alike. Christian stewards might educate industry to the necessity of balancing public and private needs, so that the profit motive is always weighed against a product's long-term effect on the quality of human life.

Christian giving also requires that through our government we assume responsibility for international needs. The poverty gap is mainly between nations today. When the United States with a small percentage of the world's population controls a high percentage of the world's wealth, it is obvious that we cannot ignore this claim on our giving resources. The world is now our neighborhood. Modern transportation and communications have altered all the dimensions of planetary life. At one time our caring was first hand within our own communities. We must still serve our neighbor across the backyard fence. But now our neighbor may be in Biafra, Hong Kong, Peru, or Jordan. Money, when given through proper agencies, may extend our love around the world. At one level, that may be done through the church; at another, it may be done through the state. Aid to emerging nations is an important aspect of corporate stewardship. But it is no more acceptable for the state than for the church to give out of self-interest. At many levels, the United States can share her wealth and technological capacity with emerging nations out of nothing more than human concern.

It is better to give than to receive. Indeed it is! And at many levels and in many ways—to the glory of God and the service of brother man!

FOOTNOTES

[1] In their present form, Old Testament tithing requirements almost certainly represent rabbinic conflation of originally diverse traditions that cover a long period of history characterized by many political, cultural, and religious changes that alter the pattern of giving.

[2] For the best biblical study of money, see Otto A. Piper, *The Christian Meaning of Money* (Englewood Cliffs, N. J.: Prentice Hall, Inc., 1965). Two other useful books are Luther P. Powell, *Money and the Church* (New York: Association Press, 1962), and Robert J. Hastings, *My Money and God* (Nashville: Broadman Press, 1961).

[3] Helpful discussions of Christian stewardship are found in T. A. Kantonen, *A Theology for Christian Stewardship* (Philadelphia: Muhlenberg Press, 1956), and Helge Brattgard, *God's Stewards*, trans. Gene J. Lund (Minneapolis: Augsburg Publishing House, 1963), pp. 22-64.

[4] For brief discussions of the Old Testament tithing system, see Max Seligsohn, "Tithe," *The Jewish Encyclopedia* (New York: Funk and Wagnalls, 1905), XII, 150-152; J. A. MacCulloch, "Tithes," *Encyclopaedia of Religion and Ethics*, ed. James Hastings (New York: Charles Scribner's Sons, 1951), XII, 347-350; Richard L. Scheef, Jr., "Stewardship in the Old Testament," *Stewardship in Contemporary Theology*, ed. T. K. Thompson (New York: Association Press, 1960), pp. 17-38. Numerous major stewardship books also have discussions.

[5] For excellent discussions, see Helge Brattgard, *op. cit;* Holmes Rolston, *Stewardship in the New Testament Church* (Richmond: John Knox Press, 1946); Warren A. Quanbeck, "Stewardship in the Teachings of Jesus," *Stewardship in Contemporary Theology*, ed. T. K. Thompson, *op. cit.*, pp. 39-53; and Holmes Rolston, "Paul's Philosophy of Stewardship," *Stewardship in Contemporary Theology*, ed. T. K. Thompson, *ibid.*, pp. 54-75.

[6] F. C. Grant, *The Economic Background of the Gospels* (New York: Oxford University Press, 1926), pp. 92-100.

[7] *Ibid.*, pp. 95-98.

[8] On tithing in the modern church, see T. A. Kantonen, *op. cit.*, pp. 20-26; Helge Brattgard, *op. cit.*, pp. 92-94; Church of England, *The Christian Stewardship of Money* (Westminster: Church Information Office, 1959); Robert P. Roth, "A Twentieth Century Conception of Christian Tithing," *Stewardship in Contemporary Theology*, ed. T. K. Thompson, *op. cit.*, pp. 132-154; "The Teaching and Practice of Christian Stewardship," in Arthur R. McKay, *Servants and Stewards* (Philadelphia: The Geneva Press, 1963), pp. 65-70.

[9] Robert J. Hastings, "The Cashless Collection," *Church Administration,* November, 1970, pp. 32-33.

BIBLIOGRAPHY

Brattgard, Helge. *God's Stewards.* Trans. Gene J. Lund. Minneapolis: Augsburg Publishing House, 1963.

Church of England. *The Christian Stewardship of Money.* Westminster: Church Information Office, 1959.

Grant, F. C. *The Economic Background of the Gospels.* New York: Oxford University Press, 1926.

Hastings, Robert J. *My Money and God.* Nashville: Broadman Press, 1961.

Kantonen, T. A. *A Theology for Christian Stewardship.* Philadelphia: Muhlenberg Press, 1956.

McKay, Arthur R. *Servants and Stewards.* Philadelphia: The Geneva Press, 1963.

McMullen, John S. *Stewardship Unlimited.* Richmond: John Knox Press, 1961.

Piper, Otto A. *The Christian Meaning of Money.* Englewood Cliffs, N. J.: Prentice Hall, Inc., 1965.

Powell, Luther P. *Money and the Church.* New York: Association Press, 1962.

Rolston, Holmes. *Stewardship in the New Testament Church.* Richmond: John Knox Press, 1946.

Thomas, Winburn T. (ed.). *Stewardship in Mission.* Englewood Cliffs, N. J.: Prentice Hall, Inc., 1964.

Thompson, T. K. *Handbook of Christian Stewardship Procedures.* Englewood Cliffs, N. J.: Prentice Hall, Inc., 1964.

Thompson, T. K. (ed.). *Stewardship in Contemporary Life.* New York: Association Press, 1965.

Thompson, T. K. (ed.). *Stewardship in Contemporary Theology.* New York: Association Press, 1960.

Werning, Waldo J. *The Stewardship Call.* St. Louis: Concordia Publishing House, 1965.

List of Contributors

Morris Ashcraft, professor of theology at Midwestern Baptist Theological Seminary since 1959, is a native of Arkansas. His B.A. degree was received from Ouachita Baptist University, his B.D. and Th.D. degrees from Southern Baptist Theological Seminary. He has done additional study at Union Theological Seminary and the University of Zurich. He has been a pastor, a Navy chaplain, and a faculty member at Southern Seminary and Furman University.

Richard B. Cunningham, associate professor of systematic theology and philosophy of religion at Golden Gate Baptist Theological Seminary, is a native of Tulsa, Oklahoma. He received his B.A. degree from Baylor University, his B.D. and Th.D. degrees from Southern Baptist Theological Seminary. He served as pastor of First Baptist Church, Crothersville, Indiana; was professor, Chair of Bible, and director of the Baptist Student Union at the University of New Mexico. He is the author of *C. S. Lewis: Defender of the Faith* and *What Does Freedom Mean?*

James Leo Garrett, Jr., born in Waco, Texas, is professor of Christian theology at the Southern Baptist Theological Seminary. He earned the B.A. degree from Baylor University, the B.D. and Th.D. degrees from Southwestern Baptist Theological Seminary, the Th.M from Princeton Theological Seminary, and a Ph.D. from Harvard University. He has also been on the faculty at Baylor University and Southwestern Seminary. He has served as pastor of several Baptist churches in Texas and has been a lecturer. He is the author of *Baptist Church Discipline* as well as several other books and sermons.

J. Leo Green, professor of Old Testament Interpretation at Southeastern Baptist Theological Seminary, is a native of Mississippi. He received his A.B. degree from Mississippi College and his Th.M. and Ph.D. degrees from Southern Baptist Theological Seminary. He served as pastor of several churches in Kentucky and Florida. He taught for eleven years at Southern Seminary and has been at Southeastern Seminary since 1951. He has done postdoctoral research at Princeton University, Oxford University, the University of North Carolina, and Cambridge University.

William Lawrence Hendricks, a native of Butte, Montana, has been professor of theology at Southwestern Baptist Theological Seminary since 1957. He received his A.B. degree from Oklahoma Baptist University, the B.D. and Th.D. degrees from Southwestern Seminary, and an M.A. degree from the University of Chicago. He has been a pastor in Texas and Oklahoma and a counselor of boys at the Buckner Orphans Home in Dallas, Texas.

Lory Hildreth, pastor of the First Baptist Church of Texarkana, Texas, was born in Collinsville, Illinois. After completing an A.A. degree at Southwest Baptist College, he attended William Jewell College. He received the A.B. degree from Southern Illinois University. He also holds the B.D., Th.M., and Th.D. degrees from Southwestern Baptist Theological Seminary.

Jerry Horner is chairman of the Division of Christianity and Philosophy, Southwest Baptist College in Bolivar, Missouri. He received his B.A. degree from Union University, the B.D. and Th.D. degrees from Southwestern Baptist Theological Seminary, and has done post-graduate work at Manchester University and Cambridge University. He is the author of *Five Portraits of Christ* and *Outline Survey of New Testament History*.

Henry A. Parker has been pastor of the First Baptist Church of Orlando, Florida, since 1956. Born in Alabama, he received his A.B. degree from Howard (Samford) College, and the Th.M. and Th.D. degrees from Southern Baptist Theological Seminary. He has held several pastorates in Florida and Alabama. Among his writings are *Words to Live By* and *Peace in a Turbulent World*.

H. Franklin Paschall, a native of Kentucky, has been pastor of First Baptist Church, Nashville, Tennessee, since 1956. He received the B.D. and Th.D. degrees from Southern Baptist Theological Seminary. Union University, where he had received his A.B. degree, bestowed